Serge Daney and Queer Cinephilia

"Don't miss the *and* in the title, for this valuable book has two objectives. On the one hand, it proposes a vital, much-needed analysis of Serge Daney's thought, of his work as a critic, media theorist, and founder of the essential film journal *Trafic*, topics which all remain woefully under-discussed in English. On the other, it considers the implications of this work for queer studies, initiating a productive, cross-disciplinary dialogue around topics like aesthetics and queer biography, film history and feminism, media archeology and festival programming. The broader frame moves past Daney in order to remain close to him: by abandoning the self-sufficiency of a single approach for the vulnerability of the encounter, the editors maintain the commitments to alterity, mediation, and impurity at the heart of his understanding of cinema."
—**Sam Di Iorio**, Hunter College, City University of New York

"This international anthology helps to construct a renewal of transatlantic discourses on cinema. The contributions not only attempt to read Serge Daney from a queer perspective today, but also to understand queer theory anew, stemming from the cinephilic image theory of one of the most influential French film critics, who saw the era of post-cinema dawning as early as the 1980s."
—**Christa Blümlinger**, Université Paris-8

"This invaluable book steps in to help fill a glaring void: the lack of English-language scholarship on the most respected French film and TV critic of the post-WWII era, Serge Daney. It trains a queer and feminist lens on Daney's writings, a task both fruitful and fugitive, Daney being a gay man who rarely wrote about homosexuality–either his own or in cinema. Given that he spent the majority of his career steeped in the masculinist-heterosexual culture of *Cahiers du cinéma*, this book, by imaginatively unearthing the "queer potential" of his vast oeuvre, has produced an exciting contribution to the study of film criticism that pulses with contemporary resonance."
—**Girish Shambu,** Canisius College, Buffalo, New York

Serge Daney and Queer Cinephilia

**Edited by Pierre Eugène,
Kate Ince and Marc Siegel**

μ meson press

Funded by the Deutsche Forschungsgemeinschaft
(DFG, German Research Foundation)—GRK 2279

**Bibliographical Information of the
German National Library**
The German National Library lists this publication in the
Deutsche Nationalbibliografie (German National Biblio-
graphy); detailed bibliographic information is available
online at http://dnb.d-nb.de.

Published in 2024 by meson press, Lüneburg, Germany
www.meson.press

Design concept: Torsten Köchlin, Silke Krieg
Cover design: Mathias Bär, Thomas Köchlin
Cover image: Still from *Le Cinéphile et le village* (1993) by
Pascal Kané. The editors thank Roman Kané for permission
to use this image.
Copy editing: Daniel Hendrickson

The print edition of this book is printed by by
Lightning Source, Milton Keynes, United Kingdom.

ISBN (print): 978-3-95796-018-4
ISBN (PDF): 978-3-95796-019-1
DOI: 10.14619/0184

The digital editions of this publication can be downloaded
freely at www.meson.press.

Contents

Configurations of Film: Series Foreword

Scalable across a variety of formats and standardized in view of global circulation, the moving image has always been both an image of movement and an image on the move. Over the last three decades, digital production technologies, communication networks and distribution platforms have taken the scalability and mobility of film to a new level. Beyond the classical *dispositif* of the cinema, new forms and knowledges of cinema and film have emerged, challenging the established approaches to the study of film. The conceptual framework of index, *dispositif* and canon, which defined cinema as photochemical image technology with a privileged bond to reality, a site of public projection, and a set of works from auteurs from specific national origins, can no longer account for the current multitude of moving images and the trajectories of their global movements. The term "post-cinema condition," which was first proposed by film theorists more than a decade ago to describe the new cultural and technological order of moving images, retained an almost melancholic attachment to that which the cinema no longer was. Moving beyond such attachments, the concept of "configurations of film" aims to account for moving images in terms of their operations, forms and formats, locations and infrastructures, expanding the field of cinematic knowledges beyond the arts and the aesthetic, while retaining a focus on film as privileged site for the production of cultural meaning, for social action and for political conflict.

The series "Configurations of Film" presents pointed interventions in this field of debate by emerging and established international scholars associated with the DFG-funded Graduate Research Training Program (Graduiertenkolleg) "Konfigurationen des Films" at Goethe University Frankfurt. The contributions to the series aim to explore and expand our understanding of configurations of film in both a contemporary and historical perspective, combining film and media theory with media history to address key problems in the development of new analytical frameworks for the moving image on the move.

A Queer Serge Daney?

Marc Siegel and Kate Ince

Serge Daney is arguably the central figure in French film and television criticism of the post-war era. Starting in 1964 he wrote for the leading film journal *Cahiers du cinéma*, and was its chief editor from 1973 to 1981. He then went on to write for the daily newspaper *Libération* and to found the film magazine *Trafic*. He died of AIDS in 1992, just as the concept of queer cinema entered international film studies and just before the start of the digital era that has transformed film criticism and cinephilia. Daney's writings incorporated psychoanalytic, Marxist, post-structuralist, film, and media theory, and offer many points of connection with contemporary film and media studies. In France, Daney is acknowledged as a key influence by a broad range of philosophers, theorists, critics, and filmmakers. Despite this, his work has never been systematically translated into English, and has not received the international scholarly attention it deserves. This collection of new essays, including six contributions that have been translated from the French, investigates the contemporary relevance of Daney's work by situating critical analyses of his writings and thought alongside reflections on queer, feminist, and digital cinephilia.

It is not challenging to find generative resources in Daney's work for thinking through aesthetic and theoretical concerns in the age of digital film production, distribution, and exhibition. In the media criticism for *Libération* that formed the basis of the book *Le salaire du zappeur/The Zapper's Wage* (1988/1993), for example, Daney focused on the aesthetics and politics of television and the televisual organization and dissemination of images. Across these essays written for a daily column of the same name, he drew out both the continuities and ruptures within histories of audiovisual technologies and questions of spectatorship. Whereas the cinephile was subject to the temporal difference of the cinematic image, the television viewer (or telephile) subordinated the televisual image to the temporal logic of zapping, a process of using the remote control to spring almost instantaneously from one image to the next. Attending to the viewing of films on television, Daney highlighted questions of scale and format while also thinking through the historical implications of the younger medium in relation both to histories and aesthetics of cinema and to the political pressures of the present and future.

If Daney's comparative analyses of film and television readily lend themselves to contemporary debates within studies of digital cinema, streaming, format histories and aesthetics, post-cinema, and media archaeology, among other areas, the relevance of his work to issues of feminist and queer cinephilia might not seem as immediately apparent. Openly gay throughout his lifetime but decisively private about his homosexuality, Daney rarely touched on the subject in his approximately one thousand five hundred published articles and interviews. This is perhaps no surprise if we take as exemplary Geneviève Sellier's assessment of the climate during the formative period of *Cahiers*. She argues that the journal functioned as "a band of boys" who, in the 1950s and early 1960s, helped established film criticism as "an almost exclusively masculine activity" and advanced a "cinephilic gaze" that is "necessarily male, heterosexual, and directed toward icons, fetishes, and female sexual objects" (Sellier 2008, 28–29). The journal, of course, went through numerous phases between these early years and the later period of Daney's involvement. Along the way, it did often address some work by gay male directors like Jean Cocteau, Jean Genet, and Pier Paolo Pasolini, even if the implications of homosexuality for questions of cinephilia and cinematic aesthetics were not explicitly addressed. Besides Daney, there were also other gay male critics who remained significant to the journal and French cinephilia, including Jean Douchet (a particularly important early voice at *Cahiers*) and Jean-Claude Biette. Nevertheless, an unquestioned masculinist heteronormativity marked the core of the journal's cinephilia throughout the years of Daney's involvement.[1] Under the influence of a militant Maoist ideological perspective in the late 1960s and throughout the first part of the 1970s, *Cahiers* furthermore afforded little space for the subjective personal expressions or systematic and structural analyses of gender and sexuality characteristic of a gay and feminist criticism.[2] The journalistic environment at *Libération* in the early 1980s could not have been more different. In the path-breaking essay that opens this collection, Pierre Eugène points out that Daney's writing style changed in the last decade of his life after he left *Cahiers* to work for *Libération*, where he adopted the subjective, first-person *"je"* ("I") and abandoned the generalized *"nous"* ("we") that had previously characterized his writing. *Libération* thus represented a liberation of sorts for Daney, a context that allowed for a public reckoning with the self that may also be as characteristic of the early neoliberal moment, which developed rather differently in France (where socialist party leader François Mitterand replaced the center-right Valéry Giscard d'Estaing as President in May 1981) than in the Republican-governed US under Ronald Reagan.[3]

1   In 1967, Sylvie Pierre, one of Daney's close colleagues and future collaborators at *Trafic*, became the first woman to regularly write for *Cahiers*, "a hitherto purely masculine grouping" (Fairfax 2021, 215). In the 1970s and 1980s, she was joined by a handful of other women, including Thérèse Giraud and and Danièle Dubroux, but, as Bérènice Reynaud points out, "their witty, often acerbic, texts did not generate larger discussions on issues of feminism or sexual politics *per se*" (Reynaud 2000, 7). Among French film magazines from the 1950s to the 1980s, *Cahiers* was certainly not alone nor necessarily the most egregious with respect to a masculinist heteronormativity.

2   The journal and Daney in particular did, for example, devote attention to *Histoires d'A* (Charles Belmont and Marielle Issartel, 1973), a militant film defending a women's right to abortion. The critical emphasis, however, lay more on "revolutionary *mise en scène*" than feminist perspectives (Reynaud 2000, 7; see also Fairfax 2021, 332). In a provocative 1978 article for *Cahiers*, "Contre la nouvelle cinéphilie," Louis Skorecki evokes the latent homophilic character of male cinephilia of the early years at *Cahiers* (Skorecki 1978). Thanks to Pierre Eugène for drawing our attention to this text.

3   Reynaud points out the pressures that both Maoist ideology and the quest for generational self-consciousness had on *Cahiers* critics in the first half of

12 *Libération* was marked by the work of such activist-authors as Hélène Hazera, Guy Hocquenghem, and Michel Cressole, all of whom had previously been involved with the *Front homosexuel d'action révolutionnaire* (Homosexual Front for Revolutionary Action) and were attentive in their writing to issues of sexuality, gender, and the developing AIDS epidemic. Although Daney maintained a distance from the sexual and AIDS activism of these colleagues and refrained from the extended public critical reflection on sexuality that distinguished their important work, he nevertheless benefitted from their proximity.[4] As Eugène elaborates, it was the queer context at the newspaper that seemed to inspire Daney to write the only article in his oeuvre explicitly reflecting on homosexuality and cinematic representation, a review of Frank Ripploh's 1981 film *Taxi zum Klo* (*Taxi to the Toilet*). Significantly, Daney did not publish the text in *Libération*, but instead in the *Cahiers*—as if to interrupt and perhaps mark a distance from the heteronormative cinephilia that had shaped his intellectual development.

Since Daney almost entirely refrained from publicly addressing his homosexuality and its possible relevance to his cinephilia, his work has understandably not received much attention within queer film and media studies. There are simply too many other fascinating figures with work better primed to help us think queerly about culture, life, and sexual politics—Hocquenghem, for instance. Nevertheless, as a prominent gay critic in the predominantly heterosexual French male film culture, Daney's work contains the seductive lure of queer potential. As Andrea Inzerillo explains in his essay in this volume, it was exactly this

the 1970s, leading them to avoid the first person "I" and gravitate instead to the collective "we" (Reynaud 2000, 4). Daney's shift to the first-person singular in the 1980s can therefore also be viewed in the context of a broader rejection of or critical disappointment with this earlier ideology of collectivism.

4 Hocquenghem, who continued writing for *Libération* until 1982, was no longer a member of the paper's editorial department at the time Daney joined the staff as editor in 1981.

rich potential that motivated the organizers of Sicilia Queer Film Festival in 2012, the twentieth anniversary of Daney's death, to devote a section of their yearly event to the French critic: *Carte Postale à Serge Daney*. Their intentions were not directed at naively asserting the queerness of Daney's work as a mere result of the biographical fact of his homosexuality. Instead, they sought to use the framework of a queer film festival as a context for investigating how Daney's work could enable a rethinking of both their knowledge of cinema and their concept of queer cinema.

Beyond the queer film festival circuit, there is an academic precedent for turning to Daney to put pressure on hetero-normative conceptions of cinema and cinephilia. Geneviève Sellier and Noel Burch, for instance, discussed some of Daney's texts as an "implicit critique of the heteronormativity of the dominant cinephilia, that of *Cahiers du cinéma*" (Sellier 2018). Sellier had also argued in 2005 that Daney was the first to put his finger on and distance himself from "the obsessive masculinist principle that underlies [*Cahiers'*] cinephilia" (Sellier 2005, 69). For her part, Karen Redrobe suggests that Daney's figure of the *cinéfils* (a term he coined to link cinephilia with kinship so as to produce himself as a son of cinema) might provide a path out of the largely straight boys' club of French cinephilia. "Some versions of the *cinéfils*, including those we find in the writing of Roland Barthes or Daney, have a distinctly queer potential, often troubling normative models of relationality: homosocial com-munities meeting in the dark for pleasure, men who identify the same object as both parent and lover, and so on" (Redrobe 2015, 5). Redrobe infuses Daney's *cinéfils* with the possibilities of the *passeur*, another term Daney used late in his life to describe his work as a film critic. *Passeur* is often translated as "smuggler," but can also more generally describe one who simply passes something on as an informant or mediator. Daney used the term to refer to those other figures—solely men—who initiated ever anew his entry into the erotically charged, homosocial space of cinephilia. "Being a cinephile meant simply devouring *another* education parallel to that of the *lycée*, with the yellow *Cahiers* as the common thread and a few 'adult' *passeurs* who, with conspiratorial discretion, showed us that indeed there was a world to discover, and maybe nothing other than *the* world to live in" (Daney 2007,19, italics in original). That is Daney in his fascinating autobiographical treatise on the development of his cinephilia, "The Travelling Shot in Kapo," where he describes a cinematic initiation ritual with the relish of one titillated by participation in a secret, all-male subculture. "As for me, I immediately despised those who were too normal and sneered at the 'cinémathèque rats' we were on the verge of becoming—guilty of living cinema passionately and life by proxy....it had all the charms of a *parallel counterculture*" (Daney 2007, 19, italics in original). Whether or not Daney's *passeurs* only passed along the love for cinema or the love for the world through cinema and not, say, the erotic love for one another, his words charge this cinephilia with the sweaty, heady, guilty pleasures of all-male sex spaces.

In the discussions with Serge Toubiana that formed the basis of the posthumous book *Persévérance* (*Postcards from the Cinema*), Daney makes explicit this connection between male sex spaces and cinephilia when he suggests that cruising for sex with men and cinematic spectatorship can both function as activities that enable the production of an image.

> As soon as you see a good-looking kid in the corner—the eye moves very quickly in this type of situation—there is immediately center and perimeter, hence shot, and that makes an image: the boy's presence makes an image. That, by the way, is all I could say about everything that is of the order of erotic investment or what we were saying about character. I never identified with Cary Grant in my life, but the films in which I liked Cary Grant are the ones where his presence made an image: all the rest was organized around him. That's definitely a principle of general erotic orientation

> where eroticism is a tool and not an end. (Daney 2007, 105,
> translation modified)

Knowing that Daney did not use the term "image" lightly, this passage is truly astounding. It encourages us to acknowledge the queer potential of what has become one of Daney's key conceptual distinctions, that between the image and the visual. He produces these concepts over the course of later essays focusing on the media representation of Palestinians, Arabs, and the first Gulf War, most significantly "Before and After the Image" (Daney 1999) and "Montage Obligatory: The War, the Gulf and the Small Screen" (Daney 2006). In the former text, Daney argues that the visual is "the optical verification of a procedure of power whatever this may be (technological, political, advertising, military), a procedure which only requires, as sole commentary, a 'receiving loud and clear.' Obviously, the visual concerns the optic nerve, but for all that it is not an image. The condition *sine qua non* for there to be an image is, I think, *alterity*" (Daney 1999, 181–82, italics in original). Daney links the visual to television and advertising and to the technically perfected, slick visualization of something intended to communicate and inform quickly and efficiently. He reserves the image, on the other hand, for photography and cinema and for a temporally dense encounter with a confounding and seductive otherness. As he puts it in the later article, "as for the image—this image we loved in cinema to the point of obscenity—it … always takes place at the border of two force fields, it is meant to bear witness to a certain *otherness*; and although it always has a hard core, it always lacks something. The image is always *more and less than itself*" (Daney 2006, n.p., italics in original). As a figure of alterity, the image challenges us to contextualize it, to "*edit* it with another, with *the* other." Daney's image is both a perceptual image and the virtual image of desire produced in the face of it.

Whether or not we subscribe to Daney's distinction between the visual (of television and advertising) and the image (of cinema), it is undoubtedly the very conception of a revelatory encounter with an image, when—to use Paul Willemen's lovely formulation—"what is being seen is in excess of what is being shown" (Willemen 1994, 237), that underlies a whole tradition of French cinephilia. If we take into account Daney's remarks about cruising for sex, we must therefore acknowledge that the revelatory cinephilic encounter with an image does not simply yield a general ethical or moral position with regard to the world. Daney's image generated within and as a gay erotic encounter can reveal something quite specific about the possibilities for challenging heteronormativity, questioning gender norms, reorienting subjectivity, and stimulating unforeseen possibilities for sexual desire and pleasure.

If the *cinéfils*, the *passeur*, and the image are figures with queer potential within Daney's cinephilic trajectory, do they yield any critical value for a feminist cinephilia? What place can the *cinéfilles* claim within a cinephilia inspired by Daney? As we are unfortunately reminded time and again, gay men are not necessarily more inclined toward feminism than straight men. Indeed, as Redrobe cautions, "the *cinéfils'* view of the screen can also be rather exclusive (even the queerest of *cinéfils* tend to erase female filmmakers, spectators, and critics, if not female performers)" (Redrobe 2015, 5). Destabilizing heteronormativity and distancing oneself from dominant forms of masculinity are important critical moves that can further feminist goals, but they do not go far along the path towards a feminist cinephilia: what place do women filmmakers and female spectatorship have in Daney's cinephilic trajectory? The weekly radio show *Microfilms*, which Daney began with Brigitte Ollier in 1985, included hour-long interviews with Marguerite Duras, Agnès Varda, Claire Denis, Juliet Berto, Chantal Akerman, Marcelin Loridan-Ivens, Patricia Mazuy, Catherine Breillat, Christine Laurent, Bulle Ogier, and Dalida, as well as single episodes about cinema for the sightless ("Odile Converset, non-voyante") and the perspective of a movie theater employee ("Annick Timmermans, ouvreuse de cinema"). Daney may not have foregrounded female authorship in his writings or made observable efforts to undo the canon of male filmmakers that is all too obvious in his books' tables of contents, but his interest in certain films directed by Duras, Akerman, and Jackie Raynal is evident,[5] and Raynal and Danièle Dubroux as well as Duras wrote tributes in the special issue of *Cahiers* devoted to him in the summer of 1992.[6] A different instance of Daney's regard for women filmmakers is offered by the article he wrote for *Libération* in 1989 about the two-week old hunger strike Bulgarian filmmaker Maria Koleva had begun in protest against the failure of French TV stations to broadcast her documentaries. (Koleva, whose acclaimed autobiographical documentary *L'Etat de bonheur...permanent* (1982) and series of films about the actor and theater director Antoine Vitez whom Daney praises highly in his article, had lived and worked in France since 1971: her 1989 hunger strike lasted forty-five days.)

By combining reflections about Daney and his work with discussions of queer, feminist and digital cinephilia, we both stay close to Daney and seemingly move away from him. In doing so, our goal is to foster a dialogue between the singular, inspiring work of a fascinating film critic and the powerful perspectives in queer and feminist film and media studies. We are guided by the speculative promise that their proximity can yield a mutual enrichment. Thanks to a network grant by the United Kingdom's Arts and Humanities Research Council, we were able to host

---

5   In the interview with Bill Krohn conducted in New York in 1977 and reprinted in French at the start of *La Maison cinema et le monde* 1, Daney names Raynal's *Deux fois* (1968), Akerman's *Je, tu, il, elle* (1974), and Duras's *Le Camion* (1977) as the three "films de femmes" that have most impressed him (Daney 2001, 28).

6   In hers, Raynal, who ran the legendary Bleecker Street Cinema in New York with her husband Sid Geffen between 1973 and 1985 and continued running it after Geffen's death until forced out by its developer in 1990, recalls Daney dubbing himself an "acrobat" of the Great Circus of Cinema (*Grand Cirque du Cinéma*), and tells the story of *Cahiers du cinéma*'s first New York Week, which took place at the Bleecker Street Cinema in November 1977, and which Daney followed up with visits to four or five other US cities that Raynal had arranged for him (Raynal 1992, 17).

18   workshops over the course of three years in Paris (organized
by Pierre Eugène), Mainz (organized by Marc Siegel), and Birmingham (organized by Kate Ince) that addressed contemporary
scholarly, critical, and curatorial perspectives on Daney and
queer and feminist cinephilia. At the third workshop in Birmingham, the last to take place, So Mayer and Selina Robertson,
London-based core members of the queer feminist curatorial
collective Club des Femmes, co-established by Robertson and
Sarah Wood in 2007, presented their UK-wide touring program of
feminist films "Revolt, She Said: Women and Film after '68," whose
title features a quotation from Julia Kristeva to complement the
French name of the collective itself. The nine feature films in the
tour (accompanied by eight shorts) were Czech, Swedish, West
German, French, British, and American, and spanned the period
from 1966, the year of Věra Chytilovà's "proto-feminist classic"
Daisies to 1991 and Prathiba Parmar's *A Place of Rage*, "on the role
of queer black women in the civil rights movement and beyond,
thus affirming the tour as addressing the full extent of second-
wave feminist history from 1968 to the beginning of the third
wave in 1992" (Mayer and Robertson 2020, 77). This tour, programmed by Club des Femmes with the UK's Independent Cinema
Office and funded by the British Film Institute, was the most
ambitious initiative yet undertaken by the collective, and over the
spring and summer of 2019[7] comprised "ninety-nine screenings
at thirty cinemas nationwide, totaling 2,346 overall admissions"
(Mayer and Robertson 2020, 79), even though CdF had had little
previous profile outside London. The direct engagements with
queer film history made by the "Revolt, She Said" tour, indicated
by the "The Q with the F" title of Mayer and Robertson's workshop presentation which appears here in essay form, were the
programming of Parmar's *A Place of Rage* and of Greta Schiller's
multi-award-winning documentary *Before Stonewall* (1984),
which, unlike many of the tour's films, "had and has a transnational cinematic exhibition history thanks to the emergence

7   May 6 to August 31 (Mayer and Robertson 2020, 79).

of queer film festivals" (Mayer and Robertson 2020, 79). *Before Stonewall* was screened in a collaboration with the Leeds Queer Film Festival where it was introduced by former ACT UP New York member and academic Monica Pearl.

Queer film festivals and the cinephilia inseparable from them were also reflected upon at the Birmingham workshop by Theresa Heath-Ellul, whose essay here offers a summary of literature on the short but crowded history of queer film festivals, arguing that they "have contributed to the development of communal, interactive, non-hierarchical modes of viewing." It also considers the role—both live and online—of the clip reel as an embodiment of queer cinephilic practices. Quoting Skadi Loist and Leanne Dawson's estimation "that there are currently around 270 queer film festivals operating globally" (Dawson and Loist 2018 in Heath-Ellul 2022) and adopting Chris Straayer's approach to cinephilia as a "material [practice] initiated and constituted in the space of the auditorium," Heath-Ellul maintains that since the first gay film festivals in the late 1970s:

> Queer film festivals [have] provided a space for a more visible, communal and public practice which [has] thrived on the extra-textual dissemination of subjective knowledge and the star-related gossip which Marc Siegel, Jackie Stacey and [Patricia] White have identified as integral to queer cinephilias.

The prominence of the AIDS epidemic in queer lives in the second half of the 1980s and early 1990s—a greater number of gay male than lesbian artists and activists died from the disease (Cyril Collard, Guy Hocquenghem, and Hervé Guibert in France as well as Daney; Derek Jarman in the UK, and Jack Smith and Arthur J. Bressan Jr. in the US, among many others)—meant a visibility of gay male filmmaking that carried across, Heath-Ellul suggests, in the "over-presence" of such work and the associated cinephilic subjective knowledge and gossip in the New Queer Cinema of the early 1990s. But as Heath-Ellul also points out, Patricia White describes the significance of the lesbian clip reel as a form in the decade and argues that it "heralded a 'coming out of the closet' for lesbian cinephilia" (White 1999, 31, in Heath-Ellul 2023).

The final contributor to "Queer and Feminist Cinephilia" in Birmingham was Girish Shambu, who as critic and blogger since 2004 has perhaps done more than any other to keep conversation and debate about cinephilia going in the digital age, in concentrated form in his recently reissued 2014 book *The New Cinephilia* (Shambu 2020). Speaking to the title of his manifesto, which had just appeared in February 2019 in a "manifestoes" issue of *Film Quarterly* assembled by B. Ruby Rich (72 (3)), "For a New Cinephilia," Shambu expanded on the ten features of the old and new cinephilias he succinctly contrasts in the manifesto by focusing on the "tactics of the everyday" that might break down the remaining elements of the mythic, celebratorily aesthetic, white male heterosexual old cinephilia. Auteurism was squarely in his sights. Although he conceded that it can be benign and that "there is nothing necessarily male essentialist about auteurism" (Shambu 2019, 33), he proposed that certain male auteur directors need not be viewed at all by those supporting the new cinephilia—a tactic of refusal—that its second tactic be to "repurpose" the concept of the auteur, and its third to redirect that same concept, since women filmmakers' readier acknowledgement of the collective and the collaborative is far more in tune with the new cinephilia's values.

Our goal with both the project's workshops and this collection of essays has been to lay the groundwork for a network of researchers interested in Daney and feminist and queer cinephilia and open to considering the tension and potential that emerge when these subjects are placed in relation to one another. By uniting in one book a selection of contributions from these events with new and related texts, we intend both to document this exchange and to further a continued critical engagement with Daney and with contemporary practices in feminist and queer cinephilia.

Daney's death in 1992 occurred during the same summer that B. Ruby Rich's article introducing the concept of New Queer Cinema appeared in the *Village Voice* and *Sight and Sound*. The birth of queer studies in the academy in the US and UK found echoes in France later in the 1990s in seminar series such as the one run by Sam Bourcier,[8] but never took hold to the same extent as in the US, and the translation—literal and cultural—of central queer studies texts (Bourcier, notably, translated key essays by Monique Wittig and Teresa de Lauretis) would be significantly delayed by the difficult encounter of gender theory and gender studies with the conceptualization of citizenship adhered to by French Republicanism.[9] Despite never being involved with any form of gay or feminist activism, Daney wanted it to be known that his death was of AIDS, "so that we don't get used to it," as Serge Toubiana wrote in the first paragraph of the introduction to the issue of *Cahiers du cinéma* dedicated to him in July/August 1992.[10] Even though it wasn't expressed until the final weeks of his life, Daney's desire to make it known for posterity that he had died of the syndrome that had taken the lives of so many others, including scores of gay men, is an acknowledgement of the necessity of agitating publicly against a homophobic status quo. This desire is just one further indicator of the tension and potential explored by *Serge Daney and Queer Cinephilia* (as research project and collection of essays).

8   For information on the seminar series, see Sam Bourcier, ed., *Q comme queer: les séminaires Q du Zoo (1996–1997)*. Paris: Les Cahiers Gai Kitsch Camp, 1998.

9   Judith Butler's *Gender Trouble: Feminism and the Subversion of Identity*, for example, only appeared in French in 2005, as *Trouble dans le genre: le féminisme et la subversion de l'identité*. Paris: Editions de l'Amsterdam. In secular French Republicanism, each individual citizen is equal in their abstract neutrality, and the state does not recognize or interact with communities or groups united by racial, gender, ethnic, religious, or linguistic identity. Identity politics of the kind familiar from the US and UK is referred to as *communautarisme* and is viewed as a threat to the Republican tradition actualized (since 1958) in the Fifth Republic. French resistance to gender studies and queer theory is charted by Bruno Perreau in *Queer Theory: The French Response*. Stanford: Stanford University Press, 2016.

10   *Cahiers du cinéma* 458: 4.

We would like to thank Judith Mayne and Patricia White for their advice and comments over the course of this research project. We also thank Vinzenz Hediger, Verena Mund, and the members of the Configurations of Film Research Training Program at the Goethe University in Frankfurt am Main for their support of this publication project. Johanna Böther provided essential assistance with the formatting of the manuscript. Finally, we appreciate the productive comments by two anonymous peer reviewers.

References

Bourcier, Sam, ed. 1998. *Q comme queer: les séminaires Q du Zoo (1996–1997)*. Paris: Les Cahiers Gai Kitsch Camp.

Butler, Judith. 1990. *Gender Trouble: Feminism and Subversion of Identity*. London and New York: Routledge.

———. 2005. *Trouble dans le genre: Le féminisme et la subversion de l'identité*. Paris: Editions de l'Amsterdam.

Daney, Serge. 1993. *Le salaire du zappeur*. Paris: P.O.L.

———. 1999. "Before and After the Image." Translated by Melissa McMahon. *Discourse* 21 (1): 181–90.

Daney, Serge. 2007. *Postcards from the Cinema*. Translated by Paul Douglas Grant. Oxford and New York: Berg.

———. 2006. "Montage Obligatory." Translated by Laurent Kretzschmar and *Rouge*. *Rouge* 8. Accessed October 29, 2022. http://rouge.com.au/8/montage.html.

Dawson, Leanne, and Skadi Loist. 2018. "Queer/ing Film Festivals: History, Theory, Impact." *Studies in European Cinema* 15 (1): 1–24. Accessed October 29, 2022. https://doi.org/10.1080/17411548.2018.1442901.

Fairfax, Daniel. 2021. *The Red Years of Cahiers du Cinéma (1968–1973): Volume 1: Ideology and Politics*. Amsterdam: Amsterdam University Press.

Mayer, So, and Selina Robertson. 2020. "Revolt, She Said: Queer Feminist Film Curation and the Freedom to Revolt." *Film Studies* 22: 76–97.

Perreau, Bruno. 2016. *Queer Theory: The French Response*. Stanford: Stanford University Press.

Redrobe [Beckman], Karen. 2015. "Animating the *Cinéfils*: Alain Resnais and the Cinema of Discovery." *Cinema Journal* 54 (4): 1–25.

Reynaud, Bérénice. 2000. "Introduction: *Cahiers du Cinéma*: 1973–1978." *Cahiers du Cinéma Volume 4: 1973–1978 History, Ideology, Cultural Struggle*, edited by David Wilson, 1–44. London and New York: Routledge.

Sellier, Geneviève. 2005. "Gender Studies et études filmiques." *Cahiers du Genre* 38: 63–85.

———. 2008. *Masculine Singular: French New Wave Cinema*. Durham and London: Duke University Press.

———. 2018. Email message to Marc Siegel, October 5, 2018.

Shambu, Girish. 2014 and 2020. *The New Cinephilia*, Montreal: Caboose Books.

———. 2019. "For a New Cinephilia." *Film Quarterly* 72 (3): 32–34.

Skorecki, Louis. 1978. "Contre la nouvelle cinéphilie." *Cahiers du cinéma* 293: 31–52.

Toubiana, Serge. 1992. "Preface." *Cahiers du cinéma* 458: 4.

White, Patricia. 1999. *Uninvited: Classical Hollywood Cinephilia and Lesbian Representability*. Bloomington: Indiana University Press.

Willemen, Paul. 1994. "Through the Glass Darkly: Cinephilia Reconsidered." In *Looks and Frictions: Essays in Cultural Studies and Film Theory*, 223–57. Bloomington and Indianapolis: Indiana University Press and BFI.

HOMOSEXUALITY

MAOISM

QUEER

AIDS

1

Serge Daney and Homosexuality: A Matter of Smuggling

Pierre Eugène

This essay retraces, in Serge Daney's private history (biography and personal texts) and public history (published texts), his relationship with his own homosexuality and that of others. Daney considered his sexuality a strictly private matter, even if he was able to evoke it publicly when speaking of the HIV disease which killed him. His personal history shows that homosexuality does not constitute a particular key of interpretation for him. During his (Maoist) political years, and even at his liberating arrival at the daily newspaper *Libération*, with homosexual militants, homosexuality stays secondary if not evacuated. Nevertheless, we can find in Daney's writings a defense of the

singularity of minority lifestyles, against group representation. Hence, there is a paradoxical defense of homosexuality in Daney's texts and declarations, which has to do with the experience of otherness in cinema, against any retranscription of it into the social.

This article will give a historical and biographical overview of the subject of homosexuality in Daney's life and work. I will rely extensively on private archives and more than seventeen private notebooks written by Daney during his life, which I was able to consult while doing my PhD research.[1]

The lack of Daney's private documents prior to 1964 and between 1965 and mid-1967 actually prevents us from knowing precisely when and how Daney experienced his first homosexual encounter. But, since Daney has—like all cinephiles—a strong passion for lists, he drew up a summary of his lovers in the 1970s. At the end of his life, in *Persévérance* (translated into English as *Postcards from the Cinema*), Daney traces his first love back to his first days at primary school, when he met Michel, a child of his age (whom he will not continue to see as an adult):

> I thought that I was perhaps completely in love only once in my life, and it was with Michel: we were about seven or eight years old. I would go play at his house on rue Keller, and we would play the most miserable games without toys, just codes that we made up. I never again had that feeling of time stopping, of a remaining abundance: there's just one person there who fulfills all the possible roles and horizons. As

---

1   The documents are not only unpublished, but unknown even by Daney's friends. Daney's cousin, Arlette Bonaud kindly let me consult them when I was doing my PhD on Daney's work and life, published under the title *Exercices de relectures, Serge Daney 1962–1982* (Éditions du Linteau, 2023). She died suddenly in February 2020, and I wish to dedicate this text to her memory, with all my friendship and gratitude.

they say in the cantata: *Ich habe genug*, which means "I have
enough." (Daney 2007, 48)

In 1964, in the first available private notebook in existence, when
Daney is 19 to 20 years old, the only possible mention of homosexuality is in a parenthesis, that of an "unknown (cute) boy" in
a group of cinephiles. His sexuality seems to have been more
present in his travels than in his Parisian life. When Daney starts
his "poor man's travels" (in his own words) at the end of the 1960s,
those of a young hippie globe-trotter, his notebooks recount
without any ambiguity or expressing any shame—but rather with
the curiosity of the traveler who sees them as equal to all the
other details of the journey—his encounters with boys, sometimes indulging in casual prostitution in the same way André Gide
or William Burroughs could have mentioned in their works. Daney
would speak of this to Serge Toubiana in 1992:

> When traveling poor it was easy to meet boys on the street,
> whether in the Arab world, Sub-Saharan Africa, or Asia.
> And since they had to sell themselves as half-prostitutes,
> they served as guides … Arab boys are in general pretty
> bad lovers, but they are very touching because they have
> the same colonial culture as we do, and their relationship
> to knowledge is real … We would read Coleridge together in
> bed. It's Gide-like in the sense that sexually it's a little over-
> whelming.[2] (Daney 2007, 100)

After May '68, Daney, who was not a full member of the editorial
board of *Cahiers du cinéma* (he was more a regular freelancer),
would make a lot of trips. First a long one—which ends with
tuberculosis—in India between July and December 1968, and
then a long journey in Sub-Saharan Africa, where he would have
some casual sexual encounters with men. We have to imagine

2   Daney's mention of his Arab lovers echoes the problematic—colonialist and
     racist—perspectives of French homosexuals and Left intellectuals about
     Arab men in the seventies (something that Daney was also critically aware
     of). It has notably been analyzed by Shepard, 2017, in particular 119–22.

 the context of these hippie-style travels: Daney and his friends have very little money; they take advantage of all the encounters available; they sleep and eat in the cheapest places possible; they barter clothes and objects. They feel closer to local people than to tourists. In these hippie-style journeys, the friends want to "carpe the diem" (as Daney says), get in touch with the people, try all the local foods and some of the local drugs (an important part of the trip experience), and do all this with the intention of recording it in writings and discussing it among themselves. Daney, a completely addictive writer, would collect his thoughts and experiences in many of his notebooks (for this Africa trip, he wrote more than 150 handwritten pages). The Africa trip is recorded in one notebook in the form of a big dictionary with various entries ("Chapeau," "Abdullahi," "Oran" etc.): the left page devoted to the text, right page to the footnotes, with footnotes to the footnotes! Daney's writings take the form of self-analysis (about himself) and "wild" psychoanalysis (about others), following the fresh discovery of Lacan's and Freud's writings. It is within this context that Daney describes his relationships with men, friendly and sexual relationships, whether he travels alone or with friends (in Africa a group of three heterosexual men and a girl), who are aware of all these relationships.

In his "travel dictionary," Daney takes note of the specular proximity with the boys he meets, in which homosexuality seems for him in harmony with research into himself:

> I have to question this recent fixation to see any teenager that I am seducing as an alter ego even if—quite naturally—a certain number of conditions, points in common always allow the same type of seduction (by words, by knowledge). Why? Regret at not having been seduced at their age, at having gone through puberty alone, and desire to simultaneously be me at 26 and me at 16 years old. A new turn of self-love,

which offers itself the shortest detour (via someone else) and
enjoys taking this route.[3]

Between narcissism and encounters with others, the encounter with the desired double that a boy personifies takes the path of a *"detour,"* a kind of stroll, both a geographical and temporal journey as well as the search for a *distance,* an alterity at the heart of the desire for the same. In fact, men are described carefully in Daney's stories: singular beings with mysterious reactions, they are part of an entire landscape, discovered at the same time as their cultural, geographical, and social backgrounds. Meetings with men, experimenting with drugs, and eating local meals represent in Daney's travels many different ways to explore a country concretely. Of course, Daney's relationships with these men—and more generally with locals—remain somehow, in a certain respect, unequal and "colonialist." Without expressing his otherworldliness to others, Daney questions himself about his own "European reflexes." He measures the "distance" and the alterity between his status as a foreigner and his daily local life.

Even if age seems not to have been an obsession for Daney, the boys he met on his journeys were teenagers. It would be wrong, however, to say that Daney was a pedophile: his relationships sometimes included some teenagers and most of the time younger men. Around 1973, in Paris, Daney would meet (among others) two men in their twenties with whom he would start a serious relationship: Walter, an Afro-American man who was studying in France, and Victor, a Sino-Thai working in his uncle's restaurant. He met them both in "tearooms" (*tasses* in French). In 1988, Daney also tried to commit to a certain "Frédéric" and relates in the notes compiled in *L'Exercice a été profitable, Monsieur*: "I started to doubt my enduring capacity to see movies a few years ago, at *Libération*. At a moment when, for the first time in my life, I considered (and tried) to live with someone. An

---

3   My translation; from now on, all translations are mine if unspecified.

idea that had never crossed my mind before (maybe a little with Dany)" (Daney 1993, 105).

If some of Daney's sexual acts are now, if not considered reprehensible, at least disapproved of, we must look back to a time when attraction to teenagers did not totally separate sex acts with minors from those between adults, unlike today when sex acts with minors are severely condemned while those between adult men are slowly being accepted and normalized. Until 1981, when the decrees punishing homosexuality were abolished in France, political repression in fact put all "types" of homosexuals in the same category. On the other hand, in the 1970s, the Front Homosexuel d'Action Révolutionnaire (FHAR) activists gave equal support to sexual liberation for women, homosexuals, and young people, without any prejudice towards the great range of "sexual perversions." The best example probably remains the "Trois milliards de pervers" ("Three billion perverts") issue of the review *Recherches* in March 1973. The newspaper *Libération*, CERFI (a Centre for Psychoanalysis founded by Félix Guattari), and a large number of intellectuals were in solidarity with these revolutionaries of sexual liberation, and considered with goodwill and interest, for example, the philosophical work of René Scherer (incidentally the brother of Éric Rohmer) or Tony Duvert's novels. Daney read these works (among his huge quantity of readings), as well as *Homosexual Desire* by Guy Hocquenghem, co-founder of the FHAR; but never committed himself to sexual activism, choosing rather to stay on the more austere side of Marxist-Leninist Maoism, where sexuality was never a subject. Nevertheless, he kept living in the climate of freedom that emerged after May '68, benevolent and attentive to all possible experiences (the experience of drugs was just one of these).

In private, Daney constantly questioned his sexuality, analyzing his homosexuality as well as his "obsessive neurosis." This last issue was analyzed in several articles and associated with cinephilia and some filmmakers, like Howard Hawks! (Daney 1983b).

On the other hand, the subject of homosexuality does not appear anywhere in the articles. But in private, Daney did not reject his homosexual sensibility. He recounts for instance his "squalido-comic" adventures (an expression of his own) when looking for a place outside to make love during a casual encounter. He also recounts his frequenting of "tasses" before meetings of the editorial board of *Cahiers* in the 1970s. When he sees Eisenstein's *Battleship Potemkin* again (which he had not seen since school), he notes in private "the sensuality of the repressed masses (especially the sailors under the tarpaulin)." He also invents, with his inimitable sense for puns, the delightful expression "tasse struggle" ("lutte des tasses"), parodying the "class struggle" ("luttes des classes"). Nevertheless, Daney stays at some distance from the "tasse struggle," and observes, delighted but without participating at all himself, the 1 May Labor march, in which the crazy FHAR and the Gazolines' group[4] make a fuss.

Politics and Privacy

Daney's private life generally has no echo in his published articles. The same goes for homosexuality: no personal mention, no sign that this type of sexuality concerns him *personally*, until the 1980s. In 1971, in one of his notebooks, Daney draws links between his own name (Daney), *The Damned* (*Les Damnés*, in French) by Luchino Visconti, as well as the condition of homosexuals. He writes about *Death in Venice* (Daney 1971–1972), which had been released, and also about *The Go-Between* by Joseph Losey (2022, 127–29)[5]: two films where a young teenager faces the

---

4   The Gazolines' group [1972–1974] emerged from the FHAR. Founded by Maud Molyneux, Patrick Bertaux, and Paquita Paquin, it was constituted by transvestites of both sexes. The Gazolines, during political demonstrations, shouted outrageous queer slogans such as "proletarians of all countries, caress yourselves!" or "makeup is a way of life," scandalizing the "serious" militants and even some of the FHAR's militants themselves.

5   Originally published in *Cahiers du cinéma* 231, August-September 1971. If unspecified, the title of the article is the title of the film criticized.

 desires of adults and interferes with them. These films could have been an opportunity to study and question (homo)sexuality. But Daney (as well as Jean-Pierre Oudart, the co-author of the article on *Death in Venice*) chose to attack the bourgeois presuppositions of the films in a very hermetic text, with semiological and political concepts influenced by Barthes, Lacan, and Derrida. Daney and Oudart do question desire in Visconti's fiction, but to invoke the "denial" of the bourgeoisie's desire toward the proletariat in order to deconstruct the figure of authorship in modern cinema.

The first article in which Daney refers distinctly to homosexuality dates back to 1969: an article about *The Staircase* by Stanley Donen held in poor esteem by Daney, who explains that the film does not break (stylistically or thematically) with Donen's previous works. Donen is only, says Daney "moving from the (already ambivalent) theme of friendship to the more direct theme of homosexuality" (Daney 2022, 111).[6] This critique is part of a more general attack against Hollywood cinema, which is accused of not reconsidering its own conventional and outdated forms. Daney ends this short article with these words:

> That said, it may be that homosexuality is still a taboo subject. And so we see the *use* of such a film: to return the seen to the already seen [*déjà-vu*], to say that a [gay] couple is always a couple and that those people are indeed human and unhappy. Didn't we know that? Any film that gives such a feeling of regained security deserves to pass as a masterpiece.

The homosexual issue thus appears here as if homosexuality were absolutely unproblematic, a non-subject, nothing relevant. In 1969, for Daney and the *Cahiers* team, a film must be "revolutionary," must provoke the audience and shake its certainties. In presenting homosexuality as something "already known," Donen's film makes it acceptable and "safe" for his

6   Originally published in *Cahiers du cinéma* 217, November 1969.

public. Daney's critique is less concerned with homosexuality's representation than with how Donen's film comforts its audience.

Most of the time, Daney does not analyze the queer situations or queer themes shown in a film. For example, when he writes about Pasolini's *Theorem* (*Teorema*, 1968), Daney does not mention the son's homosexuality, but studies only the hermeneutic structure of the film (2022, 101–4).[7] The same, later, goes for *Pigsty* (*Porcile*, 1969) (2022, 108–9).[8] Similarly, several years later, when he chronicles Bill Daughton's *Corner of the Circle* (1975), a film that describes a "homosexual relationship which comes to a sudden end" (2022, 196–98)[9] in its own words, Daney, after this short summary, displays interest only in the uncommon use of the voiceover. Writing about Jean Genet's *Un chant d'amour* (1975), Daney starts his article by saying that after this movie "most films with 'love' in the title are likely to be seen for what they are: a sham" (2022, 175).[10] But his article is only concerned with the voyeuristic look of the spectator.

There is therefore no particular angle taken on homosexuality in Daney's film studies. The reason for this undoubtedly lies in the collective state of mind of the *Cahiers*. Daney has often referred to using the inclusive "we" (and not the first person singular) when writing his articles for the review. This "we" was an effect of the group dynamic. The *Cahiers* team was a kind of family, based exclusively upon male cinephilia. A similar but different "we" was also required by the political context of the 1970s and the engagement of the *Cahiers* in Maoïsm, which involved unity, a collective way of thinking and organizing, and the cardinal notion of the "masses," all of this opposed to any attempt at individualism or intimate introspection.

7   "Le desert rose", originally published in *Cahiers du cinéma* 212, May 1969.
8   Originally published in *Cahiers du cinéma* 217, November 1969.
9   Originally published in *Cahiers du cinéma* 273, January-February 1977.
10 Originally published in *Cahiers du cinéma* 264, February 1976.

The *Cahiers* Environment

If Daney's sexuality doesn't appear in his articles, it was nevertheless also not an obsession in private: as for his travels,
sexuality was a part of life that was crucial but not central. On
December 26, 1973, becoming aware that he will turn thirty in the
year ahead, Daney writes for himself in one of his notebooks:

> This "start in life" requires that I grab the problems of SEX
> (homo) and MONEY (which is missing) by the horns (not just
> via verbose theorization) in such a way that my relationships
> with the few beings I know will not be able to change (around
> the age of 40).

At the same time that Daney wanted to tackle his so called "sex
problem" and as trying out a complicated personal life with his
boyfriends, the editorial board of the *Cahiers du cinéma* was going
through some very difficult times. After its period of extreme
politicization, the *Cahiers* took account in September 1973 of the
disastrous consequences of its militant strategy, including the
failure of the Revolutionary Cultural Front launched in August.
Economically, the magazine was spent. Only very long political
texts were printed in the last issues, without any images, with no
link to cinema. The print run was minimal, and subscribers had
deserted it. This morose assessment lead to the departure of
Jean-Louis Comolli and Jean Narboni. They give the editorial lead
to Daney and Serge Toubiana. In order to get the *Cahiers* back on
its feet, but without wanting to abandon its political line completely, Daney and Toubiana would form alliances with politicized
Maoist groups. One common fight would be the "anti-retro"
campaign, against movies (like *The Night Porter*, 1974, by Liliana
Cavani or *Lacombe Lucien*, 1974, by Louis Malle) that were accused
of promoting a so-called "sexo-fascism" and falsifying history.
But the sexual issue itself was abandoned in favor of a Marxist-
Leninist revolutionary-style ideological attack. In this conflict, the
Cahiers allied with a subgroup of UCF-ML (of which Alain Badiou
was one of the leaders), which belonged to the "dogma" trend,

"dogma" meaning dogmatic and rather austere Marxist-Leninist theoreticians. They opposed another group they called the "Spontex Maos" (Spontex like the sponge brand), which was trying to provoke a "spontaneous" and provocative liberation of bodies and minds coming from the masses themselves. The "Spontex Mao" would create the newspaper *Tout* (meaning "everything": its slogan was "What we want: everything!") and would rally to the defense of minorities (feminists, immigrants, gendered minorities…)[11]. Guy Hocquenghem would be close to them at times.

Oddly, the *Cahiers* chose the "dogma" route, which completely obstructed the individual expression of desires. Partly because of their love of Jacques Lacan and Karl Marx, partly because of their political schisms, the *Cahiers* team would remain opposed for some time (between 1973 and 1976) to the writings of Deleuze and Guattari, including the *Anti-Oedipus*, that manifesto for the liberation of desire. On that matter, they were following Jacques Rancière, who broke with Althusserism at the beginning of the 1970s on account of his Maoism and would continuously attack Deleuze from then on. On Daney's part, it was only at the end of 1977, after reading Deleuze and Claire Parnet's *Dialogues*, that he would totally break with his Maoist convictions and reconsider his past, writing in his diary:

> Extraordinary liberation after reading the Deleuze-Parnet *Dialogues* (as previously, on an overcast afternoon in the Jardin des Plantes, *Rhizome*—except that no pink panther did follow then). I really want to forget—without too much drama—these last five or six years and their endless resentment and bitterness. And this time I've done it, under duress (I tried to write without the verb 'to be' and without the

11 Manus McGrogan submitted in the University of Portsmouth, in August 2010, a Phd thesis on this subject, titled: "*Tout!* in context 1968–1973: French radical press at the crossroads of far left, new movements and counterculture".

asphyxiating little letter 'I,' but didn't manage more than five lines).

This personal liberation really took effect (at least for a while) when Daney joined the editorial board of *Libération* in 1981. The main explanation for the discrepancy between Daney's public and private life (his articles on the one hand and his private writings and sex life on another) is therefore linked to the political positioning of the *Cahiers,* as well to the relationships of the members of the *Cahiers* team.

If we go back in time to the 1960s, Jean Douchet was the only out homosexual on the *Cahiers* board (in 1964, Daney mentions in one notebook a group discussion where Douchet recounts "his homosexual experiences" to him and some friends). Greatly appreciated among the cinephiles and by Daney and his friends in 1964, Douchet had also been the "official" recruiter of young critics (only men, of course) for the *Cahiers*. Jean-Claude Biette and Louis Skorecki, but also Jean Narboni and Jean-Louis Comolli were all initially approached by Douchet, who recounts inviting Daney to write in the *Cahiers* when he was 18 (Daney declined, not feeling ready yet[12]). The situation of Daney in the 1960s–1970s *Cahiers* is actually quite comparable to Douchet's, who recalls this in 2013 when he is interviewed on the subject of his own homosexuality:

> I never hid my homosexuality, which at the time was unusual. Everyone knew it and I even made sure everyone knew it so that they could leave me alone … Of course, I had some reservations about homosexuality, quite logical at the time, but no hostility to it … The *Cahiers* cinephilia was a group cinephilia with its own coherence, the "politics of *Cahiers*." Our "auteur theory" exempted us from looking at each

---

12   Daney would start to write in the *Cahiers* in 1964, after Rivette's famous "putsch" at a moment when Douchet had left with Rohmer.

other's private lives, since they had nothing to do with the cinema.[13] (Douchet 2013)

I don't know how much the *Cahiers* team knew of Daney's sexuality. Many of his friends seem to have discovered it by chance, long after knowing him. In 1974, in one of his notebooks, Daney refers to the "brand image of his double life" in the *Cahiers*, and remarks: "I need a Tadzio to positively pass on my homosexuality to the public." In the review, the only other homosexual with whom Daney would be really close was Jean-Claude Biette [1942–2003]. The two met in 1964 but really became friends in the early 1970s. A reserved filmmaker and brilliant, extraordinary critic, Biette, like Daney, was also very discreet about his sexuality. Some of Daney's and Biette's epistolary exchanges reveal them to be "accomplices in homosexuality."

Liberation at *Libération*

In May 1981, Daney left the *Cahiers* for the newspaper *Libération,* invited by its editor-in-chief Serge July. Daney started to write in *Libération* just as July relaunched the newspaper after the election of the new French President François Mitterrand, promoting Daney to director of the newspaper's new cinema section (Daney would then make a reluctant departure from the cinema section to become an editorial writer from 1986 to 1991). His arrival at *Libération* was felt as a "liberation," as he himself put it. In his writings, Daney abandons the collective and familial "we" he used in the *Cahiers* for the first person singular, as he later related to Toubiana in *Persévérance*:

> I quickly realized that it was easier to write "I" at *Libération*, and above all that I had an enormous backlog of writing.

13   He also recounts: "I never have had a problem facing up to my homosexuality. It always seems to me obvious and natural. … [when I was a teenager] I kept 'my' secret without feeling any culpability. I accepted my homosexuality; better, I needed it. It was not in me, it was me."

Everything I should have written in the previous ten years finally came out. I should also say that the film department I managed to create was 80% homosexual, which made a huge difference... —[Toubiana speaking of "Prudish *Cahiers*..."]— Yes, disembodied. There was a sort of coming out. ... But there was no longer any ideal fraternity, it was way too uncontrollable because the people were really very peculiar. (Daney 2007, 116–17)

If arriving at *Liberation* was for Daney a "liberation," it is because *Libération* was at first a new, blank space for him, which wasn't linked to a tradition or a legacy (unlike the *Cahiers*' theoretical and cinematic legacy, quite a heavy superego to deal with). Secondly, the history of *Libération* itself has a part in Daney's "liberation." Daney said to Toubiana that he brought together an 80% homosexual cinema team, but in fact, when he arrived at the newspaper, the team was partly constituted by the former "television department," created some years prior to Daney's arrival. This television department was led by a great bunch of nonconformist homosexuals and transsexuals, coming from or linked to the "Spontex Mao" groups, Situationists, FHAR, the Gazolines... They were indeed too singular to make a coherent group at *Libération,* or to accept Daney easily (the testimonies agree about the "heckling" Daney underwent from the team on his arrival). They are evoked in *Persévérance*:

> It was a lively place for people like Michel Cressole, Hélène Hazera, or Guy Hocquenghem, who fearlessly carried out work of cultural agitation, furiously and provocatively. The newspaper was theirs by right. I added to that a serious cinephilia, but written less seriously. (Daney 2007, 117)

If Daney describes his "coming out" in *Persévérance*, it is mostly because *Libération's* team allowed him to assume a subjectivity: to regain his own singularity, meaning also to become visible. Daney always claimed personal discretion, and described in *Persévérance* the way he vanished into the landscape. If one observes Daney's body in film and photographic images,[14] it is undeniable that his relationship to his own image, his own visibility, was not simple. We can notice this, for example, in an old photograph taken by his mother at the beach when he was a child, a photograph showed by him to Elias Sanbar in a filmed dialogue about photography (*Conversation Nord-Sud: Daney/Sanbar*, Simone Bitton et Catherine Poitevin, 1993). Here is a very short excerpt of the dialogue where Daney describes this image:

> All the family photos of my childhood, taken by my mother with a camera she did not know how to use at all, are shaky photos, lopsided and so on. I think that she herself had a very big problem about being in front of a camera, which she passed on to me; this picture is our common origin in relation to images, for her and myself.

Libération is therefore for Daney a way to appear, and to do so in front of a new audience. In this new context, his relationship to homosexuality changed for sure. And when a good part of the editorial team of *Libération* was sent to Los Angeles in 1984 to follow the Olympic Games, Daney would chronicle them from a gay bar, describing the reactions of the consumers in front of the television while ABC broadcast the games (Daney 2002, 930–31)[15]. But he does it *from the outside,* without mentioning his own belonging to this community. On the contrary, he qualifies the "gays" at Greg's to be television "viewers" [*téléspectateurs*], opposing them to himself as a "cinephile." Daney seems so far from the people he describes—a real stranger—that an average reader can even ask himself why he went into this particular bar!

14   I analyzed Daney and his image in Eugene 2012.

15   "Les 'Gays' fêtent l'ouverture sans cérémonie", originally published in *Libération*, July 30, 1984.

An Average but Singular Way of Life

Beginning at *Libération,* Daney would write the single article in his output explicitly interrogating the issue of homosexual identity and lifestyle. Although he wrote in *Liberation* almost every day for two years after his arrival in May 1981, Daney did not totally break with the *Cahiers.* He was still mentioned in the editorial board, writing from time to time. The Cannes Film Festival, in 1982 and 1983, would combine the teams of the review and the newspaper, and Louella Interim from *Libération* (Marc Raynal, also using the pseudonyms "Maud Molineux" for fashion and "Dora Forbes" for literature) would even write some articles for the *Cahiers.* In this context, where Daney wrote full-time at *Libération* but stayed in touch with the *Cahiers,* he would publish in the 336 issue (May 1982) an article that to me seems like an open letter addressed to his former comrades.

Daney's article is about *Taxi zum Klo* (1981) by Frank Ripploh. A milestone in the history of queer cinema, *Taxi zum Klo* was written, produced, directed, and performed by Ripploh, who fictionalized as well as documented in a precise manner his every-day life as a primary school teacher and a lover of *"tasses"* and short-lived encounters. Funnily, the main character announces a separation between his public life and his private life in voice-over in the prologue to the film. In parallel, one of the most used stylistic devices in the film is the use of rather clumsy cross-cutting, putting separate parts of the hero's life in contact with one another, like rubbing two flints together. This separation breaks up and Ripploh's character ends up showing off in front of his pupils in his morning class, dressed like an exotic princess.

Daney thinks Ripploh's film is important because it avoids two pitfalls: "A leveled up idealization (the star is a sublime marginal) or a middling sociological approach (the character disappears, becoming an example or a typical case)" (2002, 113).

Ripploh avoids the "election" of marginality first of all, using a concrete, kind of documentary style, showing trivial aspects of his character's life, and de-sublimating the situations experienced by his character. Doing this, Ripploh does not lift his film into an imaginary space where fantasy, icon, idol, and emblem would rule the fiction and lose their concrete implications. But on the other hand, Ripploh also avoids generalizing homosexuality; he does not choose homosexual marginality as a sociological "topic" that would be exemplified with representative characters. His characters are average and singular at the same time.

Of William Friedkin's *Cruising* (1980), Daney observed that the director was respectful and tolerant towards the homosexual world, but also observed: "Friedkin is very cool. Problem is, he doesn't show [anything]. Not really. His well-intentioned and vaguely sociological tolerance doesn't go very far because his subject (scandalous as it is) interests not cinematically but *ideologically* [...]" (2022, 276–77).[16] Daney attacked the movie *Christiane F. – Wir Kinder vom Bahnhof Zoo* (Ulli Edel, 1981) in the same way, summarizing: "The real Christiane F. was a drug victim, the false one … has been a victim of the sociological gaze" (Daney 1998, 34).[17]

Ripploh does *show*: he exhibits himself, and preserves his singularity by keeping "the equation 'I equals I'" active as well by presenting a "desperately average" way of life. This ordinary and un-fantasmatic story, this kind of documentary filming avoids the promotion of marginality. On the other hand, the body of Ripploh himself and the pornographic scenes of the film prevent, Daney explains, a sociological approach that could be called for by these "average situations." What is important is not the fact that these situations are shocking, but that they exhibit in a way that

16   "Ripploh s'amuse", originally published in *Cahiers du cinéma* 317, November 1980.

17   "Moi, Christiane F, droguée, prostituée", originally published in *Libération*, August 14, 1981.

exceeds straightforward representation. These "stripped bare" situations preserve the scenes to be viewed only as a general illustration of "gay sexuality." The explicit sexual scenes make the spectator "participate," in a way, in what he is looking at. He is involved, even reluctantly. The showing of Ripploh's body, the exhibiting of his sexuality is what best preserves Ripploh's character to be a "statistical sample". Neither "sample" nor "star," Ripploh exhibits himself and his body *speaks for him,* prevents him from being spoken by someone else.

Daney describes the aesthetic of Ripploh's film as a "cooling machine." The gay aesthetic Ripploh invents is not flamboyant, fierce, and proud, but "grey" (average) and serious (precise). "Cool" but so "serious" and so "grey" that it leads to a dry-witted humor,[18] funny and disturbing, which also highlights his own singularity.

Daney himself is using discreet humor in his article. At the very beginning of it, he starts writing from the point of view of the *Cahiers* (reminding them and us of their group debate), and then switches immediately to the first person singular: "Here is a movie suitable for restarting a debate the *Cahiers* are right to be fond of and that relates to the status of singular objects in the cinema. I summarize it." In the first sentence, Daney remains in the *Cahiers'* group. In the second, he steps outside it, and will stay outside throughout his article. Maintaining a relationship with his former comrades, keeping a kind of dialogue going, he seems to discreetly request what he writes about Ripploh: "that we can watch him exist, quite simply, without holding any discourse on his existence."

Here is what Daney expects for the visibility of homosexuality on screen: not that it would be defended, or even understood, but simply recognized as singular. Highlighted by a body, made

---

18   Daney conceives humor very close to the definition in Deleuze's *Présentation de Sacher Masoch*: "twist the law by excessive zeal" by "deepening the consequences."

visible in a singular way. For Daney, homosexuality can only be a matter of practice, not a social identity. Identity is a matter of words; and every time a body appears, what it shows exceeds all the qualifiers.

The Paradoxical Experience of Homosexuality

Many other things could be said about Daney and the topic of homosexuality (his relation to AIDS, for example), but I wanted, in this last part of this essay, to question a paradox that Daney himself remarks on at the end of his life. During Cannes 1982, a month after the publication of his article on *Taxi Zum Klo*, Daney writes about modern cinema in one of his notebooks:

> Personally, I imposed this [modern] cinema on myself, I didn't like it spontaneously. I resorted to the heroism of the artist-man, severing the history of Cinema. But I did not look so much at the pretext for his heroism: Woman. For moral reasons, I elected as my greatest filmmakers those who are incapable of *representing* homosexuality: Mizoguchi, Rossellini, Godard.

Subsequently, this reflection can be found in the notes collected in *L'Exercice a été profitable, Monsieur*:

> With O.[livier] S.[éguret]. ... For him, Rossellini is an enemy. In the sense that we are homosexual and that it is clear (almost threateningly so) that Rossellini is the most "normal" of men. When he says "the Man" [*L'Homme*], it is the human, statistical, heteronormative species, the species that must be led towards ever more humanity. The fags in Rossellini are those who take advantage of the turbulences in history to act (the Nazi teacher in *Germany Year Zero*; a woman—which one?—in *Rome, Open City*); my vague memory of a sentence in an interview on the shocking, because sterile, side of love between men ... Perhaps it is this idea of transmission that

is so essential to him that it needs transitive people. (1993, 233–34)

Roberto Rossellini, whose homophobia is well known, is nevertheless the filmmaker Daney interests himself in the most at the end of the 1980s and in the 1990s. Rossellini's lifelong questioning of pedagogy and communication echoes Daney's interrogations, at this moment, about the concept of *experience* (found mostly in Giorgio Agamben's works): the experience given by the cinema associated with the didacticism inherent in cinema's recording of reality. Daney tries to conceptualize this definition of a cinema *supporting* and *supplying experiences* at the end of its life, noting however that it is strangely to the detriment of the representation of homosexuals by the cinema. This is what he explains in an interview published in 1991:

> I have always been grateful to the cinema for giving me the chance to live in the world of the real Marilyn Monroe. ... I liked the cinema for giving me first-hand information about the lives of those human beings. I was such a bad advocate for myself that I did not even mind the cinema not giving me information about people like me, for example homosexuals, whose films were not spoken about before the 1970s. (2015, 195)[19]

In *L'Exercice a été profitable, Monsieur,* Daney develops this idea:

> I remember an old debate with M[ichel] C[ressole] about an old Bolognini that I of course found over-indulgent, but which indulged in the subject of boys on screen and their beauty. It is precisely because they are beautiful (I must have said) that it is important that they also be offered to an audience untouched by this beauty. Proselytism or a crazy belief on my part that cinema can "convert" us. In so saying, I defined in my own way what I expected from the cinema: that it should

19   "Les Cahiers à Spirale." Interview by Arnaud Viviant originally published in
      Les Inrockuptibles, March-April 1982.

allow me to participate in those areas of life that "do not concern me." I want these boys not to be just the narcissistic objects of the filmmaker for the same reason that I do not want women to be filmically forbidden to me. A desperate belief that cinema transcends personal "tastes" and that I will prefer a hetero-hetero film by Rossellini to a homo-but-indulgent film by Reichenbach. ... The cinema does not give me another world, it gives me *this one*: which is quite enough, quite beautiful and sufficiently interesting ("one world at a time" [in English]). (1993, 246)

Jean-Claude Biette said something similar in one of his articles:

Loving a man and a woman is a capital test for a filmmaker: it consists of going behind the mirror of his sexual tastes. This criterion ... may be the only one that allows us to establish the authenticity and the greatness of a filmmaker. (Biette 1998, 119)

Daney presumes that a filmmaker should never try to limit the curiosity and desire of his audience. Cinema is for everyone, even those who aren't concerned by what they are shown. A second point is that Daney is persuaded that filmmakers can "convert" people: a good film could "realize" every kind of *desire,* making it perceptible by his audience. In order to do that, filmmakers have to *convince*, *prove*, and *show* (which is not a straightforward representation, but a way of showing things). In a 1976 article Daney says something that I find very accurate: "We should know by now that it is not people who communicate, but objects (state-ments, images) that *are being communicated and communicate by themselves*" (Daney 1976). A distance is needed in the film, for the filmmaker, and for the audience, that transcends their own ideas, desires or emotions. This distance is what *constructs a look at beings and things, and that allows them to be seen in a certain way and to exist.* All this was already summarized in an essential sentence of Daney's article on Ripploh's film: "Cinema is not made to promise, but to keep [*"tenir"*]." "Keep" understood cinematographically as "record" ("*retenir*"), politically as "keep going" ("*tenir bon*") and concretely as "hold up" ("*tenir debout*").

To "keep" the representation going against pressures of all kinds means *to give it a consistency, to embody* characters and situations, to make them exist on screen and to surpass the simple level of *representation: to make them exist out of the screen,* the way a true character can continue to live on in our minds after a film is finished. This explains Daney's reluctance to promote a "gay point of view" on films, as well as the following vilification in *L'Exercice était profitable, Monsieur:*

> A protected minority, with its rights and its fads ["lubies"] (a lobby), which uses a film to commune with—and—to consolidate itself as a group, not to "see itself" as if it was becoming exterior to itself. (1993, 246)

This cinema, which thinks of its audience as a limited, peculiar group of people animated by a cause (be it homosexuality or something else), is wrong, says Daney, because it doesn't attend to the fact that every experience exceeds interpretation. The cinema cannot be *useful,* it can only ever be experienced. For Daney, if a film becomes just a way for a group to recognize itself in it, just a way to "communicate, commune, and consolidate" the group—no matter what minority the group is—these objects are not films, but something else. Films have Daney's priority above any utilitarianism. The quote mentioned above ("We should know by now that it is not people who communicate, but objects (statements, images) that *are being communicated and communicate by themselves*") implies that cinema is an *external* object facing us, that we cannot assimilate totally. This is why Daney will always consider that *fantasies* and cinema are slightly antithetical to one another. Cinema vouches for the heterogeneity of interpretations: it has to fabricate otherness, unfamiliarity (and the uncanny, *Unheimlich*): a kind of queerness, in a way? The experience of otherness is for Daney the only virtue of cinema and defines all its virtualities.

Dispossession

The cinema experience is therefore for Daney not a form of possession but of *dispossession* (which includes the meaning given by the images). When Daney compares himself to Douchet in *Perséverance*, he says he is not "hedonistic" like him, but is

> Someone who would never own anything, who detested the idea of ownership, who truly owned nothing in the world except for books and records, in short someone who could only own himself and experience the simple pleasures … or simple happiness. (2007, 54–55)

A cinephile is someone that finds everything in films. He doesn't need to possess things, just his look, memory, and emotions. I very much like this quote where Daney, in *Persévérance,* distances himself from Henri Langlois on this precise subject of possession:

> There is *Psycho*'s mummy at the Museum of Cinema [in Paris], and I find pitiful the exhibition of that poor model that scared me so much the first time I saw Hitchcock's film, and which exists only inside the film and during the time of the screening! All true cinephiles are like me, but this screen memory of the shot of *Psycho* has a big defect: it generates no market, it is only deposited in the memory (or the speech) of griots like me who exhaust themselves to celebrate it. On the other side, the real mummy, it's an entrance fee, it's money. (2015, 17)[20]

In this quote, Daney opposes true objects (in museums, in the shops) and the "free of charge" world of the movies, which takes place in an uncommercial and very intimate space: memory. The cinema experience is an intimate experience that can be only experienced "within the time of the screening," lived with the spectator's own body, emotions, and memory. If cinema is a

---

20   "L'amour du cinema." Interview by Olivier Mongin, originally published in *Esprit*, August–September 1992.

  shared experience of the same representation, this experience is made by one individual, not in a group mediation. That is the reason why for Daney, cinephilia is quite similar to smuggling. It is the encounter with a form of otherness (if the film is good) that allows someone to escape from all group dynamics and rules. A priceless (in every sense of the word) experience, that can only be felt through films and that offers a world full of divergences of interpretation from which cinema gets its real value. If Daney has not promoted "queer films" in the sense we consider them today, this seems nevertheless like the idea of a queer cinema, which dispossessively gives its spectator a new world full of desire: a look onto the one he is already living in.

Translated into English by Pierre Eugène and Kate Ince

References

Biette, Jean-Claude. 1988. *Poétique des auteurs*. Paris: Cahiers du cinéma & Éditions de l'Étoile.

Daney, Serge. 1971–1972. "Mort à Venise: le Nom-de-l'auteur" (with Jean-Pierre Oudart). *Cahiers du Cinéma* 234–35: 79–93.

———. 1976. "La re-mise en scene (Notes)." *Cahiers du cinéma* 268–69, July–August 1976: 20–26. Translated by Stoffel Debuysere (modified) in https://www.diagonal-thoughts.com/?p=2022.

———. 1993. *L'Exercice a été profitable, Monsieur*. Paris: P.O.L.

———. 1998. *Ciné journal. Vol. 1: 1981–1982*. Paris: Cahiers du cinéma. (first edition 1986. Paris: Cahiers du cinéma)

———. 2002. *La Maison cinéma et le monde : Les années Libé (1981–1985)*. Paris: P.O.L.

———. 2015. *La Maison cinéma et le monde : Le moment Trafic (1991–1992)*. Paris: P.O.L.

———. 2007. *Postcards from the cinema*. Translated by Paul Grant. Oxford/New York: Berg.

———. 2022. *The Cinema House & the World, Vol. 1, The Cahiers du cinéma Years, 1962–1981*. Translated by Christine Pichini. South Pasadena: Semiotext(e).

Douchet, Jean. 2013. *L'homme cinéma, entretien avec Joel Magny*. Paris: Éditions Écriture.

Eugène, Pierre. 2012. "Apparitions de Serge Daney." *Trafic* 82: 94–102.

Shepard, Todd. 2017. *Sex, France, and Arab Men*. Chicago: The University of Chicago Press.

2

Carte Postale à Serge Daney

Andrea Inzerillo

Why does a queer film festival dedicate a whole section to Serge Daney? The Sicilia Queer filmfest forges a bond between film critics, film theory, and film programming and tries to explore the hidden links between the thought of Serge Daney and the concept of "queer" in cinema. Maybe this concept should be thought of as a mobile vector? Can we use Daney's writings in order to ask questions of contemporary queer cinema? Here we explore three possible uses of Daney in the context of an international queer film festival.

La fatica di rientrare nella media e la felicità di non riuscirci. (The effort to be part of the average and the happiness at failing to do so.)
—Nino Gennaro

At first, I thought of dividing my text into two parts: a first (let's say) of testimony, and a second, more theoretical one. Then, while writing this essay, I've come to understand that these two aspects are not easily distinguishable. They are intertwined in the theory and practice that characterizes the work I am about to present to you.

The festival I am the artistic director of, the Sicilia Queer film-fest, has a section dedicated to Serge Daney. How come a queer festival dedicates a whole section (the History of Cinema section) to Serge Daney? I will try to answer by telling you a bit about the story of this section and above all about the ambition it has. I hope that in doing so I will be able to offer some possible ideas regarding the crucial question about what relationships can exist, or can be created, between Daney and the concept of queer.

It seems to me that Serge Daney put special emphasis on the relationship between cinema and ethics, showing how the seventh art is nothing—that is, it ignores the deeper value of what can be found in the images and turns into that "visual" about which Daney writes in his last writings—if it does not care about humanity. That's why I'd like to begin by telling you that the History of Cinema section was born when three friends met. Three people of different ages and backgrounds, but all of them readers of Daney. Three people who wanted to remember him on the twentieth anniversary of his death, and did that at a newborn festival, sending him—from Palermo—one of those *cartes postales* (postcards) he used to love so much, thus bringing him back into public discussion: this was the original idea. Daney's writings have virtually disappeared from circulation in Italy, and we wanted to get them back, to read them again, to translate them, and start to spread them—even in collaboration with some journals, like the Italian *Filmcritica* (a historical periodical founded by Galvano Della Volpe, Roberto Rossellini, and the recently deceased Edoardo Bruno). We wanted to create opportunities for discussion in the name of Daney. During Sicilia Queer 2012, as part of the homage to Daney, a round table dedicated to the transformations of film criticism in the age of the internet was a nice opportunity for a comparison between industry players. Here's what we wrote in the catalog that year:

> The challenge is, obviously, trying to share a passion—which is actually vital more than intellectual—with a larger audience. To do this, we need to start from cinema: the films Daney loved, for the simple reason that sometimes the classics are more contemporary than our contemporaries (for instance Laughton, Fassbinder); the films Daney "made," since the video-interview by Régis Debray or the *Histoire(s) du cinéma* by Godard not only star him as a character but they also show a strong moral influence from the great critic; and finally the writings on cinema that Daney kindled, since it is undeniable that some of the most important philosophers of the twentieth century have begun to take an interest in cinema because of him. Few things can explain such an unusual figure as a *passeur* as the writings in which philosophers talk about him, like the text Jacques Rancière gave us, where he reconstructs the strange alchemy he shared with the founder of *Trafic*.

Quickly retracing the path taken in recent years within the section *Carte postale à Serge Daney* will show how it will always be a question of ties, connections, deviations, and detours, which all start from Daney, and intertwine at several levels in a pro-grammatically unorthodox way. In fact, I wanted to title this essay *Postcard to Serge Daney, or How I learned to Start Programming and Love Queerness (Never Merely as an End, but Always as a Means to an End)* to give the exact sense of how little orthodoxy characterizes our work (and I will do nothing but address only that).

I will focus on three operations that seem significant to me for the meeting between Daney and (Sicilia) Queer, with the idea that this may not just be a lesson, but an attempt, an example among many.

A first, quite canonical possible use of Daney tries to give him back what he offered to his readers. Reading Daney's works is exciting because it is a constant discovery, an unlimited source of ideas. Thanks to him we have discovered (or rediscovered) films and authors that we had not watched carefully, or that we had not watched at all. Consequently, we should use his writings as a real mine. When Patrice Chéreau died in 2013, it was natural for us to check if and what Daney wrote about Chéreau. We thus found an article published in *Libération* on May, 19th 1983, and imagined paying Chéreau homage by projecting *L'Homme blessé*. A canonical film for a queer festival, a less canonical reading by Daney: all in all, a rather ordinary operation, I would say.

As ordinary as the operation may be, at least on paper, to pay tribute to a director like Chantal Akerman, who died in 2015, by screening a film that has as much to do with queerness (and feminism) as *Je, Tu, Il, Elle*, a series of events and coincidences led us to make this tribute less predictable and perhaps much more interesting than it might have been. In fact, in 2015 the fourth volume of *La Maison cinéma et le monde* was published including a text titled "Laissons passer les barbares," which contains three conversations between Daney and a young man named Philippe Roux. In the introduction, Roux writes that between 1989 and 1992 he used to meet Serge Daney regularly and had some conversations with him.

Roux was more or less my age when I started looking for him, to find out that he now works at the Museum of Modern Art in Saint-Étienne. I got in touch with him, told him about our project, asked if there were any unpublished conversations. He answered with a "no" (if I remember correctly) and asked me to tell him more about what we were about to do that year. I told him about the idea of celebrating Chantal Akerman and that I didn't think Daney (who had conversations with Akerman in his radio show *Microfilms*) wrote anything specific about the film we wanted to screen. Roux told me that in *De(s)generations*, the magazine he is Chief Editor of, and that owes so much to Daney, two philosophers (Alexandre and Daniel Costanzo) had dedicated an article to the politics of Chantal Akerman's gestures. It seemed clear to me that the tribute to Chantal Akerman by Sicilia Queer 2016 could only be this: an article we managed to find thanks to an indication given to me twenty-five years earlier by Daney himself, through a bizarre détour.

A second possible use: classics of the history of cinema, which although not queer in the proper sense of this word, can be read this way, and about which Daney has provided some hints. I strongly believe that a queer festival should shun any kind of didacticism. That's why presenting films seemingly distant from LGBTQ themes within a queer festival always looks to me like an operation of particular interest. Indeed, over the years I've come to realize that this is one of the things that seem to be among the most anomalous from the outside, but all the more original within the proposal of Sicilia Queer. And this is surprising for me: films such as *The Celluloid Closet* by Rob Epstein and Jeffrey Friedman showed how, throughout the twentieth century, cinema had to say without saying, to show without showing, through real compromise formations. There are films, such as *Le Trou* (*The Hole*) by Jacques Becker, which are exemplary from this point of view. The story of a jailbreak, an all-male film in which a group of prisoners, half-naked for virtually the entire duration of the film, dig a hole in the cell and plan their break out. A claustrophobic film made up of bodies, sweat, and matter, which is literally a film about coming out, and which, from this specific point of view, possibly takes on further possible meanings. In *L'exercice a été profitable, Monsieur*, Daney writes that for him Gaspard, the protagonist of the film, is homosexual and that the reading he (Daney) gives of the film is affected by this intuition. And he adds:

> Homosexuality is at the center of this film, but in a very strange way, something between Hawks and Melville, between the ideal of brotherhood and the simplicity of intact bodies. What to me and to Jean-Claude Biette seems to be extraordinary is that Becker's eyes, at the end of the Sixties, were as open as possible, the most attentive, the least didactic. *Le trou* is not a film about the prison-breakout paradigm, it's not Bresson, it's a film that works (I cannot find a better word) with the idea of freedom. (Daney 1993, 356–57)

In 2018 we decided to screen another classic that stands in the wake of Becker's film: *The Servant* by Joseph Losey, a British masterpiece by the American director written by Harold Pinter. Here, the story of the relationship between servant and master has a clear subtext of homosexuality. We were looking for something to go along with the screening (besides an article on Losey's cinema that Daney wrote in *Libération*, June 23 and 24, 1984), and while dialoguing with one of our guests (Luciano Barisone) during the early phase of the making of the festival, we came to learn about an extraordinary film on another servant, a butler actually, clearly homosexual. (The story of the film is about something else: it's a conversation the director has with a man who used to be the butler in his house, and at the same time a reflection on time, memory, and cinema.) By choosing to screen *Santiago* by João Moreira Salles as well, we therefore set up a cinematic diptych that seemed to us to be a way of exploring homosexuality in the cinema in a way that can dialogue with the way Daney himself talked and wrote about cinema.

I am fairly aware that the third possible use is the most questionable of all. Yet, I am also convinced that the first two move exactly on this very line of thought, and that the third is only a little more audacious. It is about extending (some might say improperly) the concept of queer to works that, according to most people, have nothing to do with it. However, perhaps, it is also thanks to Daney, to the rigor and the necessity he fostered in order to establish a dialogue with moving images—as any critic, spectator, or cultural operator who proposes to think with images should do—that it is possible to rethink such a complex and not so clear-cut definition as that of queer. In 2015 we decided to invite the French actor Melvil Poupaud as special guest of the festival. Poupaud is, among other things, the protagonist of two important films of contemporary gay cinema, *Le temps qui reste* (*Time to Leave*) by François Ozon and *Laurence Anyways* by Xavier Dolan. Thanks to these roles, he is therefore a well-known figure in the imagery of gay cinema. His book *Quel est Mon noM?*, published a few years earlier, tells among other things about his childhood, and his relationship with Serge Daney, who was a friend to him and almost a spiritual father. We also knew—and that was one of the strongest reasons why we wanted to invite him to the festival—that Poupaud was the actor in ten films by Raúl Ruiz, whom we thought to be representative of a spirit that had a lot to do with the concept of queer in the sense of insubordination, anti-conformism, opening up of new spaces, difficulties in framing, and overcoming rules and categories.

Poupaud was therefore the perfect link between several things that were important for us, and we talk about all this in the interview published in the catalog, where we also get him to tackle his relationship with Daney and Ruiz. Ruiz's cinema was for us exemplary of a work that is kind of forgotten, and which it was necessary to rediscover. We believed a queer festival could not be free from trying to constantly rethink the concepts of the center and periphery of cinema itself, looking to what deviates from the norm not only in terms of content but also in terms of form (productive, distributive, artistic) and of position in the world film scene. Such an attitude more generally characterizes our whole approach, although we are aware of the fact that not all the movies we present during the festival—indeed, just a minority of them—work in this direction.

By dedicating the *Carte Postale à Serge Daney* to Raúl Ruiz, and by inviting Poupaud as special guest of the *Presenze/Presences* section, we had the possibility to present to our audience some works that Ruiz had made in Sicily; to retrieve and digitize some old archives from the Sicilian Regional Film Library (a cycle of splendid lectures that Ruiz held in Palermo in the 1990s, together with Enrico Ghezzi, Pascal Bonitzer, Alberto Farassino, and Alessandro Rais, among others); and to present the work of Melvil Poupaud, which represents a cinematographic UFO, precisely due to the influences I just mentioned. We presented a series of short films that Poupaud made since his childhood (we chose three, one of which was a tribute to Eric Rohmer), and a feature film called *Melvil*, a movie the critic Olivier Père considered "the best secret in the alternative French cinema, one of the last movies to be truly underground." In the festival catalog (which is something we work a lot on from a graphic point of view, and which also wants to make a visual contribution to the festival's conceptual process), we also published some of the postcards that Daney had sent to Melvil Poupaud.

I'm not sure if I have sufficiently clarified this third point, which is essential for the explanation I am trying to provide, and which tries to hold several things together. Serge Daney's writings and journals are what led us to Ruiz (and Poupaud), and it is Ruiz (and Poupaud) who allow us to think that the risk of extending the concept of queer beyond the borders of sexuality may not be just a risk. Thus, the section dedicated to Serge Daney becomes crucial within the festival to help us understand that maybe the concept of queer should be thought of as a "mobile vector," a tool capable of taking on intrinsically political issues. Maybe we should acknowledge this as a device that becomes ineffective when it assumes a standardized form. Initially, as we know, the term was an insult, and became—as a result of a resemantization operation—a operator of liberation. Should people be careful not

to use it in a too narrow, stiffening sense, which might turn it into
"a model," making it "academic" and inevitably neutralizing it? If
such reasoning is accepted, if it is tolerable, then it can be easier
to understand what leads us to broadly extend the spectrum
of the term "queer" in this as in other sections of the festival.
This is what allows us, for example (and this is the last example
I will give), to pay tribute to an author like Buster Keaton on the
50th anniversary of his death, focusing our interest on his "odd-
ball glance" in the wake of the indications provided in an article
from July 2, 1982 where Daney reviewed a fine book by Robert
Benayoun entitled *Le regard de Buster Keaton*.

Three possible uses of Daney within a festival such as Sicilia
Queer. It is not difficult to imagine the outcomes: we could clearly
work on classic films like *Johnny Guitar*, *Suddenly Last Summer*,
or *Tea and Sympathy*, or dedicate the section to the discovery of
lesser known but not less important authors such as Margarida
Cordeiro and António Reis, whom Daney loved and who are not
very well known to the general public, to see if and how they can
interact with the concept of queer. On the other hand, we have
always considered the space of the festival as an open workshop,
as a place in which it is necessary to experiment, to make pro-
posals, to try something new. I think it is appropriate, however, to
stop here with the "patrolling" part and head towards a possible
conclusion, where I will try to propose some (maybe temporary)
working hypotheses. I examined Daney's writings to find some
ideas that could lead us towards the hypothesis of this book:
a relationship between Daney and queerness. I cannot even
remotely expect to have exhausted the reading (nor the understanding) of all of Daney's writings, but I've soon realized that
maybe that was not the direction in which to look. I might even
think I found something (for example, an article from August 5,
1982 where Daney talks about the role of the star in cinema, and
in particular of Marilyn), but I might have had to bend Daney's
writings in a direction that risked sounding too contrived. Or
I could have simply mentioned *Persévérance*, trying to draw

 inspiration from what Daney says about himself and his homosexuality in the dialogue with Serge Toubiana. But even in this case I don't think I could have grasped anything essential. Even trying to focus on the question of desire, which is perhaps one of the characteristics bringing together several of the movies we today ascribe to a queer gaze, I would have felt forced to recognize that for Daney it is a question that characterizes all cinema, and not just a specific part of it, which is the part we are interested in here. I therefore asked myself if this relationship should not be investigated by trying to adopt a different perspective, more focused on method than on content.

There is a beautiful line in *Persévérance* (Daney 1994, 78), which tries to define what cinema is:

> Cinema is not a technique of displaying images, it is an art of showing. And to show is a gesture, a gesture that forces us to see, to look. Without this gesture, there is only an image factory. Now, if something has been shown, someone needs to answer back. Well, there may have been so many other ways to spend your life with cinema, this was mine.

If Daney is part of the history of cinema, it's because he showed us something about cinema itself. While telling the story of his "baptism of cinema" where he went together with his mother and aunt, he says that talking about a movie can be as beautiful as seeing it. Following Bazin, we know Daney considered cinema an impure art. From a certain point of view, I wonder whether the question of impurity is connected with the concept of queer. We could try to see where the hypothesis that impurity is another way of saying queer leads us. What is queer cinema? If, for example, we say that queer is that cinema that calls into question a naturally presumed heteronormativity of the world, we feel that the definition is incomplete. We're missing something and we're not satisfied: queer cinema is not just that. If it is difficult to fix something like a queer canon, we can try to make the two concepts work together: impurities and queer, and see if and how they can create something. The question of whether Daney's writings and the concept of queer can find a meeting point should therefore in my opinion be placed not so much in terms of acknowledgment (where can I find explicitly LGBTQ issues in Daney's writings?) or a coincidence (where is Daney's thought the interpreter of the LGBTQ demand?), but in terms of a working platform. Why Daney? Maybe the first answer is that in questioning the forms that queer cinema can take nowadays—in the impossible questioning about its defining, established, canonical essence—we immediately saw Daney as a traveling companion with the ability to question images. A spiritual son of André Bazin, founder of classical cinephilia, and at the same time a much closer son, a militant more than a theoretician. A traveling companion to be questioned more in the method than in the content, one we knew to be close to the issues we could have encountered, even if he had not explicitly treated them. It is not enough.

Why Daney? Second possible answer. For a festival like ours, to dedicate a whole section to Daney means to praise mediation. In an era when all forms of mediation are about to be dismissed in order to have a "direct grip on things"—as an Italian writer recently wrote in *The Game*, a book about the digital revolution—talking about Daney is a statement of intent: we need a *passeur* (a smuggler), the need for mediation is not exhausted. Festivals, catalogs, workshops, and conferences are attempts to understand the world around us, experiments to dialogue with the contemporary world and perhaps even more with the world of the future. Establishing a dialogue of this kind, beyond time, beyond the narrowness of the space in which we operate, seems to me to offer a necessary perspective on what a non-nostalgic form of cinephilia can create in a world totally dominated by the present.

There is a world within the history of cinema which has always been hidden, underground, secret, and that has been revealed since the 1990s (set free possibly by the AIDS crisis itself, first in the US, then in the rest of the world). Daney himself was taken away by that very disease, which set one more country free in the chart of global cinema, and we can only imagine how he would have treated such a world: certainly with the same unbending sincerity—without any community solidarity, in short—through which he confronted other geographies of cinema. In the beautiful documentary Serge Le Péron dedicated to Daney, *Serge Daney le cinéma et le monde*, director Olivier Assayas says that for Daney films are only symptoms of cinema. This also is an interesting point for us: what are queer films? what is queer cinema? and what is the relationship of this with cinema *tout court*? is it possible to say that queer cinema in some way represents a renewal, an innovation, something beneficial not only for society but for cinema itself? These are some questions we can ask ourselves starting from Daney.

Daney asks questions to cinema, therefore also to what we today call queer cinema. In *Persévérance* he talks about boredom in front of images that are just beautiful and about interest in the "right" movies. I think this is an important question that can work as a guideline for the direction of queer cinema, especially when the borders of the LGBT film industry and the possibilities of queer cinema become blurred and risk getting off track. Can we say *Je, Tu, Il, Elle* is not just a beautiful film, but a "right" film? Can we use Daney as a guideline, as a source of criteria for judgment, as a call for rigor in our gaze as spectators—beyond what he is talking about? I think so. And this is something of no little value to me.

References

Daney, Serge. 1982. "Le regard du muet." *Libération* (July 2, 1982): 24.
———. 1982. "Le dernier plan du star-system." *Libération* (August 5, 1982): 20.
———. 1983. "L'effet de coulisses de *L'Homme Blessé*." *Libération* (May 19, 1983): 19.
———. 1984. "Joe Losey : cinq paradoxes." *Libération* (June 23 & 24, 1984): 27.
———. 1993. *L'Exercice a été profitable, Monsieur*. Paris: P.O.L.
———. 1994. *Perséverance*. Paris: P.O.L.

———. 2015. *La Maison cinéma et le monde, Vol. 4, Le moment Trafic 1991–1992*. Paris: P.O.L.

Poupaud, Melvil. 2011. *Quel est mon noM?* Paris: Éditions Stock.

QUEER FILM FESTIVAL

QUEER CINEPHILIA

SPECTATORSHIP

CLIP REEL

3

Clip Reels and Community: Queer Cinephilia at the Queer Film Festival

Theresa Heath

Despite the current global proliferation of queer film festivals, the practices of queer cinema audiences are under-researched, and traditional models of cinephilia and spectatorship have centered the straight, white, western male. Nevertheless, queer audiences are among the most adept and committed of cinemagoers, developing highly active, creative ways of engaging with the film text. This chapter will briefly review the scholarship on feminist and queer cinephilia and spectatorial practices before examining the role of material space and, specifically, the queer film festival in the facilitation of queer cinephilias. Acknowledging extra-textual practices of gossip and fandom,

I argue that queer film festivals have contributed to the development of communal, interactive, non-hierarchical modes of viewing as articulated by scholars such as Girish Shambu and So Mayer. Finally, I examine the role of the clip reel popular at queer film festivals, arguing that this found-footage form embodies queer cinephilic practices and is central to understanding the way in which queer audiences engage with cinema.

According to film festival scholars Skadi Loist and Leanne Dawson, there are currently around 270 queer film festivals operating globally, a figure which attests to the centrality of cinema and cinemagoing to queer communities (Loist and Dawson 2018, 3). Nevertheless, the practices of queer cinema audiences are under-researched and, as Girish Shambu and Patricia White note, traditional models of cinephilia and spectatorship center the straight, white, western male (Shambu 2013; White 1999, xii). Underrepresentation in the annals of cinephilia is particularly apparent in the case of queer women who, as White argues, are often conflated with queer men in terms of their relationship to film (White 1999, 30). Furthermore, queers have not enjoyed the same sense of 'ownership' in film exhibition space as their straight counterparts. Cinephiles proprietorially describe how their viewing practices entail sitting in a favored spot in the auditorium, legs stretched out or draped over the chair in front (Keathley 2000, 42), a privileged mode of spatial occupation which may not be afforded those marked as visibly queer and/or female. Nevertheless, queer audiences are among the most adept and committed of cinemagoers, considering the level of engagement demanded of those for whom cinema has posed something of a conundrum. How to construct a relationship with a medium that has been an instrument of demonization or erasure? How to articulate a queer love of cinema within an apparatus which historically privileges straight white men? And, for women – particularly those who inhabit additional vectors of sexuality, race, ability, and class – how to construct a relationship with the image that encompasses both agency and desire and is not defined by narcissism or masochism?

Chris Straayer argues that "homosexual desire incites a critical disruption that uncovers radical viewing practices and generates momentous questions about textual flexibility" (Straayer 1993, 3). Building on this claim to the disruptive potential of non-heterosexual spectatorial positions, this article begins by briefly reviewing the scholarship on queer cinephilia and spectatorial practices, arguing that queer audiences have developed highly engaged, creative ways of engaging with the film text. Given that cinephilia is structured by both diegetic and material space, I next examine the role of the queer film festival in the facilitation of queer cinephilias. Acknowledging extra-textual practices of gossip and fandom, in addition to subjective knowledges, I argue that queer film festivals have contributed to the development of communal, interactive, non-hierarchical modes of viewing that undermine traditional renderings of cinephilia and are expansive and exclusive. Finally, I examine the significance of the clip reel, popular at queer film festivals, arguing that this found footage form is a crystallization of queer cinephilic practices, and central to understandings of the way in which queers audiences engage with cinema.

Queer Spectatorship

Cinephilia is bound to theories of spectatorship since our position as spectator structures how and why we watch film, and the affective experience produced by our relationship to the screen. Queer cinephilia and spectatorial practices have developed along complex lines, adapting to discursive and material exclusions as well as the heterosexual bias of early models of spectatorship.

Queer audiences are, like all demographics, intersected by axes of gender, class, race, sexual orientation, and ability, and the relationship to the moving image is structured according to a variety of often highly contingent subject positions. For lesbians and bisexual women, the eroticization and fetishization of the woman on screen may be both pleasurable and problematic, and queer women have had to work particularly hard to seek out images and construct meanings that speak to them. Meanwhile, as Roger Hallas argues, the relationship between gay male audiences and cinema is heavily indebted to nostalgia and feelings of loss wrought by the AIDS epidemic, resulting in unique structures of feeling (Hallas 2003, 89).

Despite profound differences, it is possible to identify points of commonality within queer audiences, the lived experiences of whom have been historically written or censured out of film or buried in the subtext. Queer audiences have learned to read against the grain, deploying highly inter/active ways of seeing in order to produce meaning outside of the film text – as Daniel Harris notes, "film became a form of 'found' propaganda that the homosexual ransacked for inspiring messages, reconstituting the refuse of popular culture into an energizing force" (Harris 1997, 15). Queers have thus become adept at identifying what Christian Keathley terms "the cinephiliac moment," a transient instance that produces scopic pleasure but is not necessarily memorable for the non-cinephile (Keathley 2000). For Paul Willemen, the cinephiliac moment performs a revelatory function, constituting a "momentary flash of recognition, or a moment when the look at something suddenly flares up with a particularly affective emotional intensity" (Willemen in Hallas 2003, 95). Within this moment lies the possibility of identification, of recognizing who one "is."

Queer cinephilia, almost by definition, lies in fleeting glances, gestures, and coded references, gaps, or spaces in the film text where queer meaning can be found or inscribed. It is the moment when Greta Garbo's Queen Christina kisses her maid on the

lips, or when a cross-dressed Marlene Dietrich rakishly flicks the
brim of her top hat. Queer audiences have additionally learned
to isolate these moments from narrative developments such as
when, for example, Garbo's Christina falls in love with the (male)
Spanish envoy, or when lesbian characters predictably die at the
end of the film. Developing such reading practices is a high-stakes
game, since validation and subject constitution lies in the ability
to identify and piece together these moments. Hallas argues that
this active approach has resulted in a "fetishistic preoccupation
with the moment, the detail, the fragment; and the perfor-
mativity that contributes to identity formation" (Hallas 2003, 93).
Historically, the queer spectator has elevated this panoramic yet
forensic look to a kind of superpower, locating queerness in the
seemingly most barren situations, bypassing narrative linearity
and closure to find pleasure in "those great moments, those interstices that were often, ironically, the source of a film's real power"
(Hallas 2003, 91).

These active reading practices stem from a desiring gaze that is
both erotic and constitutive of subject formation. However, the
heterosexual bias of classical models of spectatorship posits
a unidirectional flow of desire from male spectator to passive
woman-on-screen, which would appear to foreclose the possibility of queer and, specifically, lesbian pleasure or desire. As
Teresa de Lauretis writes in *Alice Doesn't*:

> the position of woman in language and in cinema is one of
> non-coherence; she finds herself only in a void of meaning,
> the empty space between signs - the place of women
> spectators in the cinema is between the look of the camera
> and the image on the screen, a place not represented,
> not symbolized, and thus pre-empted to subject (or self)
> representation. (de Lauretis 1984, 8)

In order to account for female visual pleasure, Mulvey famously
suggests the notion of trans-sex identification in which the
female spectator oscillates between both masculine and feminine

perspectives (Mulvey 1981, 14). Rather than bestow agency on the female spectator, however, this dual position offers only the occupation of positions of regressive, passive femininity on the one hand, and pre-Oedipal masculinity on the other. Later in *Alice Doesn't*, de Lauretis re-formulates Mulvey's construction arguing that, rather than oscillating between gendered poles, the female spectator inhabits both simultaneously. Yet again, however, this double identification has negative implications; it is a "surplus of pleasure" by which cinema seduces women into complicity with the production of cinematic and social hegemony (de Lauretis 1984, 143).

Opposing dyadic models based on binary constructions of sex and gender, Straayer deploys a queer approach to spectatorship, arguing that "a false sexual polarity *only ostensibly* governs subjectivity. This conclusion makes possible a radical assertion of multiple 'deviant' subjectivities outside the patriarchal and heterosexist confines of binary opposition" (Straayer 1996, 3). Complicating boundaries between the abstract spectator and the material woman in the audience, Straayer argues that the disciplinary look to which lesbians are subjected in the public space of the cinema marks them out *as* lesbian, perversely acknowledging the existence and possibility of the lesbian spectator. According to Straayer, queer women in fact deploy an active, desiring gaze, commensurate with queer reading practices in general, which requires exchange and sets up "two directional sexual activity" (Straayer 1996, 10). Straayer thus builds on traditional models of spectatorship, re-harnessing the power of the policing, homophobic gaze to leverage space for lesbian spectatorship, which disrupts binary understandings of masculine and feminine behavior and desire.

The Queer Film Festival Context

As Straayer highlights, cinephilia and modes of spectatorship are material practices initiated and constituted in the space of the auditorium. With the emergence of queer film festivals in the mid 1970s, queer audiences were able to view what queer images were available and to explore modes of spatial occupation previously denied to them. Prior to these events, queer cinephilia was a largely private experience conducted in the safety of one's home, private screening, or imagination. Queer film festivals provided a space for a more visible, communal, and public practice, which thrived on the extra-textual dissemination of subjective knowledge and the star-related gossip which Marc Siegel, Jackie Stacey, and White have identified as integral to queer cinephilias. Queer film festivals facilitated space for cinemagoers and functioned as a platform for queer filmmakers, thereby contributing to the development of queer film culture and community and providing impetus for the emergence of the New Queer Cinema in the 1990s. Shaped and informed by the AIDS epidemic and energetic political response of the community, New Queer Cinema was aesthetically and formally radical and rearticulated queer subjectivities as visible and active.

In the intersection of diegetic and material space mobilized by queer film festivals, spectatorial practices formed part of the community and identity-consolidating function of these events, facilitating an expansion of both the cinematic imaginary and material queer communities. In centering queer characters and subjectivities, NQC and the film festival context intervened in classical models of spectatorship, constructing alternative relationships which circumvented patriarchal spectatorial regimes. Straayer argues that "independently structured glances between women on the screen … are outside convention and therefore threaten. The ultimate threat of eye contact between women … is the elimination of the male" (Straayer 1996, 13). Despite the over-presence of male directors in the NQC, work by filmmakers such as Cheryl Dunye, Sadie Benning, and Maria Maggenti depicted queer women liberated from film configurations that privileged male characters and appealed to queer women and their shared experiences. Meanwhile, the queer space of the festival auditorium ensured that the lesbian spectator was now constituted on her own terms, rather than as the result of a homophobic gaze.

While large, national film festivals perpetuate hierarchical structures that generally work to separate high profile film-makers, actors, and industry moguls from the general public, queer film festivals tend to dissolve boundaries between film-maker and attendee, not least because films are often a collaborative effort involving those in the community. Comparatively egalitarian and accessible social events, workshops, and panels demonstrate a shift from the auteurism of traditional models of cinephilia and a move towards more interactive, communal models. Furthermore, queer film festivals may center documentary, short, amateur, and/or experimental work, forms often ignored by cinephiles but that are more accessible to queer women, people of color, and/or the trans community. In this way, unique queer canons are constructed which further decenter notions of the auteur. Materially, too, queer film festivals undermine the sanctity of the cinephile temple. Festivals such as Scottish Queer International Film Festival (SQIFF), Leeds Queer Film Festival, Glitch QTIPOC Film Festival, and Wotever DIY Film Festival have all extensively engaged with queer crip subjectivities and politics on both representational and material levels. At SQIFF, this has resulted in the implementation of a comprehensive range of access measures, including captioning on all films, comfortable seating options, quiet spaces, gender neutral toilets, and relaxed viewings. Attendees are encouraged to move around, make noise when necessary, and generally develop more tolerant, compassionate viewing practices. The expectation that abled audience members will adapt to the needs of disabled attendees stands in marked contrast to the cinephilic entitlement that has led to reports of neurodiverse audience members being forced to leave screenings due to perceived inconsiderate behavior (Marsh, 2015). SQIFF also programs a significant proportion of queer crip cinema, thus politically aligning both diegetic and material space.

Clip Reels

Since the New Queer Cinema, queer images have proliferated, and with them a growing divide between representations of assimilated, neoliberal gays and lesbians and radical, sub-cultural queers. Predictably, it is cinema centering what Stuart Richards defines as "homonormative" that is most likely to garner commercial success and large scale distribution (Richards 2017, 156). The task of many well-established queer film festivals such as London's BFI Flare is now to appeal to a range of increasingly diverse stakeholders, balancing radical work alongside that appealing to more mainstream tastes. Despite the breadth of queer cinema today, however, the programs of queer film festivals highlight a persistent return to classical cinema. This nostalgia for classic forms and reading practices is best evidenced by the continued popularity of clip reels, lectures, or presentations at these events.

Clip reels are collections of curated queer moments – explicit, implicit, or wishfully queer – edited together in creative ways, usually to a soundtrack. Hallas argues that clip reels form a central component to gay film spectatorship, constituting "perhaps the most transparent instance of cinephilia" (Hallas 2003, 2). White similarly describes the significance of this form, arguing that the lesbian clip reel heralded a "coming out of the closet" for lesbian cinephilia (White 1999, 31). Early examples of lesbian clip films include Kaucyila Brooke's and Jane Cottis's *Dry Kisses Only* (1990), an exploration of lesbian subtext in classic cinema; Cecilia Barriga's *Meeting of Two Queens* (1991), which casts dyke icons Greta Garbo and Marlene Dietrich as lovers, and Pratibha Parmar's *Jodie: An Icon* (1996), an homage to Jodie Foster. Central to this work is the reappropriation of the image and engagement with the mechanics of stardom that relies on gossip, rumors, and subjective knowledges for its erotic charge. Lesbian clip reels have played a central role in the constitution and consolidation of identity mobilized at queer film festivals; as White argues, "these texts … build group identifications. The exhibition of such works in the context of lesbian and gay film festivals … makes particularly clear how concrete audiences serve as contexts for such identifications" (White 1999, xx).

Karl Schoonover and Rosalind Galt posit the notion of hetero-synchronics to describe post-classical film structures in which heterosexual desire organizes apparently disparate strands into the delivery of the happy heterosexual ending. They argue that, in contrast, "queer structures of feeling simmer in less synchro-nous text" (Schoonover and Galt 2016, 272). In the clip reel, the linearity of classical cinema is fractured as images are detached spatially and temporally and reorganized according to queer desire. Apparently disparate images are wrought into sequences which may or may not possess narrative coherence, thus also rejecting the ultimately unifying impulses of post-classical cinematic forms. The queer clip reel therefore denaturalizes narrativity, emphasizing the role of editing in the construction of narrative. Classical linearity and post-classical heterosyn-chronics are mocked and parodied since the audience are aware of both the manipulation of the images in the context of the clip reel, and the constructedness of the original sequence. In a further twist, the gossip, fandom, and subjective knowledges associated with lesbian clip reels lend this form a type of veracity since everyone "knows" that these icons were "really queer" all along. The clip reel is therefore the crystallization of queer cine-philic practice, a series of found images constructed playfully and ironically through queer desire and shared knowledges to produce alternative queer meanings and, in the process, expose the inherent instability and artificiality of the image.

Queer clip reels remain a staple of queer film festivals, as with Daisy Asquith's 2017 *Queerama*, which mined the BFI's archive of early and classic cinema, newsreels, television, and contemporary film set to a selection of John Grant tracks. The clip show or lecture also remains popular on the queer film festival circuit, as in the case of BFI Flare programmer Emma Smart's 'Lethal Lesbians' talk at the 2018 edition of the festival. Moreover, the clip reel no longer lurks in the realms of the queer film festival or independent cinema auditorium, and thousands of independently produced queer clip reels are readily available online. Although B. Ruby Rich, most famous of queer cinephiles, has argued that VoD and other platforms encourage more individualistic viewing practices (Rich 2014), the popularity of queer film festivals has not diminished, and it is to be hoped that individual production and private viewing of queer clip reels and queer cinema in general is corollary to the communal festival experience, rather than a harbinger of its obsolescence.

Conclusion

In the context of the queer film festival, queer cinephilia tends toward the communal rather than the solitary and relies on collaborative filmmaking and reading practices. Queer cinephilia revels in the porous boundary between filmmaker and audience, eschewing auteur worship in favor of interdependent, less hierarchical modes of film appreciation. While Susan Sontag and Thomas Elsaesser may sound the death knell for traditional forms of cinephilia (Sontag 1996; Elsaesser 2005), the queer film festival, with its emphasis on sociality, community, and pursuit of social justice is, I argue, the site of a new kind of socially aware and politically active form of cinephilia and feminist cinematic engagement, as articulated by Girish Shambu (Shambu 2013) and So Mayer (Mayer 2016, 8).

Although queer cinema has, in recent years, significantly expanded and diversified, there remains a persistent nostalgia for classical cinema, and the specific reading practices and pleasures that this entails. In particular, the queer clip reel or show has retained its popularity despite the current proliferation of 'positive' queer images now widely available. Structured by historical modes of spectatorship and developed as a strategy against representational and cinematic erasure, the clip reel is a product of this engaged, queer, cinephilic gaze, a collection of moments shattered temporally and spatially and re-organized into a highly ironic, alternative queer narrative. Given current debates regarding the homogenization of queer culture and lifestyles, the clip reel may represent a yearning for, or return to, a more anarchic and disruptive form of politics and cinematic engagement.

References

Dawson, Leanne, and Skadi Loist. 2018. "Queer/ing Film Festivals: History, Theory, Impact." *Studies in European Cinema* 15 (1): 1–24. Accessed October 29, 2022. https://doi.org/10.1080/17411548.2018.1442901.

Elsaesser, Thomas. 2005. "Cinephilia or the Uses of Disenchantment." In *Cinephilia: Movies, Love and Memory*, edited by Marijke de Valck and Malte Hagener, 27–44. Amsterdam: Amsterdam University Press.

Hallas, Roger. 2003. "AIDS and Gay Cinephilia." *Camera Obscura* 18 (1 (52)): 85–126.

Karl Schoonover, and Rosalind Galt. 2016. *Queer Cinema in the World*. Durham: Duke University Press.

Keathley, Christian. 2000. "The Cinephiliac Moment." *Framework* 42. https://www.frameworknow.com/journal-archives-posts/42.

Lauretis, Teresa de. 1984. *Alice Doesn't: Feminism, Semiotics and Cinema*. Bloomington: Indiana University Press.

Marsh, Sarah. 2018. "BFI Apologises after Woman with Asperger's Ejected from Cinema." *The Guardian*, April 30. Accessed April 30, 2018. https://www.theguardian.com/society/2018/apr/30/woman-with-aspergers-ejected-from-cinema-for-laughing-at-western.

Mayer, Sophie. 2016. *Political Animals: The New Feminist Cinema*. International Library of the Moving Image 33. London and New York: I.B. Tauris.

Mulvey, Laura. 1981. "Afterthoughts on 'Visual Pleasure and Narrative Cinema' Inspired by 'Duel in the Sun' (King Vidor, 1946)." *Framework: The Journal of Cinema and Media* 15/17: 12–15.

Rich, B. Ruby. 2014. "The New Queer Cinema: Back to the Future." Lecture at University of Hamburg, October 15.

Shambu, Girish. 2013. *The New Cinephilia*. Montreal: Caboose Books.

Sontag, Susan. 1996. "The Decay of Cinema." *The New York Times Magazine*, 25 February.

Straayer, Chris. 1996. *Deviant Eyes, Deviant Bodies: Sexual Orientation in Film and Video*. New York and Chichester West Sussex: Colombia University Press.

Richards, Stuart James. 2017. *The Queer Film Festival: Popcorn and Politics*. Framing Film Festivals. New York: Palgrave Macmillan.

White, Patricia. 1999. Uninvited: Classical Hollywood Cinema and Lesbian Representation. Bloomington: Indiana University Press.

FEMINISMS

CURATION

ETHICS

COLLECTIVE

REVOLUTION

AUDIENCE

[4]

Revolt, She Said: Queer Feminist Film Curation and the Freedom to Revolt

So Mayer and Selina Robertson,
Club des Femmes

During summer 2018, Club Des Femmes (CDF), in collaboration with the Independent Cinema Office funded by the British Film Institute, curated a UK-wide touring season of films considering the aftermath of May 1968. "Revolt, She Said: Women and Film after '68" comprised nine feature films and eight accompanying shorts, exploring the legacy of '68 on contemporary feminisms, art, and activism transnationally. In this paper, two members of CDF unpack the queer feminist ethics and affects of the tour, through the voices of multiple participants, and framed conceptually by Sara Ahmed's "willful feminist" and Donna Haraway's "staying with the trouble."

[Fig. 1]: "Revolt, She Said" banner. Image courtesy of Club des Femmes and Independent Cinema Office.

Introducing "Revolt, She Said"

During the summer of 2018, Club Des Femmes (CDF), in collaboration with the Independent Cinema Office (ICO) funded by the British Film Institute (BFI), curated a UK-wide touring season of films that explored the aftermath of May 1968. "Revolt, She Said: Women and Film after '68" comprised nine feature films and eight accompanying shorts, exploring the legacy of '68 on contemporary feminism, art, and activism transnationally (fig. 1). This was the largest-scale project to date for CDF, a queer feminist film curation collective that includes the authors of this piece. Founded by Selina Robertson and Sarah Wood in 2007, at a time when there was an absence of independent and feminist film curation in London, CDF state on our website that we aim "to offer a freed up space for the re-examination of ideas through art. In the age of the sound-bite, Club des Femmes is a much-needed open platform for more radical contextualisation and forward-looking future vision: a chance to look beyond the mainstream."

Until 2018, CDF had programmed predominantly in London, and as single events or single venue mini-seasons, often in collaboration with festivals or venues. "Revolt, She Said" was thus the most ambitious—and difficult—project we had undertaken on the scales of programming, geographical reach, and temporal extent. The tour ran for four months, and there were six national flagship events, each highlighting one of the feature films. These events took place at independent cinemas across the UK's regions and nations that had a pre-existing relationship with the ICO, or where CDF had a relationship with the programmers: Glasgow Film Theatre (Scotland); Sheffield Showroom (North East); Broadway Nottingham (Midlands); Watershed, Bristol (South West); Chapter Arts Centre, Cardiff (Wales); and the London Feminist Film Festival (London).[1] We also collaborated with Leeds Queer Film Festival at the Hyde Park Picture House; Lexi Cinema's London Film School; Port Eliot Festival, Cornwall; and the BFI's Woman With a Movie Camera strand. In each case, CDF provided specialist speakers, in collaboration with the venue's wishes, who could contextualize the films within both cinematic and activist frameworks.[2]

Intellectually, the tour represented an extension of our manifesto into a larger conversation about radical histories. In our funding application, we framed our program as follows:

> One hundred years after women's suffrage was achieved in the UK, 50 years after the protests of May '68 triggered resistance across the world, where is the revolutionary woman now? … My '68 [the original season title] will present an international package of films exploring the aftermath of May '68, in work by the women filmmakers who picked up their cameras in the name of activism, art and resistance. The touring programme aims to provide access to international films, spanning the second half of the 20th century,

1   Queen's Film Theatre, Belfast were keen to screen *Maeve*, but were unable to participate due to refurbishment works falling during the dates covered by the tour's funding. We also approached HOME in Manchester, with whom CDF have a pre-existing relationship, but they had their own '68 program in place. All of these relationships, and the nationwide programming for "Revolt, She Said," are tribute to an emerging wave of feminists of marginalized genders working as programmers and educators at independent regional venues.

2   Additionally, Mayer and Robertson travelled to several regional non-flagship venues to introduce screenings.

to explore the legacy of '68 on contemporary feminism and activism around the world.

The program began before '68, with Věra Chytilovà's Czech new wave proto-feminist classic *Daisies* (*Sedmikrásky*, 1966), which was the tour's best-known film. This was followed by two key films made in 1968 itself by prominent northern European women filmmakers, but barely known outside their home countries: *The Girls* (*Flickorna*, Mai Zetterling, 1968) and *The Cat Has Nine Lives* (*Neun Leben hat die Katze*, Ula Stöckl, 1968). We celebrated a prominent European feminist auteur, who was marking her 90th birthday in 2018, by touring one of *her* favorites of her films: Agnès Varda's *One Sings, the Other Doesn't* (*L'Une chante, l'autre pas*, 1977). Subsequent films mapped the impact of feminism in the UK, with three films that combine elements of documentary and experiment in different measures: *Riddles of the Sphinx* (Laura Mulvey and Peter Wollen, 1977), *Maeve* (Pat Murphy and John Davies, 1981), and *Carry Greenham Home* (Beeban Kidron and Amanda Richardson, 1983). Our most recent films were both American-made documentaries by British filmmakers that looked back at US civil rights history: Greta Schiller's *Before Stonewall* (1984), on pre-'68 LGBTQI+ lives, and Pratibha Parmar's *A Place of Rage* (1991), on the role of queer Black women in the civil rights movement and beyond, thus affirming the tour as addressing the full extent of second-wave feminist history from '68 to the beginning of the third wave in 1992.

Today the public memory of May '68 is predominantly one of male revolt, heroism, and failure, traditionally emblematized by explosive masculinist cultural and political activism. The majority of 2018's 50th anniversary film programming in the UK reflected only these histories. CDF wanted to revive the rich and under-acknowledged connections between feminisms, film, and the revolutions of May '68 and their aftermath. As Anna Coatman notes in her feature on the tour for *Sight & Sound*, "'Revolt, She Said' aims to shift the focus away from the riots in Paris to show how people were agitating for change across the world throughout the late 20th century... challeng[ing] conventional narratives about radical political movements, reminding us of the women and queer artists, activists and filmmakers who have been written out of them" (Coatman 2018, 14). We named the tour after Julia Kristeva's book *Revolt, She Said*, and her recollections acted as our manifesto:

> May '68 in France expressed a fundamental version of freedom: not freedom to succeed, but freedom to revolt. Political revolutions ultimately betray revolt because they cease to question themselves. Revolt, as I understand it—psychic revolt, analytic revolt, artistic revolt—refers to a permanent state of questioning, of transformations, an endless probing of appearances. (Kristeva 2002)

This reflected our intention to counter these cinematic histories and public records with a curatorial response that re-framed '68 within a narrative of women's film histories and feminist activisms.

Conceptualizing the tour within this framework of continual revolution liberated us from the pressure to program films from '68 alone, when few women filmmakers were working, but created its own challenges. The date of the work reached back to 1966, with original—and sometimes the only available—formats that included super 8, 16mm, 35mm, DVD, and U-matic video. Moreover, the omission of women's heritage cinema from the canons of mainstream film histories has had a generational impact on preservation, restoration, and digitization. Further obstacles ensued because of the nature of the film season: a feminist film tour by its very definition appeals to a niche audience. As Pamela Hutchinson wrote in *The Guardian*, our summer tour represented a perhaps-welcome challenge to normative programming. "The summer season at the movies is traditionally a time for tentpoles and blockbusters, but this year's wonder women don't wear bulletproof bracelets. Independent cinemas are offering a sizzling summer of radical, intersectional film as an alternative to the franchise releases [... with a] revival of radical movies made by feminist and queer filmmakers from the 60s" (Hutchinson 2018). During one of the hottest summers since 1976, we achieved something quite remarkable with the ICO (not least due to Hutchinson's influential article which appeared in print and online): between May 6 and August 31, 2019, we programmed ninety-nine screenings at thirty cinemas nationwide, totaling 2,346 overall admissions, although CDF had had little previous profile outside London.

Within this expanded vision, we worked to maintain our commitment to creating open, non-hierarchical spaces in which to explore film, aesthetics, and actions. We wanted the tour to be about making connections around the UK with audiences, cinemas, and allies, creating conversations in the present that explore histories of transnational women's cinema. As we endeavored to take responsibility in our curatorial arguments regarding our relationships with communities, venue programmers, and audiences, Laura U. Marks's definitional article on the role of the ethical curator acted as a framework. She notes that ethics:

> might sound rather puritanical, as though making, programming, and watching cinema is our common moral duty. But ethics, or the exhortation to justice, is nothing without beauty, for beauty is the invitation to the soul... ethical relationships amongst artists, programmers, and audiences involve discourses of beauty, emotion and love. Politics, broadly understood, is hollow without these. (Marks 2004, 36–37)

Our trouble was how to hold onto these feminist curatorial strategies and commitments when we were working in unfamiliar spaces, on a national level, with a scale of budget that we had never worked with before.

This engaged us in an unprecedented level of outreach that became deeply informative and inspiring, as CDF collective member Jenny Clarke describes of her online community-building for the tour (Clarke 2018). Yet, due to our ethical commitments, we also found that we encountered *ourselves* as "difficult women"—not with audiences, but when dealing with institutional gatekeepers in terms of accessing film material and clearing rights from national film archives, sales agents, and distributors, and then programming in institutional spaces with different policies and ethics to our own. At times we found the complexities of working in multi-partner collaborations—where everyone is functioning on tight budgets, with limited time and capacity—demanding, in the relationship between our collective ethics and practical delivery.

We were inspired to continue, however, thanks to the historical and enduring examples of the filmmakers themselves, who were often working counter to national and commercial structures and cultural imperatives (as we discuss below), although this has also contributed to the punitive neglect of their films. We also were following theorists Sara Ahmed and Donna Haraway, whose recent work is concerned with difficultness in different ways. In *Living a Feminist Life*, Ahmed centers the incendiary figure of the "willful feminist," arguing that: "Willfulness is used to explain how subjects become the cause of their own unhappiness. Perhaps then feminism involves being willing to be willful. To claim to be willful or to describe oneself or one's stance as willful is to claim the very word that historically has been used as a technique for dismissal" (Ahmed 2017, 77).

The filmmakers of "Revolt, She Said" and the protagonists, aesthetics, and subject positions they generated, were—and remain—willingly willful not only as an activist strategy but as the necessary precursor to action. As Rebecca Liu observes of the program for *Another Gaze*: "The films of 'Revolt, She Said' are more interested in depiction than prescription; we do not necessarily come out of them with a greater sense of how to emancipate ourselves from the patriarchy.... But an indirect kind of answer comes in the form of the films' depiction of relationships between women, in all their messy, liberating, frustrating glory" (Liu 2019). Both messiness and connectivity are central to Haraway's conceptualization of *Staying With the Trouble*, where "trouble" refers both to the complex and often degraded ecologies in which we move, and to the beings and networks that remain within these ecologies and generate new and sustaining relationships, a process she refers to by the willful metaphors of composting and cat's cradles. Borrowing a key phrase from queer online culture (Merriam Webster), "Revolt, She Said" was willfully conceived as a "hot mess," a composting of films in order to regrow the seeds of '68 into new forms capable of staying with the trouble. Willfully, we worked in a cat's cradle of venues, speakers, critics, and audiences, and we have woven as many of their voices as possible into this account of our collective labor.

Growing Daisies

Daisies was where we started: it is one of the few feminist films with a place in the international canon, as well as in our personal (anti-)canons, because of its willful trouble. The protagonists of the film, referred to as Marie 1 and Marie 2, could be cast as the origin points of the contemporary "hot mess," such as the willfully lost protagonists of London-based queer films such as *Break My Fall* (Kanchi Wichmann, 2011) or *Stud Life* (Campbell X, 2013). In fact, *Daisies* bears out the origin of "hot mess" in the class politics of food, as the Maries express their frustrations with state control through food transgressions such as ordering vast meals at the expense of sugar daddies, gleefully dismembering sausages, and finally laying glorious waste to the wastefulness of a state banquet with an epic food fight. The Soviet authorities banned the film two years later on the grounds of food wastage, a censorious irony that could not disguise the film's role as a seed of the Prague Spring.

As film critic Carmen Gray wrote about *Daisies* for our *Revolt, She Said* zine (produced as a paper publication available at all the tour

[Fig. 2]: Still from Daisies (*Sedmikrásky*) by Věra Chytilová (Czechoslovakia, 1966) © Filmové studio Barrandov/NFA, 1966. Courtesy of Second Run.

venues, and online): "the antics of the Maries create and affirm space for personal freedom—an act that confers dignity on their audience, through methods of outrageous anarchy.… In professing no coherent strategy but uncontainable energy for rule-breaking and pure being, they don't fight for systemic change. Yet they inspire hope for it, by confirming that anything, even if just for a moment, is possible" (Gray 2018) (fig. 2). Our zine was a key strategy in planting the seeds of revolution and "confirming that anything, even if just for a moment, is possible." We used online publishing to confront the difficulty of getting press coverage (for touring programs, retrospective programming, and feminist cinema *tout court*), as well as the temporal difficulties of academic publishing.

With her "uncontainable energy for rule-breaking and pure being," Chytilová represented the kind of trouble we wanted to get into when resisting what Kristeva calls "political revolution": the strict masculinist-Marxist (often militant and militarist) model. Anti-state Czech director Chytilová famously referred to herself as an "individualist" rather than a feminist. Thus, to select her film for a feminist program was itself a willful act; the same was true of the short that we programmed to screen before *Daisies*, Chantal Akerman's debut *Saute Ma Ville* (*Blow My Town Up*, 1968), with its willful protagonist, played by Akerman herself. At the start of Anglo-American second-wave feminism, these two European directors explicitly set themselves against it. Akerman refused to screen her films in feminist and/or LGBTQI+ film festivals throughout her career, and the response to CDF's programming request was initially negative on that basis, when we approached the Belgian Cinematheque, with whom she had a close personal relationship and who control her estate. CDF continued the conversation by explaining our prior relation-ship with Akerman's work, having screened *Je tu il elle* (1974) as a collaboration with the radical Fringe! queer film festival in 2011. By staying with the trouble, we learned of Akerman's own love of *Daisies*, which helped us secure the rights and authenticated our intuitive montage pairing, affirming our willful feminist film genealogy.

A Second Life for *The Cat*

Akerman and Chytilova have both sustained auteurist canonicity, although often at the expense of being tokenized and depo-liticized. Writer/director Ula Stöckl is a cautionary example of an even more extreme erasure. Unlike her West German con-temporary Margarethe von Trotta, who has an international film festival and European arthouse profile, Stöckl has little traction outside of Germany; yet her 1968 film *The Cat Has Nine Lives* is considered to be West Germany's first feminist film. The Deutsche Kinemathek's 2K restoration of *The Cat* was long overdue, screening at the Berlinale in 2015, and in the Feminist Film Classics sidebar at the Seoul International Women's Film Festival 2017. Based on Stöckl's lived experiences but combining disruptive, non-linear action and dream sequences that form an episodic narrative, the film explores the relationships between four women. They creatively express their frustrations and desires as they experience their powerlessness to effect real change in their everyday lives. Shot in Technicolor and Cinemascope, Stöckl's film offers a riveting premonition of the feminist film culture that was to emerge in West Germany in the seventies; at once visually stunning, fashion-forward, drily affectless, and bitingly witty about patriarchy, the film also seems premonitory of television shows such as *Girls* (Lena Dunham, 2012–17) and *Fleabag* (Phoebe Waller-Bridge, 2016–).

Even with these reference points, we knew it would be difficult to create a critical audience for a film that was invisible outside of its original production context. Although Stöckl, together with Danièle Huillet and May Spils, became West Germany's very first professional female directors, they were constantly being overshadowed by their male partners and collaborators, as Julia Knight elucidates: "Stöckl... suffered from trying to explore the concerns of women too soon. With the women's movement barely in its birth throes when she made her directorial debut, a critical audience had not yet emerged capable of appreciating her work" (Knight 1992, 11). Apart from an interview that Stöckl gave to ground-breaking feminist film magazine *Frauen and Film* in June 1977, there is very little critical writing on the film. Therein, Stöckl states that because her film received negative reviews at its festival premiere screening in Mannheim, the film failed to find a distributor—except one who suggested that she add some pornographic scenes to make it more marketable! (Hillier, Lenssen and Strempel 1977, 3–11).

We therefore commissioned Berlin based writer/director Kanchi Wichmann to respond to the film for our zine, and her comments spoke to the film's complicated nature as a time capsule.

> In Stöckl's world women are comrades, soulmates, living and loving in glorious technicolour whilst men are bumbling fools, dressed in muted greys and browns and awkwardly

trying to hang on to their sense of entitlement. As gratifying as it is to see this cinematic reversal of the cultural norms of the era, there are times when the film falls into the trap of reinforcing the very gender binary her characters seek to escape. (Wichmann 2018)

We were conscious that *The Cat* needed careful handling, and realized we were fortunate to have collaborated with Dr. Annie Ring previously on a 35mm screening *The German Sisters* (1981) by Margarethe von Trotta. We invited her to give a contextual introduction to the film for a flagship screening at the BFI. She later remarked: "Audience members told me afterward that my introduction helped them to approach the film with knowledge of its context, and that my suggestions of film-theoretical ways of reading it make it easier to access a very experimental and mysterious work" (quoted in Pirkaalainen 2018).

Rather than explaining away the mystery, we expanded it by programming it with Swedish experimental filmmaker Gunvor Nelson's similarly dreamy short film *My Name is Oona* (1968), in order to maintain the position that subjective, interior films have a place in a radical/revolutionary program. A masculinist bias within histories of films and film movements was palpable in our discovery that *Oona*'s composer was listed online as Steve Reich, although (as the film's distributor FilmForum told us) the score was the work of the filmmaker. Undertaking such detail-oriented work seriously is part of the ethical complexity of queer feminist film curation; so is admitting a mistake or ignorance, and correcting it.

Here Come *The Girls*

Sometimes learning that a film exists is the beginning of that ethical work: none of us had seen *The Girls*, despite Simone de Beauvoir calling Zetterling's riotous third feature "the best movie ever made by a woman," and engaging the filmmaker to adapt *Le Deuxieme Sexe* for television (in Brison 2003, 197). A feminist manifesto/re-working of the Greek comedy *Lysistrata* (Aristophanes, 411 BCE), *The Girls* should be better known, not least because of Zetterling's cinematic and theatrical collaborations with Ingmar Bergman. Zetterling also lived in the UK for many years, making work funded by the BBC and the BFI.[3] A transnational film career presents its own difficulties: on the BFI Filmography, *Scrubbers* (1982) appears as her only directorial credit. We were, however, able to turn to her digital archives as an extensive resource; we watched filmed interviews from the 1960s, read recent scholarship on her work, and even perused her books on health, food, and cookery.

Despite its absence from the record, *The Girls* feels more contemporary than *The Cat*, because it frames its performers Liz (Bibi Andersson), Marianne (Harriet Andersson), and Gunnila (Gunnel Lindblom) as willful characters experiencing what Ahmed calls "feminist snap." They are "difficult women" who engage in confrontations with their audiences, as well as with neglectful husbands and boyfriends at home. Their articulate rage offers an historical reminder that actors were using their visibility, intelligence, and creativity to challenge patriarchal hierarchies long before the Time's Up movement. Through the women's relationship with the play's director, the film delivers an insightful and funny critique of Bergman, known for his intense and vexed relationships with the female performers whom he called "my actresses." Zetterling's sly analysis chimes with Jane Magnusson's documentary *Bergman: A Year in the Life*, which premiered at Sundance 2018, and takes its own critical look at his domineering relationships with his female collaborators and family members.

The Girls follows the theater troupe through wintry rural Sweden, and we found parallels in our own experiences with the difficulties and rewards of travelling to regional cinemas

3   In 2017, the Edinburgh International Film Festival programmed Zetterling's 1982 prison drama *Scrubbers* as the only female-directed film in their Retrospective program.

and feminist communities with our curatorial work. Thanks to support from the Swedish Film Institute, the film was the first to be confirmed for our season, but its absence from the Anglophone feminist canon made it a challenging selection for our opening flagship screening event at the Glasgow Film Theatre as part of the Radical Film Network's "Mayday '68" weekend. We had had only six weeks to program and organize the tour after our funding was confirmed, and the task at hand felt immense. Then, when we arrived in Glasgow, we faced the first heatwave of the summer, with people wanting to find the beach beneath the pavement rather than in cinemas!

Even with these circumstances, we found great pleasure in working on building our feminist networks and making new friends, in particular our Glasgow speakers Samar Ziadat, founder of Darshidi, artist filmmaker Margaret Salmon, and Kathi Kamleitner and Lauren Clarke, founder-members of Femspectives. Like the women in *The Girls*, we had to take an improvisational approach to being where we found ourselves, albeit with the added advantage of fifty years of feminist consciousness. That is: we did not have to throw pies at the patriarchal screen, we just had to get the conversation started. As Anna Backman Rogers writes of *The Girls* for our zine: "The film is ripe with Zetterling's own excoriating sense of humour and feminist rage—and for this, she has been chastised as vulgar and lacking in subtlety. It is, indeed, an unruly and disobedient work of art and it must be experienced as such" (Backman Rogers 2018) (fig. 3).

As a choice to screen before *The Girls*, Ayoka Chenzira's satirical, bitingly relevant short animation *Hair Piece: A Film for Nappy-Headed People* (1982) was our most ambitious attempt at montage programming, a term coined by Laura Mulvey (2015). Borrowing Sergei Eisenstein's revolutionary concept for film editing, Mulvey describes how the juxtapositions between films in a program can engage an audience politically. We sought a conversation between two formally and contextually diverse films that shared

[Fig. 3]: Still from *The Girls* by Mai Zetterling (*Flickorna*, Sweden, 1968). © AB Svensk Filmindustri, Photo: David Hughes, Stills Archive: The Swedish Film Institute.

a focus on intergenerational dialogue and on fashion and textiles. We also wanted to confront the whiteness of feminist cinema before the 1980s, and the way in which the canon has been shaped by access to materials, digital restorations, and dominant concepts of political relevance. Programming *Hair Piece* acted as a feminist rememory of our frustration at not being able to access the feature-length work of women filmmakers from the Global South. Filmmakers whose work we tried to access for the tour included: Franco-Guadaloupean "matriarch of African cinema" Sarah Maldoror, whose epic *Sambizanga* (1972) existed only in a single archive print that was touring elsewhere; and Afro-Cuban filmmaker Sara Gomez, whose singular fiction feature *De Cierta Manera* (*One Way or Another*, 1974) we screened at the Barbican in 2017, but could not tour on 35mm. As our tour came to a close, it was with huge satisfaction that we discovered Chenzira's *Hair Piece* has been acceded to the Library of Congress (Cannady 2018).

One Sings for Reproductive Justice

There were further resonances between CDF's counter-programming and currents of attention to feminist film in wider film culture. Over the twelve years of CDF's curating, we have seen neglected films that we have championed find a place in the archives; for example, Lizzie Borden's *Born in Flames* (1983), which CDF screened in our inaugural Dykesploitation program in 2007 from a heavily-worn 16mm print, received a restoration and 35mm transfer in 2016 by Anthology Film Archives in New York, in collaboration with the filmmaker. Borden contributed to "Revolt, She Said" with a personal reflection on *Maeve*, a coeval film directed by one of *Born in Flames*'s key cast members, Pat Murphy. In particular, Borden draws attention to the need to re-screen *Maeve* in 2018, the year of the campaign to #RepealThe8th, and subsequently the #NowForNI campaign to extend the United Kingdom's abortion laws to Northern Ireland.

While *Maeve* does not address reproductive rights directly, another of our features put abortion front and center. We chose Varda's *One Sings, the Other Doesn't* for its political timeliness. A heartfelt introduction by a speaker from Pro-Choice Nottingham introducing our flagship screening at Broadway Nottingham meant that the planned panel discussion became an inter-generational consciousness-raising group, with testimonial about experiences of abortion, single motherhood, marriage, divorce, adolescence, and finding feminism. The panel, including critic Christina Newland and programmer Sophia Ramcharan, had to find a feminist form to hold the difficult and necessary weight of this revelatory discussion in the time allotted.

One Sings produced the most personal responses of any film on the tour; as Jemma Desai noted for our zine, "*One Sings, The Other Doesn't* opens with an inscription [*pour Rosalie*]. Rosalie is Rosalie Demy: Agnès Varda's daughter" (Desai 2018). Desai notes that it is this intense intimacy that engages the viewer, as Varda shows her understanding that the "act of watching is a form of correspondence. This time I watch *One Sings, The Other Doesn't* as a form of correspondence with my daughter." This intergenerational continuum subtends from the film's central relationship between two women friends whose trajectories tally with one of the central arguments of the #RepealThe8th campaign: that access to abortion is an issue of economic class. One, Pomme, can afford to travel outside France to access a termination; while the other, Suzanne, cannot. It is Suzanne who becomes first an activist and then a healthcare provider to ensure that other women do not face the same experience, while Pomme shares the broader message of feminist autonomy and revolution through street theater and folk song.

Despite this personal-political consonance, we faced the difficulty of attuning audiences to a film infused with Marxism (including a song quoting Friedrich Engels) and Brechtian devices (such as the street theater) that fit neither with expectations of Francophone avant-garde work such as Jean-Luc Godard's more aggressive filmmaking, nor with Varda's recent auteurial reputation that had seen her refigured in (and for) the mainstream media as a grandmotherly figurehead of the Nouvelle Vague. We wanted to honor Varda's own willful critique of the ways in which older female artists are depoliticized and marketed as non-threatening. This is particularly dismissive as Varda insisted on her own difficulty; for example, by choosing to screen a new 4K restoration of *One Sings* at the Cannes Film Festival in 2018—on the beach!

Posing Riddles

1977 was a willful year: it was only in formulating the "Revolt, She Said" program that we realized *One Sings* was coeval with a foundational British feminist film, one whose difficulty is signaled in its very title: *Riddles of the Sphinx*. Connected by its co-directors Laura Mulvey and Peter Wollen to the height of film theory and theory film, *Riddles* experienced a similar split critique to *One Sings*, typed as too abstruse by feminists, and as too feminist

[Fig. 4] Still from *Riddles of the Sphinx* by Laura Mulvey & Peter Wollen (UK, 1977). *Riddles of the Sphinx* is released on DVD/Blu-ray by the BFI. Image courtesy BFI.

by avant-gardists. Yet our flagship screening at the Watershed Bristol, which we chose for the city's long association with alternative politics and experimental electronic music, ended with a cinema full of warm, supportive laughter at the final self-reflexive riddle, as an old mercury-ball toy maze is tilted over and over: an analogy for filmmaking, feminism, and the difficulty of situating the film itself.

As our panelist, scholar and curator Kim Knowles, said,

> The idea has always been that Laura Mulvey is a theorist, primarily a theorist and not a filmmaker, and I guess that's how, for me, initially I approach the film. When I came to it as a film student, having encountered [her essay] "Visual Pleasure and Narrative Cinema," I thought, okay, *Riddles of the Sphinx* is going to be a quite dense, a politically and theoretically dense film, and what's surprising is that it isn't. It has that accessibility. I find it striking how accessible it is, but surprising how absent it is from the histories. (quoted in Judah 2018b)

Despite the BFI's distribution of *Riddles* on DVD, it proved difficult
to obtain digital materials to screen on our tour, exemplifying a
general lack of access. Yet, as Grace Barber-Plentie pointed out
for our zine, perhaps this difficulty generates a useful encounter
because of its complexity:

> It's disheartening to think that in 2018, *Riddles* can still feel
> fresh and unique and new…. But maybe this is the problem
> of being the first, or at least a pioneer of something….
> With renewed interest in the film in 2018, the Sphinx is re-
> emerging. It was never defeated, never fully gone, just lying
> dormant. It is resurrected. (Barber-Plentie 2018)

That sense of resurrection was apparent in the energy that our
panelists brought to their fresh readings of the film. As filmmaker Esther May Campbell said at Watershed, "it's really clear—
[Mulvey's] understanding of what she's communicating to the
audience and how she's asking the audience to think and put a
narrative together. Sometimes it shifts from being illustrative and
then it becomes narrative and then it goes meditative and then it
goes narrative again, but I was bowled over" (in Judah 2018b).

Our third panelist, programmer and critic Lorena Pino Montilla,
noted that, for her as an immigrant from Venezuela, the film
resonated most strongly as a documentary of the changing
Britain of the late 1970s, from the freshness of its concerns with
divorce, working motherhood, mixed-race and queer relationships, and union politics, to its textural details of cigarette
packets, kitchen colorways, and vibrant clothing (fig. 4). For all
three panelists, these accessible elements were connected to,
and shaped by, the film's political and theoretical arguments. *Riddles* emerged from our discussion as, in fact, a film with nothing
to hide but rather one that has been hidden. The laughter that
greeted and celebrated what remains freshly recognizable in the
film, as it speaks to intersectional politics of labor, racialization,
and sexuality within the feminist movement, was a delight that
should not have surprised us, but was a welcome surprise.

Remembering *Maeve*

On 8th August, 2018 we were no less surprised and delighted to read that possibly our most "willful" title on the tour was featured in the London *Evening Standard* as a highlight of the London Feminist Film Festival, with a prominent still from the film in the print edition (Paskett 2018). *Maeve*'s "willfulness" meant that, due to complications over territory rights and materials, the film was not able to join the tour until 1 August. Our difficulties in exhibition reflected, in minor key, the acute difficulties of the film's production history. As Borden points out: "While we played with fake guns and planted fake bombs in downtown Manhattan [for *Born in Flames*], Pat travelled in and out of a real war zone. I don't think that we really understood that or how major it was that *Maeve* had opened the Edinburgh Film Festival [in 2018]" (Borden 2018). Although *Maeve* was only able to tour for one month, we secured nine screenings of the film; Filmhouse Edinburgh tweeted their original festival program note to mark this thirty-seventh anniversary screening!

When co-director Murphy contacted us to let us know of her availability to present the film at the Rio Cinema, we had to act fast to re-arrange the panel. The final difficulty came on the day of the screening, as festival scheduling inevitably led to overrunning. We did not have enough time to unpack the film fully with our multigenerational audience of feminists of all genders, particularly from the London Irish Women's Network, in conversation with our post-screening panel. We were, however, delighted to hear production and reception stories from Murphy, her co-director John Davies, the film's director of photography and producer Robert Smith, and Irish artist filmmaker Michelle Deignan. Not only did the screening act as a reunion for the production team, who hadn't seen each other since the release, but also Murphy connected with old friends such as Felicity Sparrow (founder member of feminist film distributor Circles), after many decades away from London.

As is the case with so many women filmmakers on our tour, Murphy's career was cut short due to the lack of institutional support. On the film's release, Claire Johnston offered a Marxist feminist analysis of *Maeve* in *Screen*, wherein she read the film as a search for a positive imaginary for women outside of a nationalist culture, thereby enabling women to enter language and history on their own terms—but beyond this, *Maeve*'s feminist reception is sparse, and the film has not entered national film histories (Johnston 1981, 54–71). *Maeve* is a critique of supposedly "radical" (nationalist, liberationist, leftist) politics that remain cis male-led today. Programming it within a post-'68 season was an important discursive intervention: reminding audiences that May '68 (when the Troubles began) also meant revolt against the rule of patriarchy as well as political occupation and colonial rape culture. The gaps within our program show that the full history of post-suffrage women's and feminist protest in the UK remains to be documented.

Carrying *Greenham Home*

"The women of Greenham Common taught a generation how to protest," noted Beeban Kidron, who made *Carry Greenham Home*, her first film, while living on-site with co-director Amanda Richardson during their final year at the National Film and Television School (Kidron 2013). Prior to CDF's theatrical screenings, *Carry Greenham Home* had previously only been been available to women's and community groups: first on video (its shooting format), then DVD, and now streaming. This allowed the film to reach the "large potential audience for feminist films" described by Annette Kuhn in the 1980s, which "exists among women who rarely visit film theatres, and who certainly do not normally consider going to see films in non-commercial cinemas" (Kuhn 1994, 187). Grassroots circulation, however, meant there was no academic writing about *Carry Greenham Home* as a film prior to So Mayer's 2017 article, which followed on from CDF's screening of the film at the Rio Cinema in Hackney (Mayer 2017, 67–76).

[Fig. 5] Still from *Carry Greenham Home* by Beeban Kidron & Amanda Richardson (UK, 1983). Image courtesy of Contemporary Films.

Programming the film within "Revolt, She Said" was a willful act that drew on the film's grassroots history while arguing for its aesthetic and theoretical place in our anti-canon (fig. 5).

Ahmed speaks of willful objects carrying affects: we feel this when carrying a feminist film, collective or community out of its grassroots "home" into institutional spaces. There was a difficulty in managing and mediating audience expectations concerning this film because of the closely guarded history of Greenham. Recent years have seen richly textured academic studies from Sasha Roseneil and Anna Reading (both speakers at CDF's 2016 screening) that cover the diversity of Greenham women, including trans women (Roseneil 2000; Reading 2015, 147–65). There remains a significant overlap, however, between traditional "ownership" of Greenham, and the historical radical-feminist community, which in recent years has become transphobic by definition in its organizing and self-constitution. This produced a number of difficult face-to-face encounters during a summer of rising tensions in 2018, fueled by social media disinformation and intense discussions around the Gender Recognition Act con-sultation (Finlayson, Jenkins and Worsdale 2018). This points to the difficulty *of* feminist community as reflected in the film. As documentary critic and programmer Sophie Brown writes for our zine: "The film observes women trying out alternative systems to exist together. There are clashes, dissonances and varying scales of radical beliefs, but they work hard to upload their shared goal of peace" (Brown 2018). We tried to learn from the film how to handle these fractures in our community as programmers committed to trans inclusion.

Placing feminist collective Sheffield Film Co-op's short film *A Question of Choice* (1982) with *Carry Greenham Home* acted as a reminder of the difficulties that have always been inherent in telling feminism as a single story. Workers' rights were at the heart of '68 politics, but little attention was paid (as *Riddles* also points out) to working mothers with caring commitments. The short observational documentary explores the lack of job pro-spects for Sheffield women with families to support. Shot one year after *Carry Greenham Home*, the film shows that there were multiple feminisms and women's experiences operating in the UK at the same time, drawing attention to the often-forgotten axis of class, which remains under-discussed in feminist film theory and history. Margaret Dickinson's and Angela Martin's oral history projects with the founding members of the Sheffield Film Co-op are vital contributions to unpacking these feminist theory and activist practice histories (Dickinson 1999; Martin 2014). Part of the difficulty, in multiple senses, of CDF's work, lies in maintaining the connections between feminist film scholarship in print, and print traffic of films, as theoretically-informed programming is viewed as willful in an anti-intellectual mainstream. Our pro-grams, however, often pay tribute to scholars such as Dickinson who have kept films alive through their writing, even when they are hard to see.

Going Back *Before Stonewall*

"We needed to write ourselves as queer people into the history books," said Greta Schiller, the director of *Before Stonewall* (1984), about her multi-award winning documentary.[4] *Before Stonewall* is a cinematic journey into the archive that unearths queer lives before the Stonewall Riots in New York City, 1969. Unlike many of our films on the tour, *Before Stonewall* had and has a transnational cinematic exhibition history thanks to the emergence of queer film festivals. Now available online through UK distribution by Peccadillo Pictures, it has become part of LGBTQI+ social and film history and popular culture. We had to find a way to re-contextualize the film for contemporary audiences, including situating it within and against Donald Trump's extremist homophobic and transphobic rhetoric, which feels like a 1980s revival. On a panel, Schiller noted that the film was made in the climate of homophobia intensified by the Reagan administration, which ignored and exacerbated the AIDS crisis.

For our zine, writer-director and programmer Jason Barker remembers watching the film for the first time when he was 28 years old:

> I remember thinking the early part of the 20th century seemed like a very, very long time ago. I probably had a patronising attitude about the people in the film—bless them! I'm pretty certain I would have watched the film marvelling at just how far gay and lesbian rights had come since then. I'm older now. Nearly 50 and it feels like time has sort of folded in on itself. Now when I watch *Before Stonewall* I don't think that we have come so far at all. Queerness feels as precarious and as precious as ever. (Barker 2018)

4   Schiller was speaking at the 2018 Berlinale, on the panel "40 years of queer programming" to mark 40 years of Panorama, the section of the festival historically closely associated with the Teddy, the festival-wide award for best LGBTQI+ film.

Queer cinema itself remains precarious and precious: in particular, the histories of queer archival production. Pre-digitization, archive documentary filmmaking was immensely labor-intensive for researchers and film historians such as Schiller, including the emotional labor of bringing the previously hidden and taboo into view. This affective and intellectual labor was celebrated within the emerging network of queer film festivals, which supported a golden era of painstakingly researched LGBTQI+ history documentaries including *The Times of Harvey Milk* (Rob Epstein, 1984), *The Celluloid Closet* (Rob Epstein and Jeffrey Friedman 1995), and *A Bit of Scarlet* (Andrea Weiss, 1997). Today's mainstreaming of New Queer Cinema, which arguably has diluted much of the political potency of many queer film festivals, has erased a certain queer urgency of earlier work.

In an era of cinematic and archival abundance within the total saturation of the military-entertainment complex, CDF's difficulty was to remind audiences that attending a film screening can be political act. This was memorably enacted at the Hyde Park Picture House, in collaboration with Leeds Queer Film Festival, when we invited former ACT UP New York member and lecturer Monica Pearl to introduce *Before Stonewall*. Her words, quoting civil rights activist and Congressman John Lewis, were live-streamed on the cinema's Facebook page; audiences then stayed afterwards to ask questions about a history taking place before many of them were born. As Pearl remarked later on:

> This is precisely why it is so important to share these kinds of stories in cinemas. It creates a gathering of like- or similar-minded people who may nevertheless be very different in attitude, age, demographic, or experience who are eager for intelligent discussion outside of an academic arena. I am not sure if it brought new audiences to that cinema, but it created a gathering that, without that screening, would not have happened. We could easily call it, therefore, a political event. (in Pirkaalainen, 2018)

 Recognizing a screening as a political event both pays tribute to the canonical film history of May '68, specifically the precursor protests against changes to the management of the Cinémathèque Français. Both the documentary method of *Before Stonewall* and our programming strategy align more closely with Kristeva's continuously transformative psychic and artistic "revolt" as an unfolding, rather than contained, political event.

Holding *A Place of Rage*

Before Stonewall's gathering strategies—in terms of its interviewees and its original release—link it intimately to *A Place of Rage*. Like Schiller's film, Parmar's draws on archival footage, but embeds it within living conversations with Black lesbian feminist leaders, Angela Davis, June Jordan, and Alice Walker. Although focused on the US, the film is also a testament to a transatlantic feminist anti-racist decolonial consciousness, although one that is less visible on-screen. At our flagship screening at Chapter Arts Centre, Cardiff, in August 2018, panelist Yasmin Begum, a writer and activist, noted that: "Watching the film made me think of activists who have gone before me, like Betty Campbell, the first Black head teacher in Cardiff. Growing up I didn't see many Welsh women of colour."[5]

As Nazmia Jamal notes in her piece for our zine (fig. 6), Parmar was a key contributor to 1980s documentation and creative practice by, for, and about women of color in the UK, and particularly queer women of color. Noting also that Parmar's work was difficult to access only twenty years later, Jamal writes that:

> By the time I started working at LLGFF [London Lesbian and Gay Film Festival, now Flare] in 2008 I'd seen *A Place of Rage* and perhaps one or two other films by Pratibha. I used my new "film job" to watch every tape of her work I could lay my

5   Tweeted by Chapter Arts: https://twitter.com/chaptertweets/
     status/1025095104703483907

[Fig. 6] "Revolt, She Said" zine. Image courtesy of Club des Femmes and Independent Cinema Office.

> hands on. At the time I was particularly keen on her queer desi work, like *Khush* (1991), or the work she made about being a woman in Britain. (Jamal 2018)

While Kali Films, Parmar's production company with her producing and life partner Shaheen Haq, has distributed *A Place of Rage* on DVD in the US, they have only recently made the film available for international streaming on Vimeo. Thus, even though it is a more recent film, we faced the same challenges of access to physical materials and to building an audience as with the older films in our program.

We therefore faced a dual challenge: we needed to care for a film that has been neglected and decontextualized in what remains a violently homophobic and racist environment, without smoothing out or excusing the film's willingly willful rage; while simultaneously working to reach beyond the entrenched white, middle-class dominant audience for cultural cinema. We thus programmed the film in Cardiff with three speakers of color with personal and political connections in the city.[6] As Jamal noted, "the audience was clearly very different to Chapter's usual crowd and several were Black women or women of colour who were involved in local organisations working with [Black, Asian and minority ethnic] women or children" (in Pirkaalainen 2018). Screening the film in 2018 and 2019 drew on and drew attention to how the queer feminist leadership and practices of Black Lives Matter have centered Davis, Jordan, and Walker, retaining their nuance, their radical self-care, and their individuality as part of their exceptional political and cultural intelligence; precisely, their willfulness.

(In)Conclusion: "A Permanent State of Questioning"

Characterizing willfulness, Ahmed in fact turns to a definition of womanist by Walker, as referring to "outrageous, audacious, courageous or *willful* behavior… responsible. In charge. *Serious*" (Walker 2005, xi, quoted Ahmed 2017, 78; emphasis in the original). Ahmed's invocation of Walker's work in 2017 signals the ways in which the willful feminist's responsible, serious archival behavior must act, continuously, as a counter to dominant culture's repeated dismissal of feminist work, and especially work by women and feminists of color. Given the complexity and vulnerability of *A Place of Rage*, we were particularly outrageous and audacious in pairing it with another film that challenges the complacencies of a white-dominated feminist film canon and spectatorship.

Nice Colored Girls (1990) by First Nations Australian filmmaker and photographer Tracey Moffatt is described by Tara Judah for our zine as

> umami: Moffatt gives us sweet tang in the "nice" girls of the title, cut in contrast with the "nasty" girls of the 1982 number one pop song she employs, Vanity 6's "Nasty Girl." Far from being about sex, the film reveals how sexualized bodies have historically been used as items for white pleasure and how they are now contested spaces, their owners expected to seize leverage for agency and survival. (Judah 2018a)

In an umami echo of our oldest film, *Daisies* (1966), the most recent also shows young women on a night out in the city, rolling an older man for food, drink, and money, but the stakes here are higher. As Judah says, the young First Nations women's "existence relies on their successfully navigating the rules of a game called postcolonial inequality." The final screen marks the young women's revolution as exceeding the frame. It requires activation by audiences, willing us to willful action. It is a difficult sensation. As Marks concludes her thoughts on ethical curation, suggesting that critical times call for critical curatorial measures: her project "was so successful precisely because its political stakes were so high…. In a country where political crisis is relatively explicit, where artists and curators operate in an environment of evident social and political injustice, clear and compelling arguments are more obviously called for" (Marks 2004, 46).

"Revolt, She Said" reflects the emergent political crises in the UK, and learns its necessity for argument from filmmakers in times and places where "evident social and political injustice" had called for "clear and compelling argument." We are, once again, in a place of rage, and the riddles of the sphinx still call for answers; we return to the difficulties of articulation and action that have confronted subsequent generations recognizing the crisis of capitalist colonial heteropatriarchy. As Coatman writes of *The Cat Has Nine Lives*, "it feels insurrectionary [… because t]he 'natural' order is starting to break down" (Coatman 2018, 15). To compost; to be willingly willful in the destruction of our happiness, Club des Femmes started to break it down in 2018 with the films of "Revolt, She Said." With this paper, we continue "probing… appearances."

Club des Femmes is a queer feminist film curation collective whose members include Jenny Clarke, So Mayer, Selina Robertson, Alex Thiele, and Sarah Wood. "Revolt, She Said" was programmed collectively by CDF with the support of the Independent Cinema Office and BFI, awarding funds from The National Lottery. Thank you also to all at the ICO, and to all of our venue partners, speakers and panelists, zine contributors, and audience members throughout the summer of 2018. Special thanks to our programming focus group participants Marta Genova (London Feminist Film Festival), Melissa Gueneau (Broadway), Tara Judah (Watershed), Mikaela Smith (Showroom), and Claire Vaughan (Chapter Arts Centre) for their insights, which helped inform this essay.

Films for the tour were provided by Cinematek (Cinémathèque Royale de Belgique); British Film Institute; Cinenova; Contemporary Films; Czech Film Institute; Curzon/Artificial Eye; Deutsche Kinemathek; Filmforum; Kali Films and Pratibha Parmar; Peccadillo Pictures; Second Run DVD; sixpack films; Svenska Filminstitutet; and Women Make Movies.

References

Ahmed, Sara. 2017. *Living a Feminist Life*. Durham and London: Duke University Press.

Backman Rogers, Anna. 2018. "The Girls." *Club des Femmes*. Accessed October 23, 2023. https://www.clubdesfemmes.com/culture-club/anna-backman-rogers-on-the-girls/.

Barber-Plentie, Grace. 2018. "Riddles of the Sphinx." *Club des Femmes*. Accessed October 23, 2023. https://www.clubdesfemmes.com/culture-club/grace-barber-plentie-on-riddles-of-the-sphinx/.

Barker, Jason. 2018. "Before Stonewall." *Club des Femmes*. Accessed October 23, 2023. https://www.clubdesfemmes.com/culture-club/jason-barker-on-before-stonewall/.

Borden, Lizzie. 2018. "Maeve." *Club des Femmes*. Accessed October 23, 2023. https://www.clubdesfemmes.com/culture-club/lizzie-borden-on-maeve/.

Brison, Susan J. 2003. "Beauvoir and Feminism: Interview and Reflections." In *The Cambridge Companion to Simone de Beauvoir*, ed. Claudia Card, 189–207. Cambridge: Cambridge University Press.

Brown, Sophie. 2018. "Carry Greenham Home." *Club des Femmes*. Accessed October 23, 2023. https://www.clubdesfemmes.com/culture-club/sophie-brown-on-carry-greenham-home/.

Cannady, Sheryl. 2018. "National Film Registry Turns 30." *Library of Congress*. Accessed October 23, 2023. www.loc.gov/item/prn-18-144/library-of-congress-national-film-registry-turns-30/2018-12-12/.

Clarke, Jenny. 2018. "Revolt, She Searched." *Club des Femmes*. Accessed October 23, 2023. https://www.clubdesfemmes.com/culture-club/revolt-she-searched-by-jenny-clarke/.

Coatman, Anna. 2018. "Kicking Against the Pricks." *Sight & Sound* 28 (9): 14.

Desai, Jemma. 2018. "One Sings, the Other Doesn't." *Club des Femmes*. Accessed October 23, 2023. https://www.clubdesfemmes.com/culture-club/jemma-desai-on-one-sings-the-other-doesnt/.

Dickinson, Margaret. 1999. "Sheffield Film Co-op." In *Rogue Reels: Oppositional Film in Britain, 1945–90*, 289–303. London: BFI Publishing.

Finlayson, Lorna, Katherine Jenkins, and Rosie Worsdale. 2018. "'I'm Not Transphobic, But...': A Feminist Case Against the Feminist Case Against Trans Inclusivity." *Verso*. Accessed October 23, 2023. www.versobooks.com/blogs/4090-i-m-not-transphobic-but-a-feminist-case-against-the-feminist-case-against-trans-inclusivity.

Gray, Carmen. "Daisies." *Club des Femmes*. Accessed October 23, 2023. https://www.clubdesfemmes.com/culture-club/carmen-gray-on-daisies/

Haraway, Donna. 2016. *Staying With the Trouble: Making Kin in the Chthulucene*. Durham NC: Duke University Press.

Hillier, Eva, Claudia Lenssen and Gesine Strempel. 1977. "Gespräch mit Ula Stöckl." *Frauen und Film* 12: 3–11.

Hutchinson, Pamela. 2018. "Angry Young Women." *The Guardian*, July 13. Accessed October 23, 2023. www.theguardian.com/film/2018/jul/13/club-des-femmes-radical-feminist-queer-film.

Jamal, Nazmia. 2018. "A Place of Rage." *Club des Femmes*. Accessed October 23, 2023. https://www.clubdesfemmes.com/culture-club/nazmia-jamal-on-a-place-of-rage/.

Johnston, Claire. 1981. "Maeve." *Screen* 22 (4): 54–71.

Judah, Tara. 2018a. "Nice Coloured Girls." *Club des Femmes*. Accessed October 23, 2023. https://www.clubdesfemmes.com/culture-club/tara-judah-on-nice-coloured-girls/.

———. 2018b. "The Riddles of Film History in 360 Degrees." *Watershed*. Accessed October 23, 2023. www.watershed.co.uk/articles/the-riddles-of-film-history-in-360-degrees.

Kidron, Beeban. 2013. "The Women of Greenham Common Taught a Generation How to Protest." *The Guardian*, September 2. Accessed October 23, 2023. www.theguardian.com/uk-news/2013/sep/02/greenham-common-women-taught-generation-protest.

Knight, Julia. 1992. *Women and the New German Cinema*. London and New York: Verso.

Kristeva, Julia. 2002. *Revolt, She Said*. Trans. Brian O'Keeffe. Cambridge: Semiotext(e).

Kuhn, Annette. 1994. *Women's Pictures*. London and New York: Verso.

110 Liu, Rebecca. 2019. "Finding Your Rage." *Another Gaze.* Accessed October 23, 2023. www.anothergaze.com/finding-rage-club-des-femmes-revolt-said-programme.

Marks, Laura U. 2004. "The Ethical Presenter: Or, How to Have Good Arguments over Dinner." *The Moving Image: The Journal of the Association of Moving Image Archivists* 4 (1): 36–37.

Martin, Angela. 2014. "Becoming Sheffield Film Co-op." *Women's Film and Television History.* Accessed October 23, 2023. https://womensfilmandtelevisionhistory. wordpress.com/2014/04/04/becoming-sheffield-film-co-op/.

Mayer, So. 2017. "'That's Why We Came Here': Feminist Cinema(s) at Greenham Common." *Angelaki* 22: 67–76.

Merriam-Webster. 2018. "The History of 'Hot Mess'." *Merriam-Webster.* Accessed October 23, 2023. https://www.merriam-webster.com/wordplay/the-history-of-hot-mess.

Mulvey, Laura. 2015. "Curating Now: Film Curating as Montage." Lecture. London: Birkbeck University of London. Accessed October 23, 2023. https://youtu.be/ yUvK_8aLg8Q.

Paskett, Zoe. 2018. "The Women Ready for their Close-Up." *Evening Standard*, 8 August.

Reading, Anna. 2015. "Singing for My Life: Memory, Nonviolence and the Songs of Greenham Common Women's Peace Camp." In *Cultural Memories of Nonviolent Struggles: Powerful Times*, edited by Anna Reading and Tamar Katriel, 147–65. Basingstoke: Palgrave Macmillan.

Pirkaalainen, Maria. 2018. "Revolt, We Said: Sharing Women's Revolutionary Films around the UK." *Independent Cinema Office.* Accessed October 23, 2023. www. independentcinemaoffice.org.uk/blog-revolt-we-said/.

Roseneil, Sasha. 2000. *Common Women, Uncommon Practices: The Queer Feminisms of Greenham*. London and New York: Cassell.

Walker, Alice. 2005. *In Search of Our Mother's Gardens*. Phoenix: New Edition.

Wichmann, Kanchi. 2018. "The Cat Has Nine Lives." *Club des Femmes.* Accessed October 23, 2023. https://www.clubdesfemmes.com/culture-club/kanchi-wichmann-on-the-cat-has-nine-lives/

This section presents some of the contributions from the first workshop in the *Serge Daney and Queer Cinephilia* project, which took place in Paris in 2018 and addressed Serge Daney and his legacy. The main topic of the event was the dimension of otherness in Daney's writings: cinema considered as the "other" as well as a means of perceiving otherness; criticism considered as a median position, a mediation—or, to put it like Lacan: the "other of the Other." Over these two days, which brought together academics, young researchers, film critics, and independent scholars[1], an important part of the exchanges (not transcribed here) focused—not fortuitously—on translation. Daney is still very little translated into English, and the question of exchanges between the French cinephilic spirit and more culturalist English-language film studies has to be investigated, as well as the differences between film cultures. Each of the following authors sheds light on a dimension in Daney's work that opens itself to an elsewhere, a form of otherness, a future. Garin Dowd and Bamchade Pourvali show how Daney's ideas trace important paths for rethinking a new cinephilia, one that he had not experienced, as well as entire cinematographies that will bloom after his death. Claire Allouche evokes Daney's unflagging curiosity for world cinema, a topic he significantly brought to the attention of his French readers. While Daney wrote numerous texts on tennis, Hervé Joubert-Laurencin studies his sole article on table tennis (its miniature twin), and the entanglement between television and sports precisely analyzed by Daney. This section ends with two contributions about *Trafic,* the critic's final project, a journal he founded shortly before his death, which was continued afterwards by his friends from the editorial board. A text by Simon Pageau revisits the spirit that animated the journal's first issues during Daney's lifetime. A round table with the editorial board revisits the history of this journal and its evolution after Daney,

1   Claire Allouche, Raymond Bellour, Christa Blümlinger, Hervé Joubert-Laurencin, Laurent Kretschmar, Simon Pageau, Sylvie Pierre, Bamchade Pourvali, Patrice Rollet, Jonathan Rosenbaum, Marcos Uzal, Dork Zabunyan.

with its constant desire to remain faithful to his former choices. After thirty years, the initial project of the quarterly journal ended in December 2021, with a last issue, *Trafic* no. 120. A new version of *Trafic* as an annual journal was launched in December 2022, under the title: *Trafic, l'almanach du cinéma*, with a new editorial board composed by Raymond Bellour, Bernard Benoliel, Christa Blümlinger, Jean-Paul Fargier and Judith Revault-d'Allones. Unfortunately, the editor ceased publication after this sole issue, following the sudden death of the copyeditor, Jean-Luc Mengus, who had accompanied the journal since 1993.

Pierre Eugène

COMMUNITY
____

CINEPHILIA
____

THE IMAGE
____

5

Cinephilia Falls to Earth: Thinking the Image after Daney

Garin Dowd

This essay explores the posterity of Serge Daney's writings by proposing a series of provisional categorizations in the manner of Daney, who often worked with tripartite distinctions. To think the image after Daney is here to think both in his aftermath and in his lineage (i.e. with him). It is to continue to think with the repertoire of concepts and approaches enshrined in his writing and to think with the conflicted practice of cinephilia that we find in his understanding of his own career as a critic. To think the image after Daney, I propose, is paradoxically to continue to think about the contemporary in a manner attentive to and following his own already retrospective disposition.

"Les films du cinéma atterrissent à la télévision comme s'ils venaient d'en-haut, d'un écran dans les hauteurs ou d'un ciel."[1]

Cinephilia after the End of Cinema

On my visit to Paris in the year of the 50th anniversary of the events of May 1968, the vitrines of the Champo cinema were adorned with publicity materials to mark seasons devoted to Fassbinder and Wenders respectively. Around the corner in another cabinet on rue Champollion a period poster featured painted representations of John Wayne and Maureen O'Hara in Ford's *The Quiet Man/L'Homme tranquille*. Beside that, behind another pane of glass, Nastassja Kinski in *Paris, Texas* was represented by a low-resolution image on A4 paper, which had clearly been printed by the cinema rather than either drawn from a repository or derived from an archival negative as might have been the case thirty years before. Posters dating from the original French release dates of Wenders's *Les Ailes du désir/ Wings of Desire* and Fassbinder's *Veronika Voss* adorned other surfaces around the curved corner on which Rue des Écoles's much loved *cinéma d'art et d'essai* stands.[2] A little further up the rue Champollion the Reflet Médicis cinema had, in its main poster glass side by side, a period poster for *La Fiancée du pirate/A Very Curious Girl* by Nelly Kaplan and one for the 4K restoration of *La Chair de l'orchidée/The Flesh of the Orchid* by Patrice Chéreau.

A few people positioned at different points along the frontage of the Champo looked at posters and read printouts of reviews

1   "Cinema films land on television as if they came from on high, from a screen in the heights or from a sky."

2   On the mannerism of *Veronika Voss*, see Daney 1986, 109.

and historical source materials.[3] They joined each other to wait
until it was time to queue for the 11.30 Friday morning screening
of Wenders' *The Goalkeeper's Fear of the Penalty*. Others began to
arrive. Eventually a queue formed and the staff placed a sign on
the pavement of Rue des Écoles to control its direction.

All the films and all the filmmakers represented on the walls of
the approximately 150 square meters of façade embracing two
cinemas on this one corner of Paris at some point came under
the scrutiny and received the critical appraisal of Serge Daney.
The manner, however, of the presence of the majority of the
films mentioned both on the walls of the exterior and within the
salles (movie theaters) has radically changed since the period in
which Daney and his contemporaries—and certainly the cinephiles of his generation—might themselves have frequented such
cinemas. The Champo retains its vitrines; it retains moreover
the preference for analog publicity (for example, original posters
from the French releases) when it is accessible. Even though
some of the publicity materials appearing behind the glass may
these days be printed out from a digital source which can make
the presentation seem amateurish, the vitrines of the Champo
continue to reflect a time that at first glance resembles and thus
includes Daney's time. The queue, the line, the *file d'attente* on the
rue des Écoles may even have comprised members of a queue
that formed there for the first run of *Wings of Desire*, the same
and different.

Daney, our contemporary?

Writing in his journal in 1990, having viewed Straub and Huillet's
Moïse et Aaron (Daney 1993, 256), Daney recounts that there were
ten of them in the *salle* at the Panthéon, adding the question:

3   Daney, in recalling the role played by the ritual of attendance at the 9
     o'clock screenings in the company of his mother in the cinemas of the 12th
     arrondissement, remembers how they would often look at the photos out-
     side and end up missing the film due to their hesitation (Daney 2015, 190).

 were we/they errant spectators or a virtual sect? Elsewhere Jean Douchet, in the *Cahiers du cinéma* special commemorative issue on Daney (no. 458), recalling the Cinémathèque française, recounts how within its walls and before its screen, first of all one belonged to a tribe, then a group, then in turn a sub-group, and finally a tendency, as in the phrase "tendance Rossellini, tendance Godard" and of course immortalized in the negative formulation in the title of Truffaut's famous attack on the *qualité française* (Truffaut 1954). Rarely, in such a community, did one belong to oneself.

Thinking the image after Serge Daney is a notion which must consider heterogeneous temporalities, depending on the Serge Daney one has been able, according to linguistic aptitude, to encounter. For the non-reader of French, it has been considerably more difficult to follow Daney in his manner of thinking the image, to follow him at the time of writing and to continue to be influenced or inspired by him after his death. The translations are scattered and to date the only book to be published in English is given the title *Postcards from the Cinema* (Daney 2007), which contains merely the sketch of a possible book by Daney rather than one signed by him during his lifetime.[4]

But there are other ways in which following Daney in France, following his writing, has become difficult. Some of the books in which his texts were collected are now out of print. While the books were always already collections of articles, they were encountered by a generation as *books*.

In fact, mimicking Deleuze's three phases of cinema for Daney (which in turn is an enumeration made by Deleuze in tribute to Daney's own penchant for thinking in threes), as outlined in his preface to *Ciné-Journal* (Daney 1986), one might say that there are, in France and for those who read French, three phases of

4   Semiotext(e) published recently the first volume of a translation of *Le Maison cinéma et le monde* (Daney 2022).

following Daney as a reader: first, there is a reading that goes 123
in tandem with publication, in *Cahiers* and then in *Libération*;
second, there is the retrospective reading of the collections *as
collections* (a period that may be complicated in that the reader
of the first category may overlap partially); third, there is the
encounter with the writings as presented in the four volumes of
La Maison cinéma et le monde, a period that of course also is that
of the period post-Daney and manifest in a form that in fact does
not reprint many important texts from the individual books published during his lifetime.

Hence those who come after in this context may consist of
a following that is contemporaneous—Daney leads, readers
follow—but equally a following that is retrospective, just as it also
embraces one that is posthumous. Is the Daney encountered in
each of these different temporalities of engagement the same? A
focus on the *passeur* and the allied theme of community makes
this question relevant.

To explore temporal complications further, there is a pre-68 and
a post-68 *Cahiers* or a *Cahiers* under Daney's editorship as one
that needs to be set apart; a *Libération* phase; a tennis-journalist
phase overlapping with a *zappeur* phase; and of course, finally, a
Trafic phase (encompassing both the period of its planning and
his brief tenure at the helm).

One might then—to broaden the perspective and to add yet
another tripartite distinction—consider the question of the
status of the cinematographic and the audio-visual image during
each of these phases—phases that are marked by three distinct
modes of engaging with his writings (contemporaneously, retrospectively, posthumously) in turn symbolized by the article in its
original form, the article collected in *La Rampe* (Daney 1983), for
instance, and the article as collected in the four P.O.L. volumes
(Daney 2001–2015). The first phase would loosely coincide with
the continuation of the development of what Deleuze identified
as Daney's preoccupation with the great pedagogical lines; the

 second with Daney's exploration of the new image regime of television and video. The third is our period, the one Daney could not have foreseen, the one of streaming, Netflix, boxsets (without boxes), and films produced by Amazon.

As a way of approaching these themes one can propose that there are (again) three modes of encountering the work of Daney, and therefore three modes of disseminating his thought—three modes of its *passing* which includes being passed on, as we say in English of the act of bequeathing upon death. (I say this because, in taking up the baton of *Trafic*, Raymond Bellour, Sylvie Pierre, and the other editors have enabled Daney's final project to be passed on to us as an inheritance.) At the same time I want to invoke the idea that there are at least three communities in the village named Daney, born in different decades and belonging to different generations. I want to think about the specificities of these readerships both in terms of their relationship to the historical period, considered especially in terms of technological communications developments (but also political developments), and to the mode in which Daney was writing as their con-temporary (magazine, newspaper, book), to their relation to the technology and/or to the mode, and whether this relationship was one of contemporaneity or retrospection.

With and After Daney

Thinking the image after Daney? In terms of an encounter through English, the time lag between a possible and an actual *being-with* Daney can be immense, for reasons well doc-umented. But there are isolated signs of some catching up. In a 2016 article for the art theory journal *October* James Tweedie asserts that Daney is a precursor of media archaeology. Tweedie challenges the widely held view that Daney disdains television. He acknowledges inconsistencies in Daney's view of the medium, but asserts that the rediscovery of film on television forms part of an already anachronistic view of cinema, both in terms of an acknowledgement that we are already at the end of cinema, with something such as Pasolini's *Teorema* in 1968, and in the era of the victory of mass industrial cinema. Hence the rear-view mirror (*rétroviseur*) idea, which Tweedie adopts from Daney as the organizing metaphor for his reappraisal.

In a much earlier appraisal, on the tenth anniversary of Daney's death, Jean-François Pigouillié, who contributed to *Cahiers* in the 1990s, presents a quite different argument about Daney's posterity, suggesting that in the issue of *Trafic* devoted to Daney in 2002 it is really only the notions of the *ciné-fils* (cine-son) and of cine-biographical relations that endure (Pigouillié 2002, 84). He complicates this perspective by what he regards as Daney wanting to maintain at all costs a strict correspondence between his life and that of modern cinema.

Both articles, however, share an acknowledgement of the indelible presence of the melancholic disposition in the Daney version of cinephilia and both in distinct ways attest to the figure of anamnesis and, hence, to the ultimately psychoanalytic tenor of the late writings and thought of Daney.[5] Pigouillié even goes so far as to diagnose narcissism in the error that he attributes to Daney, of mistaking the year of Rossellini's film *Rome, Open City* as 1944. This may be historically correct, but Pigouillié is guilty of his

---

5   Very Oedipal, for example, is how he characterizes his early ritualistic film viewing (Daney 2015, 190). Elsewhere, he comments that the salary paid to him for his work in *Libération* was modest but enough to keep a psycho-analyst from abject poverty and to keep at bay transference from the couch (Daney 2015, 105). In another interview he improvises a psychoanalytic "reading" of how Straub and Huillet play out a Lacanian theater through their work (Daney 2015, 111). The specifically Lacanian tenor of many articles such as for example on *Le Diable probablement/The Devil Probably* (Robert Bresson, 1977) is noteworthy, as indeed is Daney's comment that he is more Lacanian than Deleuzian. In a characterization that recalls aspects of Barthes's distinction between a normative pleasure of the text and a trans-gressive *jouissance*, Daney identifies an out voice and a through voice (482). In the out voice cinema fetishizes the emergence of the voice from the lips, from which, in his Lacanian formulation, the *objet a* separates.

 own error in claiming that Daney says the camps were *liberated* in 1944. In fact Daney only states that their existence came to the knowledge (of the Allied forces) in this year (to assert an *ethical* lapse, or worse, manipulation by Daney is unwarranted).

The one attributes to Daney a prescience that propels him into the future while the other claims that he deprived himself of his own legacy. But each ponders legacy.

Daney after Daney

The texts comprising the posthumously published volume of fragments in *L'Exercice a été profitable, Monsieur* are notable for the frequent invocation of the question of environment and location. The *salle obscure* (or movie theater—the fetishization of which Daney claimed to be not at all susceptible to, as in the famous dismissal "les salles, je m'en fous" ("I don't care about the movie theaters.") (Daney 2015, 199)[6]—is of course here as elsewhere invoked, but in macrocosm France, symbolically stood in for by the French "films of quality," which, in Daney's eyes, make such a pernicious comeback in the 1980s and continue beyond his death. The battle, in Daney's eyes, is between a voracious postmodern regime of the visual and some form of "resistance," but the latter he finds holed up or in hiding.[7] Hence the metaphor of

6   Reprised in another text: "je me suis toujours foutu de la salle" ("I never cared about the movie theater") (Daney 2015, 181). Less colorfully in the interview with Viviant he comments, "chez-moi, l'amour du cinéma c'est jamais confondu avec l'amour de la salle. Dans la salle il y avait encore trop de société, de consensus" ("For me, the love of the cinema is never confused with the love of the movie theater. In the movie theater there was still too much society, too much consensus") (Daney 2015, 194).

7   Repeatedly in the pieces collected about films on television, Daney refers to the specificity of the material viewing circumstances. He addresses his readers as fellow TV watchers (invoking a kind of community and occasionally an imagined village—a concept to which he often returned). He refers to his own susceptibility to the flow of television—the phenomenon referred to by Dork Zabunyan as the "'visionnage' distrait qui absorbe avec indifférence le défilement des images: un nouveau somnambulisme"

a new Occupation, marked superficially by films with the "aroma" of Vichy (as he states elsewhere) but more generally by all that he detests in Besson, Beineix, Annaud, and Berri.[8] Daney's pessimism is not total: within the same volume of fragments he suggests that the filmmakers he prizes have all retreated into territorial enclaves but also that there is hope to be found in younger directors of the period of the late 1980s such as, notably, Leos Carax and Wim Wenders. Cinema had lost its place by the time these fragments were written and Daney had been through the "non-legendary years" of *Cahiers* but also of French society of the 1970s. The *maison* (house) he had once shared within the hermetic cinephilia of the journal, along with the dominance of the *salle obscure*, have gone.

Hence, the pressing question of the public, which is notable in the volume, but also of habitability. The topic is there at the beginning of the journal. The question often translates as how to live in France under the new "Occupation." But it has resonances with the more abstract and macro question as posed by Godard in *Soigne ta droite: Une place sur la terre* (1987), whom indeed Daney directly cites, in stating "une place sur terre comme au ciel" ("a place on earth as in heaven").

Cinephilia

Ciné-fils: Daney made innumerable references to this, his Lacanian formulation, and as Tweedie has reminded us, through this endlessly returned-to word, he deliberately took a critical distance from the founding cinephilia of *Cahiers*. He also referred in this context, in *L'Exercice*, to being kidnapped by cinema. As

"distracted 'viewing' that absorbs with indifference the scrolling of images: a new somnambulism" (Zabunyan 2011, 169).

8   "La France est occupée et le studio représente l'Occupation dans le champ du cinéma" ("France is occupied and the studio represents the Occupation in the field of cinema") (Debray in Daney 1999a, 40).

 reflected in an exhibition at the Palais de Tokyo by Jean-Jacques Lebel, which was in its final weeks in May 2018, objects *collect us*. The objects in this case: the local cinema, the publicity material, the street corner, the films themselves. Daney was a collector but he was also himself appropriated by cinema: cinephilia is not simply a uni-directional projection of love onto an object; the cinephile is also apprehended by the object of their desire.

In the notes he was writing in preparation for the publication of *Devant la recrudescence des vols de sacs à main* (the volume that deploys the title from the public awareness message projected in the heyday of the *salle*), Daney begins by asking what it is that is in crisis in cinema at this time. The question, he elaborates, is not "the crisis in cinema" as such but *what exactly* is in crisis. The answer is divided into two: *la salle obscure* and *l'enregistrement* (recording). At one point in his deliberations he writes that in the great films everything in the *tableau* (the image) moves, but at different speeds—from which he concludes that skies, and in particular skies with clouds, are the best metaphor for such films. We shall return to these skies later.

Digital After-Images

To return to my allegory of the Champo, some of the experiences of the setting and indeed of the experience of the *salle obscure* are the same, but some have been altered by the digital revolution. The second *salle* of the Champo still has a 35mm projector but in its own description this is in order to be able to screen films not yet converted to DCP format rather than due to a commitment to 35mm in itself.

Many commentators have addressed the question of a purported loss that occurs when the defining context of cinema and cinephilia centered on materiality and projection is removed, namely the movement, migration, or mutation entailed in wresting an experience defined as requiring a viewing experience in a *salle* (such as evoked in my quotation at the start) on to platforms and portable devices. Raymond Bellour, for example (2012), in his demand that the cinematographically specific rests on regarding cinema in terms of the *dispositif*—made with projection in mind and then in fact projected—has among the more emphatic of such positions.[9]

The French film scholar Martine Beugnet, writing in English in her essay on watching films on iPhones, singles out Odin and Daney as the only French voices—at her time of writing—who ponder something other than a narrative of loss. In a footnote on Daney she points out in fact Daney's acknowledgement that the small screen could improve some films (for example *The Ten Command-ments*, and even, he quips in *Devant,* the films of Claude Lelouch (Daney 1991, 41). Readers of Daney will know that it is true to say that he insisted on his retention of cinephilic disposition as distinct from the gaze of the telephile—thus asserting on his own behalf and within viewing conceived of as an act of mourning a modality of resistance even within the field of the saturating visual.

Community

Amid the notes and drafts collected posthumously as *L'Exercice a été profitable, Monsieur* lie Daney's transcription of several quotations dated April 22, 1988 and taken from Jean-Luc Nancy's *The Inoperative Community* (1983/1991). Daney transcribes phrases that link the idea of community to mortality and finitude and, in this context, to Nancy's distinction between the individual and the singularity, the latter to be understood as entailing an

9   The sort of position with which Daney marked his divergence. For Daney there were those for whom even in a completely empty screening (ideal for *India Song* as he quips, Daney 2015, 194) the film/cinema would still be happening through the mere fact of projection, "c'est-à-dire le dialogue d'un lieu obscure et d'un lieu éclairé" ("that is to say the dialogue of a dark place and a lighted place") (Daney 2015, 177). Indeed, the same text contains Daney's claim that the *politique des auteurs* at *Cahiers* was a regime *against* the *salle* (177).

 exposure to alterity.[10] The longest passage transcribed concerns the state of *between* "you" and "I" in which such exposure is manifest as *comparution* (co-appearing). The notes, arguably, have a resonance in different planes or facets of Daney's practice and theorization of cinephilia. The community of the *Cahiers*-immersed cinephilia was the refuge in which Daney the critic was formed, while the *ciné-fils* (according to his late self-categorization) who saw himself as at a remove from the generation of the Cinémathèque rats might be thought of as exemplifying the paradox at the heart of Nancy's conception of community. Community found itself addressed by other authors in the decade, Maurice Blanchot (to whom Nancy was in part responding) and later Giorgio Agamben. As many have done before, not least Daney himself, in his "cine-biographical" final phase, one can chart his career as one whose potentiality stirred facing Preminger and Hitchcock at the age of 15, who finds its first community in *Cahiers*,[11] then breaks with the cinephilia of the latter in favor of the collective political militancy of the journal after 1969, regrouping under his editorship after 1974, only further to remove himself both from politics in the post-'68 sense and from the journal and the standard practice of the film critic in the 1980s, when he became a journalist with a remit far wider than cinema for *Libération*. During this trajectory, ideas of community (affiliation, belonging) and of emergence (becoming) recur, but each of these is characterized by the foundational melancholia so often identified by commentators on Daney.

10   "There is nothing behind singularity—but there is, outside it and in it, the immaterial *and* material space that distributes it and shares it out as singularity, distributes and shares the confines of other singularities, or even more exactly distributes and shares the confines of singularity—which is to say of alterity—between it and itself" (Nancy 1986/1991, 27).

11   In the 1992 interview with Arnaud Viviant, Daney recounts how he began to read *Cahiers* in 1959 just before the release of *L'Année dernière à Marienbad/ Last Year at Marienbad* and then started to attend the Cinémathèque immediately after.

In considering the image after Daney, and thus after his death, one wonders if the lessons of Nancy's *The Inoperative Community* resonate retrospectively. Daney regarded the cinephilia of his youth as belonging to the past, and his writings on the falling to earth of film on to television already take the form of an act of mourning.[12] The community felt by Daney was not only of his virtual sect—and he invoked mysticism over religion many times (not the "mass" of television viewing, which signaled conformity, nor of the *salle*—too much society, too much consensus, he said)—but also the films, directors, and stars whom he bumped into via the broadcasting of a film on television: "how are you?" "what's new?" "good to see you," he observes in a short entry. The community was already felt to be impossible, in this case through an awareness of a mutation in the media complex—to use Paul Virilio's term (Virilio 1994)—of which it was becoming part (symbolized by the parasitic relationship of television to cinema, the increasingly saturated field of the visual and the contamination of cinema by advertising, so scathingly blamed on Besson and Beineix).[13] *Pace* Beugnet, it is perhaps worth recalling that Daney's reflections on what constitutes cinema is not confined to the viewing context, so that for Daney, the experience of *Diva* in a film auditorium would not be an experience of cinema but only of advertising. There is no supplement for Daney in *Diva*, just the gliding of images over images. The didactic dimension

12   He makes this comment in the interview with Roger. Films are said by
      Daney to fall from the sky to television (also Daney 1991, 31), a highly
      Godardian metaphor designed to indicate a reduction in scale and in power
      (mannerism), but also to indicate a theological dimension: films "sanctify"
      television, or at least when those films are by someone such as Visconti
      (Daney 1991).

13   The interaction with Virilio, which resulted in the dialogue between their
      pieces in *Libération* on the Gulf War, also results in sporadic references to
      his writings. Virilio's observations on the "vision machine" (the title of one of
      his books) are published in *Trafic*. Daney's observations on being able to see
      what was not seen (in relation to the camps) refers to Virilio's text (Daney
      2015, 216).

 of his disdain for Beineix in particular notwithstanding, *Diva*, he remarked, was—on TV—like a fish in water.[14]

The community of cinephiles in the context of Paris—the Cinématheque, the Champo, the Pantheon, the Pagode, wherever—and the groups formed around *Cahiers*, these were already acknowledged by Daney as governed by finitude, deriving from the impending swamping of the reservoir of the visual and the cliché.

After the End/Until the End of the World

To return to a mixture of those who were there with Daney and those who came after or who did both: what, one wonders, would Daney make of the fact that the long-lost film made in May 1968 by his "petit frère" Philippe Garrel, *Actua 1*, can now be viewed by anyone on YouTube? Daney declared himself in favor of pirate videos in an interview with Philippe Roux, so one would imagine he would approve (Daney 2015, 178).

Given his interest in the concept of information (i.e. data), what would he think of films with frames in which it is impossible to perceive what is going on because so much digital information is teeming beyond the range of human perception on the screen? What for example of *Dr. Strange* or of the film in which Benedict Cumberbatch reprises his superhero in *Avengers: Infinity War*? A film, the closing credits of which list up to five separate companies of visual effects artists? Would Daney have migrated from television to streaming? No doubt the answer is yes—in

14   He would point out in an interview for *Esprit* that he watches television with a cinephile's eye always feeling implicated, "Alors qu'un téléphile est toujours à la même distance du poste, bien placé pour engranger de l'information pure, peu impliqué" ("While a telephile is always at the same distance from the television set, well placed to gather pure information, little involved") (Daney 2002, 27).

L'Exercice after all he mentions the installation of cable in his home.[15]

Analog cinephilia remains possible for, in Daney's phrase, the "nostalgique de la salle" ("nostalgia for the movie theater") (Daney 2015, 307) of our times. The Lincoln Center's Philippe Garrel season for example in 2018 showed almost everything on 35 or 16mm prints, but exposure such as this is becoming rarer and rarer with institutions such as the British Film Institute and the Cinémathèque française adopting a policy geared towards preservation of prints when a digital alternative is available. But is it possible now only as part of a prolonged act of mourning for cinema? Daney, we must remember, regarded viewing films on television as already being involved in mourning.

To return, once more, to the vitrines of the Champo in May 2018, in *Wings of Desire* Bruno Ganz plays an angel who sacrifices his guaranteed continuation in the ether in order to be on earth, where he will succumb not only to the effects of gravity but also become mortal. Wenders's film also features Peter Falk playing himself and recognized by Ganz as the actor who played Columbo. I call this an allegory of cinephilia falling to earth, or cinephilia in the era of television and latterly of streaming. It is the trajectory of Daney's own cinephilia, which ended up becoming manifest in the figure of the *zappeur* flitting about in the continuity of "life's parade" (in the words of *All that Heaven Allows*), the cathode ray tube.

Listening to the 1987 interview with Wenders on the France Culture series *Microfilms* hosted by Daney to mark the release of the film, I was struck by the remarkable felicity with which the dialogue corroborated my own projection or fabulation.[16]

---

15   Elsewhere Daney suggests that television is mutating into a "ciné-vidéo-câblo-philie" (Daney 2015, 108). His statement regarding cinema being "finished" is playfully extended into the notion that it is finite because its metamorphoses are not infinite.

16   *Microfilms*, episode 7, 1987.

  Wenders states that he made a film about angels as a pretext to show humans and to show the quotidian with fresh eyes and new images. It is in this sense that Daney thinks Wenders can in fact *resist* within the context of the regime of the visual. He directly asks Wenders about the *salle*, and Wenders ponders a possible future with an immense television screen replacing the traditional apparatus of projection. Daney goes on to talk about the vast circular screen at the Géode, not long in operation at the time. What would Daney have made of the fact that the first UK screening of Godard's *Livre de l'image/The Image Book* took place at the BFI Imax cinema—a film which one might regard as the very antithesis of the visual spectacular screened in a "cathedral" largely devoted to the merely spectacular (Godard one week, *1917* the next!)?

The conversation with Wenders turns to the question of weight and already the freeing of the apparatus of cinema from gravity. The correlation between cinephilia and the angelic is complete, and it is the gaze of the child that is enabled to see the angel. Novelty of gaze, novelty of image, restoration of the new and the fresh but also of the finite: in coming down to earth to experience the sensations of the embodied and to participate in the terrestrial community the angels are emblems of the double-edged sword of life and death, and the backward, rear-view mirror (*rétroviseur*) look of Wenders is thus co-opted into Daney's melancholic archive.

The fundamental distinction manifested in the late writings of Daney is that between the visual and the image, allied to the concept of mannerism, which he took as the key to understanding what was at stake in certain filmmakers of the period as well as in the interstices of television where David Lynch caught his attention. Daney found something in Lynch's TV work that he did not in the films—to date he had made *Eraserhead*, *Elephant Man*, *Dune*, and *Blue Velvet*. Prophetically as far as *Cahiers* is concerned, he says of *Twin Peaks* that it comes from/of cinema (Daney 1993,

333)—the return by Lynch some 25 years later would see the series top the end of decade list for the then editorial team.

Jonathan Rosenbaum, who was among the first to acknowledge Daney's importance in the coming era, notes the aspects of scale and occasion that mark the specificity of cinema and that these were crucial to the interest Daney had in films on television (Rosenbaum 2005). In his review of Coppola's *One from the Heart*—the film which famously featured the director's Zoetrope[17] experiment in directing from the interior of his famous Airstream trailer, the "Silverfish"—Daney reaches for what will become a thoroughly malleable and reproducible metaphor concerning the celestial and the earthly domains: the camera is in the sky, the characters in the rain.[18]

Daney's review of Wenders's *Wings of Desire* argues that the "desire" part of the French title gets things wrong. Daney says the film harks back to silent cinema, which knew how to film the sky, and places it with Godard's *Passion* in this respect (Daney 2015, 30). In fact, I would add that there is another important sky sequence in Godard's *Soigne ta droite*, at the beginning. This scene is itself an echo of the opening sequence of *Playtime* by Tati. Godard begins his film with a shot from a plane and a voiceover debating the location or whether there is any location. A place on earth (Daney 2015, 101) is a genuine question in Godard. Of course, in *Soigne ta droite* Godard boards a plane with his film canisters and ends up flat on his face—this is Godard's most Tatiesque film after all.

17   "L'image est (grace à la vidéo) 'bien traitée' tandis que les acteurs sont (à cause de la vidéo) 'sous surveillance'" ("The image is (thanks to video) 'well processed' while the actors are (because of video) 'under surveillance'") (Daney 1986, 125).

18   Coppola, Daney argues, shows how "le jamais-vu redevient trop vite du déjà-vu" ("the never-seen-before becomes déjà vu all too quickly") (Daney 1986, 123). "Mannerism in cinema is defined as nothing happens to the characters, what happens happens to the image. The decor and the characters do not belong to one another; they do not, unlike in Minnelli, have the same weight as one another. The camera is in the sky, the characters in the rain."

The trope returns repeatedly in Daney. For example, he likens himself to a silent era hero required to land a plane safely without even holding a pilot's license (Daney 2015, 302). Daney writes that in *Tarnished Angels*, Sirk films the aeronautic display like a domestic scene and intimate scenes as if they were dogfights. He also refers to the coming down to earth of these films, many of which land badly (like in *Tarnished Angels*). They can land badly on television for a number of reasons and with a number of consequences. Technical factors for example may impinge, such as a cinemascope film boxed in by two bands which cannot be as black as they need to be. Or they can be revealed through a particular mode of viewing to have been artistic failures, such as *Some Like It Hot*.

Image

The late writing of Daney places a lot of faith in Wenders and Carax. Another way to ponder a thinking and a practice of the image after Daney would be to consider their subsequent work in light of the faith Daney placed in them and, as I shall argue in Carax in particular, for reasons linked to the themes of cinephilia and community, the role of the *passeur* and the "end" of cinema.

Recalling that what he hoped for in these two filmmakers was the capacity for a single image—an image charged for him with salvific properties, and he invoked Godard's formula too, "just an image"—it is perhaps of note that Carax would continue to operate in the singular way Daney identified close to the beginning of his career. In this light it is fascinating to reflect that the other film at the top of the *Cahiers* top ten, in second place, Carax's *Holy Motors*, is in its way about cinephilia fallen to earth in the era of the visual.[19] The character of Merde, expanded by

19   Daney had a nurturing attitude to Carax who attended (without being registered) the course at Censier he taught with Danièle Dubroux (whose 1991 film *Borderline* made an enormous impression on Daney). But he frequently leavens his praise with statements of perplexity (Carax wastes too much

the director from his segment of *Tokyo!* (2008), did not fulfil the promise made at the end of the short film of a "Merde in the USA," but rather was absorbed retrospectively as one part in the playing out of an assignment to an actor in what can be read as a scripted reality show taking place across Paris filmed by invisible cameras. The film was also made during the hiatus in the planned film "Scars," which at the time of writing remains abandoned. It was Carax's hope to shoot on film but finances did not permit this. Daney often repeated his assertion that every film is the story of its own elaboration and to an extent the depiction of its own context of production. Arguably the context of the non-production (that is, *on film*) and the difficulty perennially experienced by the director (allied to personal grief) forms the backdrop of *Holy Motors*.

The cinephilia espoused by the early Daney was regarded by him as a specific cinephilia of *Cahiers*; Carax himself is steeped in this both due to the frequency of his appearance (as both reviewer and reviewed) in the journal (not least Daney's championing of his debut film *Boy Meets Girl* in *Libération* while he was still on the editorial board of *Cahiers*).

In this regard the film may be regarded as the falling to earth of Carax's own cinephilia in a context marked by technological constraint on the one hand (he is unable to shoot on film due to financial constraints) and opportunity on the other (at least he can make something). Carax would go on to make a film which surpasses the quintessential meta-film—at least for the Daney of 1969—in the extent to which it embeds within itself a critical reflection on the industrial and technological framework embodying at once these constraints and possibilities. Whereas in 1969 Daney argues that Pasolini's *Teorema* is the pinnacle

time trying to find out what he wants, in the interview with Viviant). He answers his own question "Who can new filmmakers copy now?" by saying they, like Godard, follow Lang. They can't copy Carax, he says (Daney 2015, 210). The reason is not entirely clear but perhaps it is because Carax already reprises and recycles aspects of Godard and Garrel.

(Daney 2022, 101–4), Carax in 2011 would, in the era named post-cinematic by some, prolong the lineage (which we in part associate with Daney) of the interrogation of the question of spectatorship in the *salles* and in the expanded vision machine of our era. The film opens with the awakened director escaping through a panel in what appears to be a hotel room to the interior of a cinema, with an inert, apparently sleeping audience incapable of registering any response to the screen. Is this Carax's depiction of the era of the end of the *salle*? The vignettes that unfold subsequently do so out of this opening, the aperture into the space of the empty historically cinematographic (the film is projecting *without an audience*, in that the people are *not spectating*): filming, production, projection. The "heavy machines" of old, referred to in the conversation between the mysterious impresario played by Michel Piccoli and M. Oscar, were also the ones that, paradoxically, produced Daney's skies; the new ones, being so small and ubiquitous in a world become reality show, leave us firmly on earth (as does the character *played by the character played* by Kylie Minogue, Eva Grace). Daney had written about reality shows in *Le Salaire du Zappeur* very early in the development of the genre or form now so ubiquitous on our television screens. The reality show is the new occupation, according to Daney. It is as if Carax's film takes up the baton from Daney in its elaboration of a metaphorical display of this.

In this period where some talk of a post-cinema or, as William Brown does in a Laruelle-inflected idiom, a *non-cinema* of the digital era (Brown 2018), one can only speculate as to what Daney would make of departures from industrial practice such as films made on smartphones (Soderberg[20]) or Godard and Wenders's mannerist use of 3D or of the dissemination and proliferation of multiple viewing contexts of our present moment.

20   "Soderberg, c'est malin" ("Soderberg's clever"), remarks Daney in 1992 (of *Sex, Lies and Videotape*), but he doesn't think he can go very far (Daney 2015, 187).

Regarding the output of our times, Daney was prescient about a transformation that he observed toward what he termed the vectorial mise-en-scène of some US cinema of the time—Daney cites Tim Burton's *Batman* in particular (Daney 2015, 163)—where we do not come across the space bit by bit (as we would in Lang). Is this now even more the case in Hollywood blockbusters? Carax's *Holy Motors* interrogates this too in its way, in the green-screen and motion-capture episode. CGI in cinema today is even more prone to deploy the potentiality of technology to render the vectorial experience that is produced by contemporary communications technologies in a media-saturated world. In CGI cinema, which is so full and contains densities of layers that although perceptible to the machine eye are imperceptible to the human, we are arguably ever more plunged into a world without the gaps of the Daneyian *visuel*.

If the community for whom Daney functioned as *passeur* is to be considered, to sound like Blanchot, unavowable or, to sound like Nancy (sounding like Blanchot), inoperative, it is so in a way that is open to an ethics. In the essay "Before and After the Image" cinephilia is linked insistently to an ethical project. There Daney defines love of cinema as the knowledge of *what to do with the image that is missing*. When the other comes to be missing, each side takes refuge in their "visual," the one in its real State, the other "in a state" of its imaging (Daney 1999, 190). Thus in the context of the audio-visual representation of the Other there is a pervasive failure to "go to the Other" (31). When this failure arises—as on television it almost always does—then we give ourselves images of ourselves as our way of failing to go to the other. The task of the critic for Daney was to enumerate and write about the ways in which this failure is endemic. Daney had produced powerful examples of the failure to go towards the other, notably the coruscating attack on a televised concert associated with *Live Aid* and television coverage of the Iraq war.[21]

The question posed by the project edited by Dork Zabunyan, *Que peut une image*, is pertinent as a reference point for this essay. It rests on two responses, in the style of Daney as identified by Deleuze: inviting an optimism bordering on naïve—an image can change everything—or on a pessimism, throwing one's hands in the air and exclaiming in defeat: "as if an image could ever do anything" (Zabunyan 2014, 4). Daney, as we know, wavers in the end, still believing in one image, *une image*. Carax's film may in its way be discussed as the answer which the future would provide.

Carax aims to show us a world where everything is image, the instantaneity being such that acting out and viewing are simultaneous; reality TV equated with reality, visual with world, or so intermingled that one cannot exit it; a world in which M. Oscar as hooded vigilante can shoot M. Oscar as banker outside Fouquet's. Does Carax manage to give us an image, just an image?

Singularity

For Daney it was still possible for a single image to produce and embody a moment of resistance to the regime of the visual, even if by depending on it cinema could still, through mannerism, effectuate some element of anamorphosis—which we might think both metaphorically, as in a distortion or stretching of normative perception and knowledge, and as manifest in images themselves, as for example in the universes of David Lynch.

In a text in which Daney is cited, Bernard Stiegler sums up for me one response to the intervening period, the period when Daney is still our contemporary:

21   Of the video clip *"We Are the World"* he wrote: "a dissolve makes the dying and the famous dance together" (34).

Controlling primary and secondary identification leads to psychic dis-identification, which in turn leads to a process of collective disindividuation, that is, to a destruction of the social body itself, and engenders disaffected psychic and social individuals. It does so in a dual sense: it engenders their disaffection [*désaffection*], ruining their affective capacities; and it engenders their withdrawal [*désaffectation*], the loss of their place, that is, of their ethos. For this amounts to the question of ethics: ethics, which is the knowledge of the abode [*séjour*]. Ethics, as the translation of the Greek word ethos, is that which gives me my place within the circuit of affects through which the process of psychic and collective individuation constitutes itself. Insofar as it establishes such places, ethics is also what weaves that process of *transmission linking together the succession of generations*. [emphasis mine] (Stiegler 2012, 7)

It seems to me that Daney's late writings are diagnosing such a dislocation—written about in Benoît Goetz's recently re-published book (original publication 2001), prefaced by Nancy, *La Dislocation: Architecture et philosophie*. Daney, in his articulation of a passing (or already past) era and his interaction as *zappeur* of the squeezed space of television, is producing an ethics, as it were, on the run and in the intermittently available loci of a topological mutation.

25 years after the series admired by Daney, David Lynch delivered a further installment of *Twin Peaks*. The first series for Daney was a moment where an affirmative mannerism could inhabit and work against the dominant culture of the televisual, whereas the second, 25 years later, occurs in a period of television characterized for many by telephilia and by the emergence of new modes of series construction and dissemination.

Agent Cooper is beyond individualization (and Daney suggests of the original series that he has something of Cary Grant in *North by Northwest*). Whereas M. Oscar individuates and disindividuates according to scripted, costumed assignments throughout the reality show that has supplanted the world and his own agency, in a different way Cooper, the agent and *agency* that is Cooper, is usurped and suspended in his inadvertent unconscious and un-self-aware fractalization, circulating the cosmos, not least in the famous episode 8 of *Twin Peaks: The Return*.

At the beginning of *Soigne ta droite*, Godard, though the voiceover, looks for a place on earth, asking the question that one might attribute to Heidegger, of the *etre-là*, being there. Already in his films identified with the question of the sublime, Godard is posing a question about what we now refer to as the Anthropocene and the ethical question of how cinema is to act when being-there is fractured and recognized comprehensively as finite.[22] The question of being there as posed by the jolt of the camera in the sky at the beginning of *Soigne ta droite* has intensified in the intervening period. Godard lies on the runway at an airport, film cans strewn around his body. No longer the same; the question of being on the planet has changed, both since Godard asked this question and since Daney pondered the stakes of being a *passeur*.

The words of Patrice Rollet sum up the introduction to the first volume of Daney's writings as collected in *La Maison cinéma et le monde* as follows:

> [H]e wrote that in it, cinema was "a home for images that 'no longer have a home'." The cinema home, like the "Sirk home" that he speaks of in *Trafic*, and not the home of cinema (its official institutions), cinema as a home for the shelterless image, vulnerable to the inclemency of history and the world, but also a home base from which one may set off again once the wind of image rises. (Rollet, in Daney 2022, 12)

---

22   In the interview with Viviant Daney cites Valéry: "Nous savons que nous sommes mortels, nos civilisations" ("We know that we are mortal, our civilizations") (Daney 2015, 195). Valery said : "nous autres, civilisations, nous savons maintenant que nous sommes mortelles".

In different ways the examples of Carax and Lynch continue to show us the after-images of the cinema as Daney understood it, now even more emphatically dislocated from both the *salle* and its official institutions.

References

Beugnet, Martine. 2013. "Miniature Pleasures: On Watching Films on iPhones." In *Cinematicity in Media History*, edited by Jeffrey Geiger and Karin Littau, 196–210. Edinburgh: Edinburgh University Press.

Bellour, Raymond. 2012. *La Querelle des dispositifs*. Paris: P.O.L.

Brown, William. 2018. *Non-Cinema: Global Digital Filmmaking and the Multitude*. New York: Bloomsbury.

Daney, Serge. 1983. *La Rampe*. Paris: Gallimard/Cahiers du cinéma.

———. 1986. *Ciné-Journal 1981–1986: Préface de Gilles Deleuze*. Paris: Cahiers du cinéma.

———. 1991. *Devant la recrudescence des vols de sacs à main: cinéma, télévision, information (1988–1991)*. Lyon: Aléas Editeur.

———. 1993. *L'Exercice a été profitable, Monsieur*. Paris : P.O.L.

———. 1999a. *Itinéraire d'un ciné-fils*, propos recueillis par Régis Debray, édition établi sous la direction de Christian Delage. Paris: Jean Michel Place.

———. 1999b. "The organ and the vacuum cleaner." In *Literary Debate: Texts and Contexts, Postwar French Thought, Vol. 2*, edited by Dennis Hollier and Jeffrey Mehlman, 474–86. New York: New Press.

———. 1999c. "Before and After the Image." *Discourse: Journal for Theoretical Studies in Media and Culture* 21 (1): 181–90.

———. 2002. *La Maison cinéma et le monde Vol II. Les Années Libé 1981–1985*. Paris: P.O.L

———. 2003. "The Screen of Fantasy (Bazin and Animals)." Translated by Mark A. Cohen. In *Rites of Realism: Essays on Corporeal Cinema*, edited by Ivone Margulies, 32–41. Durham: Duke University Press.

———. 2007. *Postcards from the Cinema*. Translated by Paul Douglas Grant. Oxford: Berg. Translation of *Persévérance*. Paris: P.O.L, 1994.

———. 2012. *La Maison cinéma et le monde Vol III. Les années Libé 1986–1991*. Paris: P.O.L

———. 2015. *La Maison cinéma et le monde Vol IV. Le moment Trafic 1991–1992*. Paris: P.O.L

———. 2022. *The Cinema House & the World, Vol. 1, The* Cahiers du cinéma *Years, 1962–1981*. Translated by Christine Pichini. South Pasadena: Semiotext(e).

Eugène, Pierre. 2012. "Apparitions de Serge Daney." *Trafic* 82: 94–102.

Goetz, Benoît. 2018. *La Dislocation: Architecture et philosophie*. Paris: Verdier.

Nancy, Jean-Luc. 1983/1991. *The Inoperative Community*. Edited by Peter Connor. Translated by Peter Connor, Lisa Garbus, Michael Holland, and Simona Sawhney. Minneapolis: University of Minnesota.

Pigoullié, Jean-François. 2002. "Serge Daney sans postérité." *Esprit* 286 (7): 61–87.

Rosenbaum, Jonathan. 2005. "The Missing Image [On Serge Daney]." *Jonathan Rosenbaum,* May 29. Accessed October 29, 2022. https://jonathanrosenbaum. net/2022/05/the-missing-image-on-serge-daney/.

Stiegler, Bernard. 2012. *Uncontrollable Societies of Disaffected Individuals: Disbelief and Discredit, Vol. 2.* Translated by Daniel Ross. Cambridge: Polity Press.

Truffaut, François. 1954. "Une certaine tendance du cinéma français." *Cahiers du cinéma* 31: 15–29.

Tweedie, James. 2016. "Serge Daney, Zapper: Cinema, Television and the Persistence of Media." *October* 157: 107–27.

Virilio, Paul. 1994. *The Vision Machine.* Translated by Julie Rose. London and Bloomington: BFI and Indiana University Press.

Zabunyan, Dork. 2011. *Les Cinémas de Gilles Deleuze.* Montrouge: Bayard.

Zabunyan, Dork. 2014. "Que peut une image ?—Les conditions d'une question." In *Que peut une image ?,* edited by Dork Zabunyan, 4–11. Paris: Le BAL / Textuel.

6

Thinking the Future of Cinema

Bamchade Pourvali

Beyond the melancholy, beyond the repetition of the 'death of cinema' feeling of the 1980s, we find in Serge Daney's writings an attention to a new cartography of cinema that was at that moment taking shape in Hong Kong and in Iran. These were two filmographies in which Daney recognized the continuation of "modern cinema." This reflection on the future of cinema in the late period of Daney's writings is coupled with his sensitivity to a cinematographic form to which he was always attentive and which he called the "essay film." The development in the 1990s of these two filmographies as well as of the form of the essay film retrospectively produces some echoes in these writings.

Serge Daney's works from the 1980s onward are infused with a certain melancholia about the crisis faced by modern cinema and its possible disappearance. But beyond that, his writings reflect on the future of this modern cinema in which he recognized himself,[1] by paying attention to the revival of Hong Kong and Iranian cinema, and the rise of a form he had always appreciated: the essay film. His writings from that time shed some light onto the 1990s debates, when Hong Kong and Iranian filmmaking would flourish, and the essay format would come to occupy a new space in thinking about modern cinema. Re-reading Daney's works from that time allows us to link these two types of cinematography, as well as the essay film, to the history of modern cinema. It also offers a more nuanced image of Daney's concerns regarding the future of cinema in general, and of modern cinema more specifically. Indeed, in the 1980s, when Serge Daney quit his role as editor in chief of *Les Cahiers du Cinéma* to oversee the cinema section at *Libération*, he did not hide his doubts about the future of modern cinema. A certain melancholia permeates his texts accompanying the *La Rampe* collection (1983). In November 1983, six months after *La Rampe* was published, Daney declared in *Esprit*:

> the question that people are starting to ask themselves is not about the future of cinema but about the potential death of this (small) part of cinema which does have a history, which conveys the seismographic tremor of what is happening elsewhere, at the same time, in "real life." (Daney 2002, 13)[2]

According to Daney, what defined modern cinema was its ability to record real life and the audience's desire to encounter real life differently when going to the cinema. Because it is definitely real

1   Because Daney was born in 1944, the year Roberto Rossellini filmed *Rome, Open City* was released, and he discovered Alain Resnais's *Hiroshima mon amour* upon its release in 1959, he identified with modern cinema.

2   Originally published as "Passion de l'image: des *Cahiers du Cinéma* à *Libération*. Entretien avec Serge Daney par Michel Crépu, Serge Delavaud, Michel Mesnil et Olivier Mongin" in *Esprit* 83: 11 November 1983.

life that Daney was talking about when he evoked Hong Kong cinema and Iranian filmmakers, and Daney viewed the essay film, which appeared as one of the outcomes of modernity in cinema, as an extension of a modern heritage.

The New Horizon of Hong Kong Cinema

Serge Daney was an aficionado of Hong Kong cinema. He enjoyed watching Hong Kong films at festivals—in Cannes, Pesaro, Hong Kong—or in Parisian cinemas such as La Cigale, located on boulevard Rochechouart, but also during the Kung Fu film festival he organized in 1983 and 1984 with two other *Libération* editors, the brothers François and Max Armanet. From 1982 to 1984, Daney often pointed out how strongly Asian cinema was represented in festivals.

In 1985, one year after the signature of the Sino–British Joint Declaration, and during the ninth edition of the Hong Kong International Film Festival, Daney published in *Libération* the essay "Hong Kong a le blues" (2002, 819–26),[3] in which he drew attention to the shift happening in the work of Hong Kong directors. The essay starts with the following observation:

> Hong Kong—Her Majesty's colony—has produced strange colonized beings. They are Chinese, but Chinese people who have not been taught their history as Chinese from Hong Kong. No textbook evokes China after 1949 in its terse summaries of contemporary history. No mention of Hong Kong. The colony does not, should not, possess a history. It is a parenthesis opened in the nineteenth century awaiting to be closed imminently. British people are not the type of people who impose their history ("Our ancestors, the Angles" is not really their style), and Chinese people have all the time in the world to impose an umpteenth rewriting of theirs (it will be the post-Deng Xiaoping history; we do not know it yet). For

3   Originally published in *Libération*, 19 July 1985.

Hongkongers born after the Second World War, the only history they have is the often bitter life lived by their parents.

Daney retraced the period of the Chinese Cultural Revolution as it was experienced in the colony:

> In the late 1960s, there was a wave of student protests in Hong Kong (1967). Faced with British bureaucracy, these students had no other recourse to maintain their Chinese identity than to declare themselves "pro-Chinese." But in China, the Cultural Revolution was happening. This joke was the price a generation had to pay to start watching (and filming) the city in which it had been born: ungrateful and unique Hong Kong, a global but showcase city. This realization is of interest to cinema critics in that it precisely needed *images*.

Daney evoked the situation of the Hong Kong new wave's filmmakers whose films seem to find a new historical horizon that was absent until then, benefitting genre cinema alone: "'New wave' filmmakers … are faced with a new challenge. They need not prove their talent by playing the game of the 'genre' movie but they need to welcome some concern for (or at least a sense of) history twelve years before the return of Hong Kong to the Chinese motherland." Then, reinstating the "retro trend" in a different context than that of 1970s French cinema for which this concept was coined, he added:

> As for Hong Kong, we need to turn to the 1940s, between the day the city was taken by the Japanese (Christmas 1941, after eighteen days of siege) and its return to the status of British colony (after 1949). This time period is at the heart of many recent films. Amnesia is no longer possible: there has been something of a retro fashion in Hong Kong cinema. … As with any retro trend, it is largely phantasmatic. It consists in pretending to process past events for the second time when they have never been processed in the first place. How can we tell Chinese stories from the 1940s in the global language

of 1980s quality cinema? How can we invent a nostalgia? ... Judging them would be silly: how many human communities *need* cinema today to play the part of their identity. Very few indeed.

Reading these lines, it is impossible not to think of a filmmaker that Daney would never know; one that would become one of the most prominent Hong Kong directors of the 1990s, and the first Chinese president of the Cannes festival: Wong Kar-wai. Wong Kar-wai was discovered internationally in 1994 with his fourth film, *Chungking Express*, and right away, was labeled as the filmmaker of the handover of Hong Kong to China in 1997. This historical moment would indeed appear in his sixth feature film, *Happy Together*, shot in Argentina. The film follows two Hong Kongese lovers, Ho and Laï, played by Leslie Cheung and Tony Leung, who have left the colony to go and work in Buenos Aires. In the restaurant where they work, Lai meets Chang, a young Taiwanese man played by Chang Chen, whom, at the end of the film, he will go to find in Taiwan when Chang goes back to look for Lai in Argentina. Through these characters, the film brings together the three Chinas: Hong Kong, Taiwan, and mainland China, since the film mentions the death of Deng Xiaoping, which Laï hears about in his hotel room in Taipei on 20 February 1997, the year the handover happened. It is hard to know if Daney would have enjoyed the works of Wong Kar-wai, a director born in Shanghai, a city which is at the heart of the Hong Kong retro trend from the 1980s. This trend in Wong Kar-wai's works is more about Hong Kong in the 1960s, the moment when he arrived in the colony with his parents in 1963. The only thing we can be certain of is that Daney would have perceived the historical dimension of Wong Kar-wai's films as he did with Tsui Hark's work.

Encounters with Abbas Kiarostami and Mohsen Makhmalbaf in Iran

Daney's relationship to Iranian cinema was not as strong, in the long term, as his relationship with Hong Kong cinema, but it is still present, sometimes in an indirect manner. Daney took an interest in Shorab Sahid Saless[4] after discovering his film *Utopia* and, on 22 February 1983, published an article entitled "L'Iranien aux dix films allemands" (2002, 657–58).[5] What Daney wrote about the film and its director is also valid for Saless's Iranian works that Daney did not know. The position and influence of Shorab Sahid Saless was decisive for Abbas Kiarostami's career. Two years later, in his account of the 1985 Locarno festival, Daney likened Amir Naderi, winner of the Montgolfière d'or for *The Runner*—the first Iranian film to be awarded a prize in an international festival after 1979—to directors from the three Chinas.[6] In 1990, Daney went to Iran for the eighth Fajr International Film Festival in Tehran. He wrote an article published in the 3–4 March issue of *Libération* entitled "Images fondues au noir dans Téhéran sans visage" (2012, 513–20)[7]. Right away, Daney wrote: "The image that Iranian directors reflect of their society is one that is harsh … but stronger than expected." Daney met the two prominent directors of the 1980s–1990s, Abbas Kiarostami and Mohsen Makhmalbaf, who were not well known outside Iran, and in Makhmalbaf's case, completely unknown by non-Iranian audiences. This was the year before *Close-Up* (1990) by Kiarostami in which Makhmalbaf played himself, was shown for the first time. Daney defined the distinctive features of these two filmmakers in an assured style, with striking and irrevocable phrases. Kiarostami is described as being "methodical and cruel, a true filmmaker," whilst Makhmalbaf is

---

4   Serge Daney nicknamed him SSS as Pier Paolo Pasolini was called PPP.

5   Originally published in *Libération*, 22 February 1983.

6   "Les Trois Chines," *Libération*, 4 December 1985, reprinted in *La Maison cinéma et le monde*, Vol. 2, 838–839.

7   Originally published in *Libération*, 3–4 March 1990.

qualified as a "Baroque mystic (à la Scorsese)." Daney added: "Kiarostami and Makhmalbaf are very different but both very interesting. Very serious, too. Convinced of the importance of Art and of cinema as an art."

Daney also identified a gap in Iranian movies that center around childhood: the absence of little girls. This would become the originality of a different filmmaker, one who, at that time, had only directed short films, a director whose name now automatically follows Kiarostami and Makhmalbaf: Jafar Panahi. His first two films, *The White Balloon*, which won the Caméra d'or in 1995 at Cannes, and *The Mirror*, which won the Léopard d'or in Locarno in 1997, both portray little girls. With *The Circle*, which won the Golden Lion in Venice in 2000, Panahi would ultimately create a new genre of Iranian cinema about women's condition, which would come to replace his focus on childhood. If Daney stopped writing about Iranian cinema, Kiarostami's works would continue to haunt him as evidenced by the following remark made during the conference at the Jeu de Paume:

> The magnificent Iranian filmmaker Abbas Kiarostami affects me very much and, at the same time, it's very strange because his work reminds me of Rossellini's. I wonder by what type of strange alchemy an Iranian can, all by himself, continually discover, rediscover, and push further the hypothesis which produced Rossellini and some other Italian filmmakers. Does Kiarostami belong in the history of cinema? I'm not quite sure, but he does belong to a certain history of cinema, which Rossellini is a part of, and which is the same as mine.

The importance of Kiarostami may seem obvious today but, at this point in time, no one had predicted with such fervor the place Kiarostami would occupy in years to come. Moreover, Jonathan Rosenbaum recently recalled the importance of Kiarostami in 1990s international cinema by comparing him to 1960s Godard (2016).

A Modern Form: The Essay Film

Talking about Daney's reflection on modern cinema amounts to talking about a cinematographic form he was always interested in: the cinematographic essay, or the "essay film" as he liked to call it, anchoring it into the history of cinema. It is well known that Daney's cinephilia was sparked at the Lycée Voltaire during Henri Agel's Latin lessons, which the latter sometimes replaced by film screenings. He would always show the same films, two essays made into movies: Georges Franju's *Blood of the Beasts* (1949) and Alain Resnais's *Night and Fog* (1956). In 1966, in the entry about Éric Rohmer that Daney wrote for the *Dictionnaire du Cinéma* edited by Raymond Bellour and Jean-Jacques Brochier, he mentioned Rohmer's works for educational television and even went on to regard the first one, *Les Cabinets de physique au XVIIIe siècle*, as Rohmer's masterpiece.[8] Of all of Godard's films, the one that Daney quoted the most is *Here and Elsewhere*, the first video film by the Godard-Miéville couple, a film that Daney went on tour with and presented around the world. In the same manner, Daney wrote a short but enthusiastic text about *We Can't Go Home Again* by Nicholas Ray (2022, 324–26).[9] He also repeatedly and enthusiastically evoked Fellini's *The Clowns* in two texts (1998, 247; 1992), but always in parentheses. Discovering Artavazd Pelechian in 1983[10] marked an important moment in Daney's work as a critic. He also liked Van der Keuken, Robert Kramer, and Hans-Jürgen Syberberg who are all essay film directors. As someone who linked experimental cinema to art history and was not too keen on Rossellini's educational films, Daney could nonetheless sense the importance of the essay film, which Bazin, Astruc, or Rivette had already written about, but which would only

---

8   Daney would once more evoke Éric Rohmer's film in "Sur Salador," *Cahiers du cinema* 222, July 1970.

9   "Nick Ray et la maison des images.", originaly published in *Cahiers du cinéma* 310, April 1980.

10 "À la recherche d'Arthur Péléchian," *Libération*, 11 August 1983, reprinted in *La Maison cinéma et le monde*, Vol. 2, 410–413.

significantly develop in the 1980s and 1990s thanks to video and
digital technology.

In Daney's text about cinema[11] for Anne Bony's book *Les années 60* (1983), the penultimate paragraph is entitled "Towards the essay film?" He wrote:

> Towards the middle of the decade (let's say *All These Women* by Bergman in 1964, *Masculin Féminin* by Godard in 1965, *Hawks and Sparrows* by Pasolini in 1966) we could have anticipated a very free cinema in which, once the conventions of the "spectacular" had been rejected, an author would no longer be afraid of regularly showing pages from his work notes or his diary, which are made out of public (belonging to everyone) and private thoughts (belonging to himself only).

In the preface to *Ciné-Journal* (1986), Gilles Deleuze wrote to Daney: "You did not give up on finding a deep link between cinema and thought … You have thus maintained the great conception of the early days: cinema as a new Art and a new form of Thought." Viewing cinema as "a new Art and a new form of Thought" and in line with the 1920s avant-gardes (a period Daney wrote about in Anne Bony's *Le cinéma des années 20*) embeds the essay in cinema. Since the 1990s, there has been a great deal of research on the essay film (Blümlinger and Wulff 1992; Liandrat-Guigues and Gagnebin 2004; Rascaroli 2009; Corrigan 2011; Bacqué et al. 2015; Papazian and Eades 2016; Alter and Corrigan 2017; Alter 2018; Hollweg and Krstic 2019). It is hard to avoid observing that Chris Marker represents a large gap in Daney's works. This can be explained by the *Cahiers du Cinéma*'s position towards Marker's *Le Joli Mai* in 1963 (Delahaye 1963) up to *Level Five* in 1997 (Jousse 1997). Daney met the "unmeetable Chris Marker" only one time. It was in Hong Kong as Daney recounted in *Persévérance* (1994) and in "Journal de l'an passé" (1991). In the

---

11   Reprinted in *La Maison cinéma et le monde*, Vol. 4, 241–248.

1990s, the dialogue between Godard and Marker would become clearer around the form of the essay film. *Germany Year 90 Nine Zero*, on which Daney wrote in "Journal de l'an passé," is a response to Marker's *Berlin Ballade*, just as *The Kids Play Russian* (1993) is a response to *The Last Bolshevik*. Indeed, Serge Daney, in *L'Exercice a été profitable, Monsieur*, writes about *Germany Year 90 Nine Zero*: "His best film, for a long time, with the good aspects of *Histoire(s) du cinéma* (1988–1998) and *Nouvelle Vague* (1990)" With this remark, Daney highlights what defines Godard's originality in terms of the film essay, the invention of a new form: the novel essay (or fiction essay) that goes back to *Deux ou trois choses que je sais d'elle* (1967). The interrogations on cinema's character developed in "Journal de l'an passé" gravitate around that question. "The loneliness of history" and "the history of loneliness" of which the Godard film speaks correspond to those of Germany, through the journey of Eddie Constantine and his character Lemmy Caution. *Les enfants jouent à la Russie* will confirm this inscription of Godard in the fictional essay and his dialogue with Marker from which he takes footage. I like to think that Daney may have written about Marker then.

As can be seen from the above examples, a large part of the critical and theoretical stakes from the 1990s which extend Daney's reflection on modern cinema was already substantially present in his work from the 1980s and the early 1990s. This is what makes reading his works so stimulating. In laying the foundation of modern cinema to come, he was, after all, and despite himself, the historian of the passage of cinema from one century to another.

Translated into English by Melina Delmas and revised by Kate Ince

References

Alter, Nora M. 2018. *The Essay Film After Fact and Fiction*. New York: Columbia University Press.

Alter, Nora M., and Timothy Corrigan, eds. 2017. *Essays on the Essay Film*. New York: Columbia University Press.

Bacqué, Bertrand, Cyril Neyrat, Clara Schulmann, and Véronique Terrier-Hermann, eds. 2015. *Jeux sérieux: cinéma et art contemporains transforment l'essai*. Geneva: Mamco, Head.

Blümlinger, Christa, and Constantin Wulff. 1992. *Schreiben Bilder Sprechen: Texte zum essayistischen Film*. Vienna: Sonderzahl.

Bony, Anne. 1983. *Les Années 60*. Paris: Du Regard.

Corrigan, Timothy. 2011. *The Essay Film: From Montaigne, After Marker*. New York: Oxford University Press.

Daney, Serge. 1986. *Ciné Journal*, Vol. 1, *1981–1982*. Paris: Cahiers du Cinéma.

———. 1991. "Journal de l'an passé." *Trafic* 1: 5–30.

———. 1992. "Journal de l'an présent." *Trafic* 3: 5–24.

———. 1998. *Ciné Journal*, Vol. 2, *1983–1986*. Paris: Cahiers du Cinéma.

———. 2002. *La Maison cinéma et le monde*, Vol. 2, *Les Années Libé (1981–1985)*. Paris: P.O.L.

———. 2012. *La Maison cinéma et le monde*, Vol. 3, *Les Années Libé (1986–1991)*. Paris: P.O.L.

———. 2022. *The Cinema House & the World*, Vol. 1, *The* Cahiers du cinéma *Years, 1962–1981*. Trans. Christine Pichini. South Pasadena: Semiotext(e).

Daney, Serge, and Serge Toubiana. 1994. *Serge Daney: Persévérance—Entretien avec Serge Toubiana*. Paris: P.O.L.

Delahaye, Michel. 1963. "La chasse à l'I." *Cahiers du cinéma* 146: 5–17.

Hollweg, Brenda, and Igor Krstic, eds. 2019. *World Cinema and the Essay Film: Transnational Perspectives on a Global Practice*. Edinburgh: Edinburgh University Press.

Jousse, Thierry. 1997. "Mr and Mrs Memory." *Cahiers du cinéma* 510: 60–62.

Liandrat-Guigues, Suzanne, and Murielle Gagnebin, eds. 2004. *L'essai et le cinéma*. Seyssel: Champ Vallon.

Papazian, Elizabeth, and Caroline Eades, eds. 2016. *The Essay Film: Dialogue, Politics, Utopia*. London and New York: Wallflower Press.

Rascaroli, Laura. 2009. *The Personal Camera: Subjective Cinema and the Essay Film*. London and New York: Wallflower Press.

Rosenbaum, Jonathan. 2016. "Philosophical Treatises of a Master Illusionist: A Conversation about Abbas Kiarostami." *Underline*, July 8.

THE GIFT

WRITING AND TRAVELLING

FILM FESTIVAL

THIRD WORLD

WORLD CINEMA

PASSEUR

GRIOT

7

Showing Cinema Where It Happens: Serge Daney, a Global Cinema Critic

Claire Allouche

By focusing on Serge Daney's festival writings, remarkable for what they catalyze in terms of reflexivity, we propose to trace here a decentered critical cartography, particularly concerning the place and analysis accorded to non-western cinematographies, which were essential for Daney's "making of the world" of cinema. This movement implies a rethinking of the term "passeur" in relation to the non-western film festivals from which Daney wrote, as a kind of image "gifter" understood according to Jacques Derrida's thinking of the gift in *Given Time: I. Counterfeit Money*. Daney's various forms of gifts in turn question the his-torical status and form of statehood of cinema

 and film criticism, as well as the cinephile's responsibility for his critical activity.

Serge Daney sometimes introduced himself as an all-surface tennis aficionado. At the beginning of this workshop, Hervé Joubert-Laurencin presented him as a table tennis player who did not know he was one. To Serge Daney's sporting qualities, involving both his sense of observation and the outpouring of words on keyboards or notebooks, I would add: Serge Daney as long-distance relay runner, Serge Daney as lead climber, linking non-hegemonic images from various places in the world, on the margins of an already recognized cinema history.

During the student seminar devoted to Serge Daney's works, organized at the ENS Rue d'Ulm by Pierre Eugène in 2016 and 2017,[1] I started to get interested in the "change" of critical angle[2] brought about by Daney's texts on non-western cinematographic production. This paper proposes to put into perspective the considerations sketched out during the following sessions: "Serge Daney, ciné-fils de la maison-monde: *Réflexions sur un cinéma tricontinental*" in April 2016 and "Serge Daney, écrits festivaliers" in March 2017, organized with Marc Nauleau.

What critical cartography of Serge Daney's work emerges when we consider all of his texts about non-western films—themselves written far from the rue Traversière, far from his office at the *Cahiers du Cinéma* or *Libération*? What historical

1   The seminar's program can be accessed through the following links: – 2016: http://dhta.ens.fr/Serge-Daney-voyage-entre-mots-et-images.html – 2017: http://dhta.ens.fr/Serge-Daney-de-l-ecran-a-l-ecrit-et-inversement.html

2   The image of the angle is at the center of Daney's account of the 1980 Rotterdam festival: "And so, in 1980, at the 9th International Festival of Rotterdam, one could feel targeted by the films in two ways. Sometimes on a right angle, frontally interrogated, perpendicular to the image, facing characters looking into the camera, positioned as judge, witness, arbitrator. Sometimes on an obtuse or acute angle, aslant in an entrelac of bodies and fictions, of 'scenes' providing ever-changing 'slots' for the spectator's eye." (2022, 473). Originally published in "Rotterdam 1980," *Cahiers du Cinéma* 310.

thread can be woven between these geographically distant texts,
whilst taking into account the singular temporality in which they
were produced? Indeed, their creation strongly depended on the
organizational frame of film festivals and the geopolitical context of the countries in which these festivals took place. To what
extent should we consider this body of texts as another form of
critical invention, sometimes more reflexive, more essentialist,
but always constitutive of the continued creation of a "global"
cinema, which goes beyond Eurocentric prominence?

"Faire monde" on Several Levels: An Incomplete Third Path

In his *Journal de l'an passé*, which opened the first volume of *Trafic*,
Serge Daney drew a direct analogy between the fragile per-
manence of cinema in time and the acknowledgment of a third
world which was persisting in a global cartographical approach:
"Because, of this, at least, I am sure: cinema cannot better endure
forthcoming societies than Africa can find its place on the map
of a world that works. A place is needed to write this, so that
oral tradition can continue. Before griots retire. A journal, for
example. A cinema journal" (1991, 5). It is interesting to note that
as "the place to write this," *Trafic* embodied from its first pages
the privileged and shared space of this fundamental union, of this
shared voice, and of this simultaneity of fact: the future of images
and the world's destiny. A world not conceived from a dominant
center but as a constant emergence, which was lacking rightful
visibility. Moreover, the future of cinema was envisaged to be in
solidarity with immaterial writing, culturally anchored outside
western issues of preservation. In Daney's mind, was the main
mission of the authors of the *Trafic* era—these active "griots" as
he called them—to be depositaries of a centrifugal memory of
cinema rather than to work towards an applied history that was
already referentialized?

 "The world," said Serge Daney to Philippe Roger in an interview entitled "Le passeur," ought to be "the 'vast' world, the world in which limits are pushed back by the camera and the world of which I am allowed to call myself a 'citizen'" (1999, 123). He added: "when we talk about 'the whole world,' we should actually say 'rich countries,' because the other ones are very far from that, they view them as quite Baroque" (1999, 123). Here he was highlighting the unequal topography of the cinematic map, organized according to an asymmetrical axis of separation, thus complexifying cinematic reception in the name of a presumed "global" entity. Thus, to take up Deleuze's formula in his letter to Serge Daney (1998), it is not really about making sure that "the world turns to film" in each and every possible location, but about keeping the overall scale of cinema as "global" in order to "faire monde," without losing sight of the historical discontinuities, the geographical gaps, the halted projects, and the living hopes for a completely different order of cinema. "Faire monde" does not involve a satisfying encounter with a presumed "cinema of the Other," with a stranger dutifully and successfully fulfilling his role by maintaining the impossibility of understanding the codes of another culture. What matters for Daney in this "faire monde" is first to construct and to help an "Other cinema" so that it can emancipate itself from Eurocentric expectations. In that, his festival writings appear to be "looking out onto" this promise of a global cinema.

"Faire monde," beyond the illusion of a lasting unity, first involves thinking about the expressions used to refer to this "periphery," this "other," which is usually stigmatized before it is aptly named. It is interesting to note the occurrences of the term "third world" in some of Daney's texts. He often uses it with defiance, either by using quotation marks, or by stressing the outdated value of this term once it is taken out of its historical context. It is with this momentum that he defended and participated in the Festival des 3 Continents, founded in 1979 by Alain and Philippe Jalladeau, who "always combatted the lazy and narrow-minded comfort of

that small term: 'third-world.' At the same time, we ought not to
lose the promise carried by this term" (Daney 2002, 837).[3] Nevertheless, in two texts written in 1981 about Filipino cinema, Daney asserted somewhat of a contradiction based on this tension between "comfort" and "promise," between the historical weight of this term and its possible contemporary echoes.

In fact, in his text from December 9th, 1985, "Nantes à l'heure de Manille,"[4] Daney wrote:

> In a part of the world that for a long time was called "third," a dying regime decided to create a brand image for itself. To sell the country off or to save its hide. In order to folklorize itself to the non "third" world, it had three types of smoke-screens: the tourist camp, the sport celebration, or the cultural event. (2002, 599)

When Daney presented the most emblematic Filipino filmmaker in his text "Qui est Lino Brocka?" published on December 10th, he declared:

> A third-world filmmaker is necessarily someone reinventing cinema for personal reasons, caught between the law of quick profit (which is even tougher than elsewhere) and the risk of a brutal confrontation with the powers in place (who are always wary of images they cannot control). That is when these filmmakers manage to move us. Satyajit Ray in the 1950s, Ousmane Sembene in the 1960s, Lino Brocka in the late 1970s and today.

In the first text, reminiscing about this "third cinema" is associated with an abusive consideration of the "cinema of the Other" from the affected country. As soon as the country no longer needs emancipatory cinema, the assumption is that all audio-visual creation is selling national imagery. At the same

---

3   Originally published in "Nantes, l'âge de raison" in *Libération*, 29 November 1985.

4   Originally published in *Libération*.

 time, Daney exposed the authoritarianism of image production in a ternary manner, as if the three blows of theater would sound anyway, a dramatic backlash against the shift from hope of a world opening up to a strongly controlled insularity. In the second text, Daney surprisingly places Brocka in a presumed aesthetic and political continuity with two filmmakers who are emblematic of the development of their country's cinema and of an unmatched western international acclaim. Because there is no obvious meeting point—either formal or social—in the films of those three filmmakers, this is surprising. The occurrence of the word "third world" nevertheless entails the unchanging effectivity of an "Other cinema," as if it were still acceptable to re-appropriate it, to transform it, to reiterate its impact from a different temporality. By unfolding a cinematic course of action running from the 1950s to the beginning of the 1980s, he renews his claim that an "Other cinema" is necessary.

Nevertheless, as far as I know, Serge Daney did not offer a different term to replace "third world" so that this evolution could begin from a critical standpoint. Implicitly, we could view Daney's critical "faire monde" as situated on the level of a post "third cinema," one which would go beyond the momentum of the 1969 eponymous manifesto by Octavio Getino and Fernando Solanas. A cinema that would respond neither to North American consumers' expectations, nor to the small elite of auteur cinema.[5] It is easy to read this between the lines of his report on the 1985 Cartagena Festival when he wrote: "Since Glauber Rocha or Fernando Solanas (late 1960s), there has no longer been a need to shake up the language of cinema to talk about shocking things.

5   "In the meantime, there exist *our* culture and *their* culture, *our* cinema and *their* cinema. Because our culture is an impulse towards emancipation, it will remain in existence until emancipation is a reality: *a culture of subversion* which will carry with it an art, a science, and *a cinema of subversion*. The lack of awareness in regard to these dualities generally leads the intellectual to deal with artistic and scientific expressions as they were 'universally conceived' by the classes that rule the world, at best introducing some correction into these expressions" (Getino and Solanas 1997, 35–36).

The Esperanto of TV films is enough. Period" (2002, 828).[6] Here, Daney indicates the desertion of the third path to the benefit of shapelessly unifying the life of images. A decade earlier, he was insisting on his responsibility as a critic to increase the visibility given to this other cinematic path when he wrote about the reception of Miguel Littin's *La tierra prometida* (1973): "We'll go see *The Promised Land* because it is Chilean or because it is beautiful, but not both" (2022, I:163).[7]

From festivals to press projections, Daney viewed the lack of consideration for this "third cinema" in the western world as constitutive of a cinematic "faire monde." Hence the necessity to support "third cinema" with more forward-thinking inter-rogations rather than stories that are completely decipherable by a western audience. During the 1985 Cannes Film Festival, Daney noted about the so-called "international competition" that "ninety years after its birth, cinema—'Cannes-able' cinema, of course—is coming back to the place of its origins, that is to say, our country. As for the rest, it has become impossible to show, or it never even existed. We are orphaned from the rest of the world" (2002, 783).[8] His use of the word "orphaned" here clearly shows a blocked cine-filiation in the most internationally visible cinema festival. Daney summons a map of the world that has been threatening to turn into a blinding outward appearance rather than a reservoir of cinematic images ever since it was a childhood memory.

On the contrary, a few months later that same year, Serge Daney would write about the Festival des 3 Continents: "In 1978, there was good reason to create a 'Festival des trois continents'. Indeed, there were no more festivals dedicated to the confrontation and

6   Originally published as "Cartagène 1985 – Cartagène ressuscitée" in *Lib-ération*, 26 August 1985.

7   Originally published in "La Terre promise: un film invisible" in *Libération*, 18 November 1974.

8   Originally published in "Géopolitique de la compétition" in *Libération*, 9 May 1985.

 competition between films from these three continents (Africa, Latin America, and Asia)." He concluded:

> What was enduring in the eyes of the organizers, the Jalladeau brothers, was the desire to prove that cinema history was neither over, nor reserved for a handful of experimental countries, nor even well known. [...] In this new context, festivals will play an essential role: that of showing. Happy Nantais who have already seen so many things! Do they know that they are unconscious co-producers of the films they discover? (2002, 837–38)

By ending his text on a question addressed directly to the audience rather than to the reader, Serge Daney was stressing the fact that the global history of cinema first starts from the space where a film is screened, in a hotspot of Nantais and international "griots," before being written in the pages of *Libération*. Thus, the audience's responsibility in the reception and the circulation of films is essential, as the best remedy against the "lack of people" which is problematic at Cannes, a festival that does not have a lay audience. In this way "the place to write this" is still first and foremost the cinema.

Beyond being acknowledged in the western world, this "Other" cinema still ought to live, be shown, be cared for, and preserved in the original areas where it was created. In his repeated praise of the Festival des 3 Continents, Serge Daney suggested that each of the three continents should have its own "Other hotspot." "Asia lacks a great festival" (2002, 600), he also noted in 1985, in Nantes. In 1984, at the Festival de Rio, he had already pointed out:

> The map of cinema festivals is both busy and gappy. Geopolitically speaking, it favors the "dialogue" between West and East but penalizes encounters between North and South. Until now, there were only four great festivals (Cannes, Venice, Moscow, Montreal)—said to be *de rang A* –, and since the disappearance of the Tehran festival (after the 1979 Revolution) and the Manila festival (after Imelda

and Ferdinand Marcos came to power), no country from the South (a better term, because of its romantic brutality, than the gloomy "third-world") has been able to organize and to "lend credibility to" a great international festival, a festival that is full of color, culture, and "glamour," and which is supported by the film market. (2002, 751)[9]

"Speaking like a geographer," echoing Gilles Deleuze's motto (Deleuze and Parnet 2008, 159), Serge Daney places his historical conscience in these unequal cartographical dynamics, where revealing a center also means taking into account the limits of its influence. This cinematic "faire monde" could be read as an attempt to inhabit cinephilia, that is to say—to use Jean-Marc Besse's words—to combine a "collective destiny and an individual experience which, in the end, take us back to the sometimes contentious organization of life, that is to say to the definition of a time, commensurate with a space and with their general orientation." (2013, 9). Thus, the most inclusive composition possible of a global cinema history stems from the critical possibility of welcoming in this cartographical pulsation.

Being a Go-between: A Gift

The relative space left to world cinemas that were not those of rich countries occupied a special place in the works of Serge Daney right up to his death. For example, in the "Journal de l'an nouveau" he wondered about the disappearance of "concrete America behind the success of abstract Americanization" (1992, 8) and he compared the American spectacle of the previous decades to a "potlatch of images which intrigued Bataille and which now concerns Hollywood's Japanese buyers" (1992, 8). The use of the word "potlatch" in this context is as disconcerting as it is revealing. Potlatch, which is a central term in Marcel Mauss's

9   Originally published in "Lever de rideau sur Rio" in *Libération*, 12 December 1984.

 The Gift (2007), expresses, in different communities from different continents, particularly in America and Oceania, a system of gifts and counter-gifts which, in itself, is not synonymous with the kind of bartering familiar from western societies. Other than the idea that there would be a sort of "mercantile theft" of the Hollywood recipe in one of the Asian countries with the largest cinema production, there remains a preoccupation regarding "images which show themselves," those that "make us think about" contemporary cinema, by working to bring closer what is thought to be "distant."

How can global cinema's tacit counter-gifts establish themselves where hegemonic potlatch is dying? How does Daney contemplate a possible extension of this for "the Other cinema"? In which terms does he describe his role? I could surmise that his work, which is continuous in time but spatially intermittent, involves a double work of cinematic programming in his works about the Other cinema: the task of receiving the preliminary work of international festival programmers, and the task of carving, within these pre-established programs, a particular cinematic substance, interrogating apparent contingencies in what they carry of signification, by multiplying questions and speculations. This preoccupation is at the heart of his text "Découverte du cinéma chinois," following the program of films put together by Marco Müller in Turin in 1982. Daney ends his text by wondering about how to make a fragment of cinema history visible in the country where the films themselves are produced:

> Things will stay like this as long as the Chinese audience
> continues to view nothing or nearly nothing of foreign pro-
> duction and while the latter is viewed behind closed doors,
> only by professionals. As if cinema could have two different
> histories: that of the filmmakers who see everything in secret

and that of their audience who sees nothing. A semi-colonial situation, again. (2002, 618)[10]

Far from moving towards a sociological study of the audience,[11] Serge Daney watches the films of the Other cinema behind those who are looking at the screen. He pays an almost ethnographical attention to emergent cinema: emergent in the sense understood by Clifford James in his work *The Predicament of Culture: Twentieth-Century Ethnography, Literature, and Art,* not as

> a practice of interpreting distinct, whole ways of life but instead as a series of specific dialogues, impositions, and inventions. "Cultural" difference is no longer a stable, exotic otherness; self-other relations are matters of power and rhetoric rather than of essence. A whole structure of expectations about authenticity in culture and in art is thrown into doubt. (1988, 14)

Serge Daney was actually interested in festivals as structures, as matrices that are porous to the current history of the world, as screens that parallel contemporary geopolitics. Daney's festival writings outside of the western world look like new takes on the world, far from the postcard fetish, or from the snapshot imagery. They recount the complexity of this ever-changing cartography in which the legend does not always match the map. Others ventured out to claim a "history of cinema" written in black and white, as is the case in *Cinémas d'Amérique latine* edited by Guy Hennebelle and Alfonso Gumucio Dagron (1981). Daney, on the other hand, first talked about mourning the cinema that no longer happened, the cruelty of the films that will never be made, a geography never exhaustively explored, before talking about inventoried filmographies, proofs of a tradition:

10   Originally published in "Découverte du cinéma chinois" in *Libération*, 31 March 1982.

11   Even more so if we take Daney's words from *Itinéraires d'un ciné-fils*, in which he explains that society is the enemy of the world. This idea can be found in other of his texts too.

What does a "Latin-American cinema" specialist look like? It looks like a man looking sadly at a map of Latin America. With its small and large countries. Surinam and Brazil. Cuba. One by one, this man crosses out the countries he no longer expects "good" cinema from, and sometimes even no cinema at all. He reviews his index cards joylessly. A monotonous diagnosis: if "good" cinema has a hard time existing in the jungle of money, it cannot exist at all in places where the military is cracking down. (2002, 480–81)[12]

Here, we witness a similar concern to the one voiced in his text "Petites guerres au Liban," which was published a year later, in which he listed the risks faced by Lebanese filmmakers at this point in time: "Is he aware that an ever-growing part of the world is less and less able to produce an image of itself? To stage itself? As if counting on cinema to hand others an image of yourself had become a luxury" (2002, 166).[13]

Considering the texts of Serge Daney, a festivalgoer on three continents, as a developing bath of emerging, threatened, or missing images, I would surmise that his critical role as a "passeur" is intensified here. Not only because he writes about "what is happening" in the thickness that separates him from screens, but because festivals represent "passages," actual moving microcosms. However, it is best not to consider Serge Daney as a "passenger" and thus, I refuse to idealize his travels into those of a "globetrotter." He is more of an image "gifter," strengthening his stance and the readability of his location for readers who might not have access to other traces of the films than through his words. Daney's critical exercise appears to be most profitable, as it allows readers to imagine films of which they are divested.

---

12   Originally published in "Le tout cinéma latino-américain" in *Libération*," 16–17 January 1982.

13   Originally published in "Petites guerres au Liban" in *Libération*," 11 February 1983. The "he" in this quote refers to Lebanese filmmaker, Maroun Baghdadhi.

The gift given by Serge Daney in this body of texts resonates with one of the variations proposed by Jacques Derrida in his book *Given Time: I. Counterfeit Money*:

> If there is gift, the *given* of the gift (*that which* one gives, *that which* is given, the gift as given thing or as act of donation) must not come back to the giving (let us not already say to the subject, to the donor). It must not circulate, it must not be exchanged, it must not in any case be exhausted, as a gift, by the process of exchange, by the movement of circulation of the circle in the form of return to the point of departure. If the figure of the circle is essential to economics, the gift must remain *aneconomic.* Not that it remains foreign to the circle, but it must *keep* a relation of foreignness to the circle, a relation without relation of familiar foreignness. (1992, 7)

Coming back to my initial premise of an incomplete "faire monde" for a critical analysis of cinema in all its complexity, I come back to the idea that global cinema "closes the loop on itself"; it does not mold itself to the globe but, on the contrary, expresses itself more through uncertain arcs.

I can see at least three possible instances in which Serge Daney gives to the Other cinema. First, Serge Daney as a psychic festivalgoer, who sees burning cinema questions behind the artifices and illusions of obviousness. His text "Carthage, An 10" (2022, 399–414)[14] could be considered seminal in this regard, as he took care to analyze all the strata of the festival and because the films reviewed do not appear to be unilateral subjects but various prisms through which to think about a continental cinema. He lists, quite exhaustively, subdivisions that will appear again in later texts with some variations. He considers, in chronological order: the historical context of the festival; his mood when he arrives; the jury's selection; the history of the festival and the way it has evolved; how censorship is influencing this festival at

14   Originally published in *Cahiers du Cinéma* 272, December 1976.

 this time; and the place of the audience and its role. The text also contains: an inventory of the screens' geography; an analysis of the films selected; thoughts about official cinema, about the limitations of national cinema and about the absence of politics; a reflection on the continental potential of cinema; a brief review of two striking films; and a prospective sentence in conclusion.

Secondly, Serge Daney can look like a "giver of presence" of the actors of this Other cinema with his presence, alternating his point of view with a listening stance. The episode of his show *Microfilms* dedicated to Fespaco (Festival panafricain du cinéma et de la télévision de Ouagadougou) in 1987 is remarkable in that, after having listened to the dreams of commercial North American cinema related by young audience members, or "little soldiers" as he called them, by the hotel swimming pool, he talked for a long time about the future of African cinema with Thomas Sankara, Burkina Faso's head of state and well-known figure in the country's first revolution, who would be assassinated that same year. Serge Daney thus shows the coexistence of an alienated look with that of an emancipating project, which is a constitutive tension in the "Long March of African Cinema." Questioning the future of cinema given to us in the present tense means to put it back in play in the midst of uncertainty, to simulate a muddled cartographic forecast.

These works by Daney can also be seen as the gift of a time for a history of cinema in continued emergence, if we view it in Jacques Derrida's sense:

> The gift is not a gift, the gift only gives to the extent it *gives time*. The difference between a gift and any other operation of pure and simple exchange is that the gift gives time. *There where there is gift, there is time*. What it gives, the gift, is time, but this gift of time is also a demand of time. The thing must not be restituted *immediately and right away*. (1992, 41)

Serge Daney thus worked on the three continents like a watchful compass, far from his status as a "slayer of preconceived notions, always seeking the right images to wage his war against clichés."[15] His festival writings show how much his geographical movements and his capacity to be analytically anchored in each cinematic place catalyze the writing of his thoughts on the discontinuities of the history of cinema and, at the same time, the political upheavals of the contemporary world. In some ways, the singular space-time of festivals gives him the opportunity to revive his acuity by displacing possible cinephile habits. They are experiences of refining his awareness of his place of enunciation, whereas Daney prefers to be disoriented by the circumstances of festivals in distant cinematic countries than to conquer any neocolonial ideal. Writing about cinema from festivals is definitely not an expression of power but the bilateral experience of a cinematic encounter, a genuine way to definitely stay a "giver of presence."

That is why it appears to us that Serge Daney also "gave" himself a text, all the while opening his perspective and ability to listen, adjusting his critical compass to that of a specific filmmaker. We could reread "Johan van der Keuken's *Vers le Sud*" and view the Dutch filmmaker as Daney's festival alter ego, who, in the early '70s was looking to "find a cinema form that would respond to the third-world sensitivity of that era" (Daney 1998, 132)[16]. In 1982, in the face of the evolution of "docu-liar's" work, Daney acknowledged that "the word 'third world' has gone stale" (1998,

15   Here, I am quoting one of Daney's three ways to "come back from a far-away place": "Until now, there were [or was (sic)] three ways of coming back from a far-away place. Three ways to show the few things one had seen—*there*. Three ways of showing one's own docu-lie, of bearing witness. There was the globe-trotting journalist, seeking easy-to-sell, never-seen, and surprising scoops and images (let's say Reichenbach's *L'Amérique insolite*). There was the famous artist, only armed with his or her gaze, one of those unique gazes that can make anything interesting (let's say Antonioni's *Chung Kuo*). And then, there was the slayer of preconceived notions, always seeking the right images to wage his war against clichés (let's say Godard for *Ici et ailleurs*)." Originally published in "L'As du cliché," *Libération*, 10 January 1983, and reprinted in *La Maison cinéma et le monde*. Vol. 2 (2002, 147).

16   "Vers le Sud.", originally published in *Libération*, March 2, 1982.

 132) and that the South is a "geopolitical and physical state" (1998, 132) that they share. Johan van der Keuken himself confided: "I don't care about the documentary, in the sense of documenting something, but what you document is actually a physical presence, not only that of the other, but my own. It might be even more important to document the fact that we were there and in which way" (1993, 78). Serge Daney, giver of cinematographies from three continents, worked (while) fully present. Jacques Derrida claimed: "'to give time' is not to give a given present but the condition of presence of any present in general" (1992, 54). "Faire monde," is not so much letting moving images emerge as it is chasing them, definitively, along a centrifugal trajectory.

Translated into English by Melina Delmas and revised by Kate Ince

References

Besse, Jean-Marc. 2013. *Habiter: Un monde à mon image*. Paris: Flammarion.

Clifford, James. 1988. *The Predicament of Culture: Twentieth-Century Ethnography, Literature, and Art*. Cambridge: Harvard University Press.

Dagron, Alfonso Gumocio, and Guy Hennebelle, eds. 1981. *Les Cinémas de l'Amérique Latine*. Paris: Lherminier.

Daney, Serge. 1991. "Journal de l'an passé." *Trafic* 1: 5–30.

———. 1992. "Journal de l'an nouveau." *Trafic* 3: 5–24.

———. 1998. *Ciné Journal*, Vol. 1, *1981–1982*, 131–35. Paris: Cahiers du Cinéma. (first edition 1986. Paris: Cahiers du cinéma)

———. 1999. *Devant la recrudescence des vols de sacs à main, cinéma, télévision, information: 1988–1991*. Lyon: Aléas.

———. 2002. *La Maison cinéma et le monde*, Vol. 2, *Les Années Libé (1981–1985)*. Paris: P.O.L.

———. 2022. *The Cinema House & the World*, Vol. 1, *The Cahiers du cinéma Years, 1962–1981*. Trans. Christine Pichini. South Pasadena: Semiotext(e).

Deleuze, Gilles. 1995. "Letter to Serge Daney: Optimism, Pessimism, and Travel." In *Negotiations, 1972–1990*. New York: Columbia University Press.

Deleuze, Gilles, and Claire Parnet. 2008. *Dialogues*. Paris: Flammarion.

Derrida, Jacques. 1992. *Given Time: I. Counterfeit Money*. Trans. Peggy Kamuf. Chicago: University of Chicago Press.

Getino, Octavio, and Fernando Solanas. 1997. "Towards a Third Cinema." In M. T. Martin, ed. *New Latin American Cinema*. Detroit: Wayne State University Press.

Keuken, Johan van der. 1993. "Le Comment du monde." *Cahiers du cinéma* 465.

Mauss, Marcel. 2002. *The Gift: The form and reason for exchange in archaic societies*. London: Routledge.

TABLE TENNIS

TENNIS

TELEVISION

LE SALAIRE DU ZAPPEUR

DECONSTRUCTION

8

Ping-ponging with Daney

Hervé Joubert-Laurencin

By commenting on the only text that Serge Daney devoted to table tennis, this essay retraces both his multiple writings about tennis, a sport that he followed very closely, and a whole series of theorizations the critic carried out in his texts: about gestures and bodies, about the way in which television films sport (imposing democratization and visibility on it), and about the fiction and suspension of meaning that is in every sport as well as cinema. Without being a specialist of the game, it is through a look trained and informed by the cinema that Daney reconstitutes certain cinematographic character-istics on the ping-pong table, bringing in all the intelligence of the sport at the same time.

    A researcher friend was kind enough to send me a snapshot of
the young Serge Daney playing ping-pong. I could not find any
photos from my childhood to return the favor, which is too bad
as it would have clarified the title of this piece right away, thanks
to a rhetorical figure of cinema called shot/reverse shot, which
parallels racket games and very much resembles my title: "Ping-
ponging with Daney." So the only thing I can do is to display a
relic: my old Nagoya "YV S" racket. At the end of my ping-pong
years, I had only kept the original Hanna blade, type Ehrlich, for
the feeling of its diagonally cut varnished handle with its eleven
holes on each side. "At the end," that is to say when my game had
reached the last stage of its evolution, which occurred between
the ages of eight and fifteen, we had to change the rubber on
my blade. This was a tricky task for which I relied entirely on my
coach, who knew about the different types of glue and which one
was best for me. So my blade is no longer covered by the sponges
of a "YV" but has the same sponge on each side: a 1.5mm-thick
Butterfly Sriver D13-L. This is a great sponge for attacking and
lifting efficiently when you master lifts and topspins, but also
thin enough to counter-attack—for example, to perform fast
and sharp backhand blocks, which were my best moves, and had
saved me during many matches. After being in a cupboard for
more than forty years, however, my old racket looks a sorry sight.
It has become impossible to play with: the wood is decaying, the
lovely deep red sponges have turned black and become cracked
and slippery, and without that adhesion would not be effective.
I think the racket would break into pieces if I were to play with
it. But holding it in my hand still feels great and brings back the
feeling of playing ping-pong, which is forever ingrained in my
central nervous system and which I only ever get in my everyday
life when my arm goes to catch something falling off the table
without me having consciously decided to do so.

So in the match I want to play against Daney, I only have old and
tattered tools, and I have not played professionally since I was
fifteen. As for Daney, my opponent today, he is not much better

off, since he is only an amateur (or at least that is what was suggested by his P.O.L publishers who, in 1994, posthumously entitled his book *L'Amateur de tennis*). The picture confirms this status: his right arm and his legs are too stretched out to be able to stop the ball except by sheer luck; the fact that his hand is blurry—other than making me think that his wrist is moving when hitting the ball, which is a mistake (one's hand should stay firm at the end of the arm and the wrist should be solid as the ball is hit except when performing a very sophisticated move)—cannot hide how badly he is mishandling the racket, which he holds like a shovel. Moreover, his free arm does not seem to know what to do and does nothing to help balance Daney's posture. In short, he is hopeless, except for the fact that his eyes seem to be following the ball, which is good.

As his picture shows, entering the game of ping-pong also means adjusting hand-eye coordination, just as you do when making or watching movies.

I brushed up a little (both for you and for myself) on my knowledge of ping-pong. I can thus summarize the Sino-Japanese situation on that front, which will help us understand the context of the only text Serge Daney ever wrote about ping-pong which, strangely enough, comments on images of Japanese ping-pong players.

Since the end of classical cinema, let us say 1959, and since ping-pong entered sport's modern age of professionalism and Olympism (around 1988), it is China, rather than Japan, which has literally been crushing all the world's other countries with its social basis of millions of players. Ma Long has been the world champion since 2015 and is the winner of the most titles in history after several of his fellow countrymen, including the good-looking Wang Liqin who was crowned world champion several times. After 1959, the Chinese were the kings of the world twenty times out of thirty, the French once, and from time to time the Swedish. Take for instance Stellan Bengtsson when I was fifteen years old, and in the late 1980s, the great blocking player Jan-Owe Waldner. The latter is my ping-pong ego ideal, as he is the all-time king of a move called the block—the matrix move of third style or so-called counter tactics. (There are three different types of play in table tennis: offensive, defensive, and counter, also called counter-attacking.)

It is well known that Serge Daney was a sports journalist for *Libération* between 1980 and 1990, but apart from a few exceptions, only wrote about one sport: tennis. However, in the middle of the decade, on the occasion of a video installation at the Centre Pompidou in December 1986, he wrote a text about ping-pong.

My hypothesis, my back-and-forth—my ping-ponging if you will—will thus be one of deconstruction. If we accept that sports journalism is generally a less legitimate activity than cinema criticism—and that it could, for that reason, allow us to better grasp Daney's writing—then ping-pong is even less legitimate than tennis and will enable us to go even further. I will start with an example of Daney's remarks about sport in general, then address the question of tennis and, finally, that of ping-pong.

Sport

In *Le Salaire du zappeur*, Daney compares football to tennis in the following terms: "It is by becoming televised that some sports (tennis especially, but the list is much longer, see golf) gained a larger audience than they had previously had" (1988, 184–87).[1] He added: "football (which *already* had this audience) has managed to become the ultimate democratic form of entertainment." This democratization is possible through the addition of "time-outs" and "the sum of *inserts* that TV-channel hoppers always relish in." In other words, "time-outs and image inserts" are the key words here. There is a topic that Daney often talked about and that is often discussed where Daney is concerned, which I cannot

1   Originally published in *Libération*, 24 November 1987.

come back to here: the freeze-frame. In this new grammar, these
"time-outs and inserts" would be the televisual equivalent of
freeze-frames. These surroundings and excesses should not be
categorized as what our little "Trumpo-Macronian" era—an era
eager for the politics of control, for a semiology of superficiality,
and which is unconscious of the unconscious—would call *storytelling*. Rather, they should be categorized as a Freudian slip, or
one of those random non-manageable signs that are specific
to TV and were described by communication sciences starting
from their prehistory in the 1950s. For Daney, this is the "vanity"
specific to football, a "playground" for big children, "the space
of a soft 'Discipline and punish,'" where "pupils' parents" are in
cahoots. Through this last expression—a very negative one for
Daney—we understand that the childish scenes football players
perform when they pretend to be injured, and the democratic
complicity that this creates with the audience, is not in itself very
good staging. What needs to be understood is that it is nevertheless staged, and that it can count as staged when faced with
the filmic emptiness that TV also creates in huge quantities. This
is why going beyond the strictly sporting subject of sports in this
medium turns out also to be a return to cinema. In this instance,
Daney adds in this short text, "*tennis players*, be they the winner
or the loser, have few moves at their disposal to behave badly."
Nevertheless, these few moves make up most of Daney's sports
commentary and the originality of it too. Actually, his only text
about ping-pong is significantly entitled: "Quelques gestes."

A first conclusion: Daney thinks sport through television; it is TV
that brings him to tennis. He is a sports poet at the time when
sport is going through its televisual metamorphosis.[2] Even though
Daney becomes a regular at Roland Garros and attends the 1983

---

2   I will not come back to what is called "acceleration," which is decided by
sports federations and famously due to the constraints of the TV calendar. It
appeared both in tennis and table tennis as they became more popular with
the public. I am truly shocked that a table tennis set is nowadays played in 11
points rather than in 21.

182 Davis Cup in Grenoble, his first tennis articles talk about his gaze being mediated by the small screen. For example, in the issue of *Libération* published on 7 July 1980, he writes: "McEnroe saves two match points, winning eight consecutive shots. Screams erupt in Wimbledon's stands while I start screaming too in front of my TV set (a small Sony color set, a very good one)" (1994, 38–39). Consequently, this experience goes hand in hand with the claim—which for Daney is not specific to sport, but to TV commentary in general—of a look formed and informed by cinema. "The benefit of clay, why I love this surface so much, much more than others (but of course my perspective is that of a cinema aficionado, who prefers a still shot to a zoom), is that it creates fiction" (1994, 15), he writes on 29 May 1980. Here, Daney equates a resounding clear rebound in Roland Garros to a still frame, opposing it to the zoom of a swift and fast ball gliding onto Wimbledon's grass (2002, 905–6).[3] Additionally, a rebound or plot twist [*rebondissement* in French—a pun already present on the first page of *L'Amateur de tennis*] would generate fiction.

These are two examples of a general approach brilliantly summarized by his masterpiece about televisual stylistics, "Nouvelle grammaire," a short article written on the occasion of his trip as a special correspondent for the Los Angeles Summer Olympics (1986, 243–45).[4] We could mull it over for several hours, and I can only refer you back to it if you do not believe how rigorous and inventive Daney's completely original theory of television is.

On that point, ping-pong as an operator of deconstruction should not let us get lost in the search for surface equivalence (the equivalent to the tennis court's variation between grass or clay can only be that of sponges, which are themselves more or less fast, glued to the flat and neutral surface of the racket's blade, the questions of the play area and the table's and balls' material and manufacturing having been standardized and resolved a long

3   Originally published in *Libération*, 29 June 1981.
4   Originally published in *Libération*, 4 August 1984.

time ago). It will only help us to understand that when tennis is
experienced through television, the court is no longer, for man, a
space in which to run, glide, and fall. Once resized onto the small
screen, it becomes a visual table to scrutinize. That is to say there
is no longer a ping-pong experience, an experience of "table"
tennis, but rather of "retable" tennis, the playing surface having
been tilted up like an altar table in sacred art (in Italian, "retable"
translates as *pala d'altare*).

Thus reduced to the classical form of western thought of the
example, tennis can become an object of discourse. I do not have
time here to go over the frequent developments of that issue that
can be found in Giorgio Agamben's various works. Thus, I will
only mention, as the Italian philosopher recalls multiple times,
that the first meaning of the German word usually translated
by "example," *Beispiel*, means: "what is played on the side," and
that this corresponds quite well to the word "paradigm," derived
from the Greek *para-deigma*: "what is shown on the side." On TV,
tennis "is shown on the side" (paradigm) and "plays on the side"
(*Beispiel*).

Thus, now that tennis has become ping-pong again through the
intervention of TV itself, this historical excrescence of the imme-
morial racket game is reconnected with its roots. But let us not
get ahead of ourselves.

A second conclusion: what is at play—both with television itself
(this object of social leveling and voyeurism as considered
by Daney, as it allows us, according to his admirable expression, "ce qui ne nous regarde pas": to "watch what is none of
our business/what is not watching us") and also, more simply,
through its mediation—is a whole issue of social legitimization
and delegitimization. To better understand Daney's ideas, it has
to be specified that he is a theorist deeply linked to the form of

 the proletariat.[5] The *tennis players* who have "few moves at their disposal to behave badly," are, whether they want to be or not, likened, through televisualization, to the popular "cinema" displays of common-or-garden football players. It is obvious that Daney is perfectly aware that, in the late 1970s, he is playing a discursive game with tennis, because this sport, which had until then been used by the petty bourgeoisie to try and marry their daughters into a higher social class, is now offered to those for whom tennis was once "none of their business." Here, ping-pong as an operator of deconstruction asserts that the original racket game is both a royal game and a people's game—a phenomenon, not of leveling or destruction, but of class deconstruction. I will not go as far as to say that Maoism can explain the world domination of Chinese ping-pong players, but I will maintain the idea that the concepts of people and elite have, for a long time, made particular sense in that huge, nationalized empire. Thus, the motto in my coach's room "Ping-pong is the game of the masses, table tennis the sport of the elite" is explained, because it refers to a sport which has kept within it a double postulation revealed by the two different names it bears. I do not know any other sport that has two names which are as equally recognized and commonly used. Here I would also note that the sociology of sport has long taught us that nations who dominate through their elite champions are also those who possess the biggest mass of players in their population." Game of the masses, sport of the elite" is thus the formula of a general rule valid for every sport, even if it is not known or explicitly said.

---

5   This, I must point out, is not linked to the leftist stance he had adopted at one point of his life, which, as far as he is concerned, was one of the stages of his progressive social legitimation as someone coming from an impoverished background.

Tennis

Serge Daney's tennis chronicles are the object of a separate work, *L'Amateur de tennis*, prefaced by writer Mathieu Lindon, who was one of his former *Libération* colleagues. It was published in 1994 by P.O.L., in other words before Daney's writings started being published in several volumes by the same publisher.[6]

Let us go back to the spring-summer season of 1981. Two articles from that time can be found in the short chapter entitled "Wimbledon, 1981" in *L'Amateur de tennis*. This chapter could have been called "McEnroe's consecration," since the first article relates the difficult victory of the capricious American against Rod Frawley: "Both players were playing the same kind of tennis and the mimetic violence was extreme" (1994, 49). After this evocation of René Girard's theory, the mimeticism motif continues in the second article which implicitly refers to the political alternation that had just happened in France, where after decades under a right-wing government, the left came to power when François Mitterand was elected President on 10 May 1981. "L'alternance du pouvoir" tells how McEnroe beat Björn Borg on 5 July 1981 after having lost against him the previous year, thus ending the Swedish player's complete domination of tennis (five consecutive victories at Wimbledon and six at Roland Garros during the previous years). *La Maison cinéma et le monde*, volume II, which was published in 2002, however, tells a truly suspenseful saga if we put the articles back in order. What happened before this shocking twist? Borg was getting bored on the roof of the Galeries Lafayette during a promotional tennis event for children.

6 The benefit of having a book is that it gives an overview of Daney articles and shows how a system constituted itself (Lindon even claims, quoting Marguerite Duras, that it is this book that makes Daney a writer). The downside is that each of the first three volumes of Daney's general works dedicates a whole chapter to the tennis articles that were not published in *L'Amateur de tennis* but does not include all the articles on the subject either. This scattered configuration does not allow a quick grasp of the timeline of the sporting stories.

 He was bored because he could not now play each serve as if his
life depended on it, but only "as if his *image*, and only his image,
depended on it" (2002, 904).[7] He did not know yet that a change
in power would happen and that he would be replaced. It was as
if the part of reality resisting in his victorious body, whichever
media is representing it, was replaced by imagery.

Björn Borg's visual and televisual becoming preceded his disappearance from sport. The following article (Daney 2002, 906)[8]
condemns the dreary and dispassionate comments from 1981's TV
journalists, which are as regular and safe as Borg's perfect game.
Daney prefers their precursors' prose, the TV sports journalists,
who saw the "the possibility of astounding twists," that is to say,
creating fiction by getting closer to reality, as reality will, in this
specific case (but this case is paradigmatic) make a spectacular
comeback with McEnroe's victory.

If we push further the logic of Daney's little scribbles about
sport that I have quoted so far, McEnroe's victory becomes the
triumph of cinema over television, of reality and storytelling over
boredom and repetition. There is also a stand-alone article in the
same chapter of volume II of *La Maison cinéma et le monde*, a little
later in 1982, about William Klein, who had filmed Roland Garros
the previous year, and whom Serge Daney critiques quite neg-
atively (2002, 915–17).[9] With great coherence, Daney reproaches
the photographer for not being able to capture "the cinema,"

7   Originally published in *Libération*, 21 May 1981. In 1969, Pasolini produced
     an analysis of the cyclist champion Eddy Merckx that is similar to Daney's
     about Borg. Pasolini says that Merckx's "explosion of vitality" is "overflowing
     but not at all shapeless." Here is his argument: on TV, "victories seem to be
     conditioned by a will to repress which humiliates the cyclists … their real
     relationship with us has irremediably gone through a process of alienation
     and falsification. Merckx is a truly great champion because he wins in spite
     of all of this. Merckx's body is stronger than the way we consume it. Merckx's
     victories are scandalous" (Pasolini 2012, 158), originally published in *Tempo*, 7
     June 1969, "Il Caos" column.
8   Originally published in *Libération*, 29 June 1981.
9   Originally published in *Libération*, 6 July 1982.

which would have enabled him to break "television-tennis," because "cinema and tennis are arts of (lasting) performance and of (passing) time" (2002, 917), whereas "photography is a practice of immediacy."

A third collection, *Ciné journal*, from 1986, includes an article that comes back to the spring 1981 French Open, entitled "Des balles si lourdement chargées." It is a summer text fairly heavily charged with erotic and sexual imagery, written a month after the end of the tournament. The balls are described as testicles, sometimes "deflated, hairy, dead," sometimes as a "concrete object, hairy and conforming to the regulations" turning into something "phantasmatic." The balls are "struck with great violence before falling to the ball boys and girls who retrieve them," "they carry hatred, phobias, desires to lose or to punish"; some men can "get into the ball and they are screaming." By offering such a fantasized description of the tennis ball, this article goes beyond the sport itself to turn it, as explained by its retrospective introductory paragraph, into a "stock of metaphors." The idea (also taken up elsewhere) of the ball "representing the gaze" is interesting, but here it is seemingly developed from a primary Lacanian presupposition, which brings together the gaze and the phallus under the designation of "objet petit-a," amongst others. "The tennis ball—Daney says in a very elliptical nod to André Bazin[10]—has no seam." Apart from the fact that a tennis ball is indeed made out of pieces of felt—yellow felt since television imposed this color so that the ball would be more visible on screen—it is glued rather than stitched together, and the use of this possibly poorly controlled allegory of Christ's unshareable,

10   Quoting the Bible (John, 19:23–24, Psalms, 22:19), André Bazin writes: "For Renoir, knowledge is achieved through love and love through the world's epidermis. The suppleness, the mobility, and the living formation of the way he stages things, are his way of draping, for his pleasure and for our joy, the seamless tunic of reality" (2018, art. n° 927), originally published in *Cahiers du cinema* 8, January 1952. This image is taken up in "Découpage," in the volume entitled *Vingt ans de cinéma à Venise* (*Écrits complets, op. cit.*, art. n° 1089).

seamless robe that soldiers cast lots for prior to his crucifixion, may link the ball, or the gaze, to a perpetual back and forth without any solution as to its continuity? The article's conclusion seems to go along with that. McEnroe's cathode-ray tube fluorescence, unlike Borg's metronomic body, which is seamless and does not know any break, produces visible humanness, the unconscious, life, what is loose—in short, it produces cinema in its way of buttressing reality. I quote: "Between two racket blows, for a time that can be infinitesimal, the American player becomes undone, dislocated, absent. I … am talking of his body and about this piece of the unconscious that passes through his body. For him, the ball is the Other, it is adversity rather than the adversary" (Daney 1986, 243–45).

Having given this idea of what Daney is doing with his descriptions of tennis, we shall now get back to the ping-pong ball, which is not made out of soft felt, nor out of marble, but out of celluloid.

Ping-pong/Table tennis/Gossima

The glued and perfectly spherical ping-pong ball is a product of the reunion of two hemispheres, like the miniature globes that you find on kids' desks. Until the International Table Tennis Federation decided recently to approve the use of PVC and plastic, the ball shared with cinema and its film, and with cartoon and its cel, the fetishism of the little celluloid skin.

Because it is colloidal (that is to say agitated by Brownian motions that can be seen under a microscope) celluloid was also favored in Auguste Lumière's medical neo-humoral theory. He was one of the inventors of cinema, the first maker of photographic plates and photographic film in the world, and thus the first photographic chemistry engineer in history. He claimed to save humankind—make it immortal even—by maintaining in the human body itself, through various ingestions and radiations, the colloidal state of its interstitial liquids, by preventing their flocculation, that is to say by impeding the immobility that leads to their biological death.

His theory fizzled out, but it clearly carries resonance relating to cinema and animation. Where this is concerned, I have studied the only Lumière film attributed to Auguste, *Les Brûleuses d'herbes*, from 1897, in which the vibratory agitation of the smoke is a wonder of cinema. Following this logic, we could claim that the very, let us say "filmic", way sports are staged, is colloidal-like. Historically, this staging only occurred with the invention of television, which is the only thing that Serge Daney is interested in. We could claim that tennis looks more like ping-pong when the balls' long trajectories and the players' coming and goings, once broadcast on a small screen, turn into Brownian motion. And finally, that in the years Daney knew it, television itself, as a fast material, was already overtaken by video art.

Thus, it seems quite logical that, in the mid-1980s, the video artist Christophe Bargues invited Serge Daney to write commentaries for his video installation entitled "Quelques gestes… de Tokyo à Yamagushi," dedicated to Japanese people playing ping-pong. It was exhibited in the foyer of the Centre Pompidou near the exhibition "Le Japon des avant-gardes" from December 1986 to January 1987.[11]

Daney's only text about ping-pong starts with an anonymous main character, which reverses the traditional story of the *tennisman*. An eighty-three-year-old amateur discovers the tennis table's moves. He is playing, Daney says, "without thinking about victory." In fact, the descriptions of Borg and McEnroe, to go back to two examples which do not constitute exceptions, do still convey the rage to win, although they are realized in opposite ways. This Japanese man from the Seibu shop club, is, on the other hand, experiencing an opening, the opening of "the door

11   Prod. Corsaire sanglot, 1986. In *La Maison cinéma et le monde* (Daney 2012, 354–63), the reproduction of this article is composed of ten "sequences," which are each accompanied by a video screenshot.

 of a world constituted of different moves." Thus, armed with my celluloid tool of deconstruction—ping-pong as an operator of deconstruction—I conclude that Daney saw reality in sport being breathed through the little interstices of timeouts and of the celebrities' fuss making (their "cinema"), and this is why he chose McEnroe over Borg. In front of the ping-pong table, he discovered that it is within sport itself that cinema can disturb television or, in other words, that the real can tear reality, gently, in the action of sport itself.

This idea is expressed from the first sequence and from time to time in the following ones, through what could be deemed a Barthesian description of Japan as an exotic civilization. Daney was writing about the art of video for the Centre Pompidou rather than televised sports for a daily newspaper. This might have induced him, maybe involuntarily, or maybe not, to act like the new Roland Barthes. Fifteen years after the publication of *The Empire of Signs* and six years after Barthes's accidental death at the exact moment his name became associated with the *Cahiers du Cinéma* through the publication of his book *Camera Lucida*, Daney sees, in these images of Japan, the signs of an "empty availability" in "spaces of inefficiency," of "suspended" moves, one "that is self-sufficient," and another one a "repeatedly tested" basic move, producing a "pleasure without trace and almost without image." In other words, variations on the central motif of *L'Empire des signes*, that is to say not *L'Empire des sens*,[12] as one could mistakenly think but the *exemption* of meaning. In this book, Barthes does indeed offer a sort of sequel to suspension as commitment, which is the idea he had noticed in the work of Bertolt Brecht. After a suspended ending, rather than a classic happy or tragic ending, the theatergoer returns home with a political issue on his mind. More than the suspended meaning, he imagines in his study the exempted meaning. Taking haiku as

---

12   The French title of Nagisa Oshima's *In the Realm of the Senses* (*Ai no Korīda*, "Bullfight of Love", 1976).

an example, he claims that artists engage in political acts when they offer the free spectacle of a fair cry, whatever it may be: "the haiku is as pure, as spherical, and as empty as a musical note; this might be why you're supposed to read it twice, like an echo … the echo only underlines the lack of meaning"[13] (Barthes 1970, 99).

But it is not the Barthesian version of Daney that prevails. This rhetorical exercise in the manner of Gide's or Barthes's way of observing little things would remain too predictable if Daney the sports journalist did not once again emerge, and if the tennis observer in him was not displaced by the proximity of the hands and table game that is ping-pong. The generosity of the theorizing machine thus gives forth nearly a dozen invaluable remarks inspired by this sport that Daney only discussed once.

Firstly—and this had already emerged in some tennis commentaries—there is "a dialogue between humans and the humble celluloid ball."

Secondly, the gaze of the ping-pong player which follows the ball all the way to his or her opponent becomes an extension of that player. This leads to dispossession: if it goes beyond mimetic rivalry and the microscopic avatars of surveillance and voyeurism that the text is talking about, it could let go of alienation and go all the way to becoming other.

In the third sequence, by describing what a ping-pong championship looks like, with its rows of tables aligned in a gymnasium, Daney, being the good formal analyst that he is, perceives what every ping-pong player inherently knows: the paradoxically collective, nearly collectivist, let us say "Chinese" nature of this racket game that is in theory an individual sport. Practicing a sport professionally can tear down the apparently clear distinction between individual and team sports. I quote:

---

13   Haïku is therefore a good parallel with table tennis. When the pure and free note of the spherical and empty ball resonates, exempt from all meaning, its double sound echoing: ping? pong!

Because there's never only one table in a room, but several, and the tables are so geometrically arranged that they offer to the audience's gaze, on top of the balls' crafted trajectories, the relentless rippling of the lines of the bodies "at work." Every player is of course "focused on his or her game," but all of them know that they are borne by the wave crashing around them.

This remarkable observation brings to my mind two memories that are very far apart from each other. The older one goes back to the first team championship I took part in during my childhood. It is the moment I first saw, suddenly and in a single panoramic look, a whole gymnasium filled with rows and rows of ping-pong tables, and that, at the exact same moment, I heard the balls, all in action at the same time. This was probably my first vision of community. The second is the very detailed memory of the first book Serge Daney and I discussed the first time we met: Giorgio Agamben's *The Coming Community* (1993). Chapter 12 of this work is a good continuation of Daney's remark about the gymnasium full of anonymous Japanese ping-pong players. Its title is "Dim Stockings" and it is about a TV ad[14] in which a group of individuals (young women wearing tights, as is to be expected) magically creates a common movement which does not belong to any one of them specifically but to all of them, including us, the audience. For the Italian philosopher, this effect unintentionally produces a new "ordinary body," "torn from the merchandise in its decline."

Because of this remark, Daney then notes the choreographic and musical aspect of ping-pong: "the spirit of table tennis … means that there's never any rest, only restful rhythms".

The sixth sequence retrospectively appears as a superb funeral oration for a strange and phobic rule of table tennis, which was

14   It also appears both in William Klein's film, *Qui* êtes-vous *Polly Maggoo?* (1966) and in Guy Debord's short film, *Réfutation de tous les jugements tant élogieux qu'hostiles qui ont été jusqu'ici portés sur le film "La Société du spectacle"* (1975).

banned in the mid-1990s, the *"obstruction"* rule: "this thing that
is so ambiguous in table tennis" Daney says, right away using
the right word, the Lacanian concept of "the Thing." "One must
return all the balls, except for the 'faulty' balls," Daney sums up
perfectly, like the good neurotic he is. He adds: "The good object
becomes the bad object, which you should not touch under
any circumstances: plague-ridden." So if a bad serve from your
opponent, which had clearly gone over the endline, unfortunately
touched your racket, you used to lose the point. Thus, players
used to withdraw their hand or even their whole body when a ball
was coming at them.

Daney uses this little ethnology of table tennis to address the
Japanese's presumed phobia of responsibility and their relationship to guilt. This orientalism is of little interest, but it nevertheless enables him to tell a legend I would call: "the legend of
the guilty racket." "There is this story of a decisive ball, very high,
judged by everyone to be a fault and which the player who was on
the receiving end of it greeted by joyfully throwing his racket in
the air, anticipating his own victory. But the pseudopodal racket,
which had an unconscious, went on to touch the ball in the air."

If we use one of Daney's observations about tennis and add it
to the commentary on this pongistic *noli me tangere*, we can
suggest that this table tennis rule paralleled the unwritten rule
beginning around the 1910s in cinema, which is the basis for
both the existence and the invisibility of the off-screen. Indeed,
players suddenly withdrawing their body to avoid *"obstructing
the ball"* meant that the table's surroundings were taboo (and it
should be added that the interdiction on touching the table in
any manner during the game is still a rule at international level).
A visible portion of the game space suddenly became invisible
by being untouchable; it was as if an inhabited and dangerous
emptiness was suddenly created. Similarly, the prohibition of the
look-to-camera in cinema creates the fourth wall of an imaginary
cube as efficiently as if a giant and metamorphic plastic one-way
mirror had been set up in a real space. With the abolition of the

 "obstruction" rule, so well spotted by Serge Daney who sees it as the Lacanian "Thing," *"Das Ding,"* table tennis lost its "off-table" and, with it, a little phobic piece of its relationship to cinema.

I will skip an observation about the sound rackets make, which goes back to the issue of rhythm already mentioned, in order to get to one last observation from the ninth sequence, which again shows Daney's very keen perception of the game. Namely, his perception of a very specific competition, the "doubles" ("men's doubles," "women's doubles," or "mixed doubles": two players against two others, playing on a table of the same size as usual), with its terribly quick disappearances and reappearances of the person who must, when it is his or her turn, answer the invitations from the whole table. Daney sees mostly joy here: a "joyous rush around the table" allows one to "dance his or her appearances." He sees "young women who are eager to rush to the ball with youth's impetuosity," because, he adds, "there's also the joy of being where the ball expects us to be."

This joy is not the silly "importance of taking part," which was the political conception of early Olympism, in my view very far from the profound reality of the game in sport, nor the enthusiasm of tiring oneself out. On the contrary, joy is the gist of sport, and more particularly of racket sports, which should really be called hand games or palm games (*jeu de paume*).

During a trip to Macao (as attested by one of his *Carnets personnels*), on 28 July 1980 at the Jai Alai Stadium, Daney attended Basque pelota games with an "audience that joins in, screaming and betting as if this was the races." One of the oddities of the history and geopolitics of hand and racket sports means that Florida in the United States of America, and Macao, which is a special administrative region of China and was under Portuguese administration at the time of Daney's visit, are the two main places in the world to which Basque pelota was exported. These two territories use the Basque words, names, and forms but they have their own off-track betting.

Daney accidentally happened upon one of the multiple games descended from the matrix of "real tennis," and which carries in its very name what Daney described, regarding doubles in ping-pong, as "the joy of being expected by the ball." Indeed, *Jai alai*, the name of Basque pelota is neither Florida English nor Macanese Chinese, but Basque and it simply means "happy game" (*jaï*: game; *alaï*: cheerful, happy). I would add that except for one letter and one phoneme (which does not constitute a pun but rather a strong proximity under the old frameworks before the invention of literature in the modern sense of the word), the *jeu* (game) itself is very similar to the poetic *joy*, the *joi* of Provençal poetry, of *trobar*, a word that the readers of Jacques Roubaud and Pasolini know well. The latter says he sings *"ab joy,"* "from joy—out of joy," and describes this very specific feeling of elation, which is very similar to the Portuguese or Brazilian *saudade*, in the following way: this "joy" is an instantaneous "nostalgia" for life, which creates a feeling, or an understanding, of the "exclusion" that "heightens the love of life." The "happy game" is, in sum, a poetic and vital "happy *joi*."

It is now time to conclude by explaining that it is not important to differentiate or hierarchize tennis, table tennis, or badminton (the three Olympic racket sports). Or Basque pelota, called *jai alai* or *chistera*, which allows us to understand that every racket is the extension of the hand and the arm, the Italian *palla tamburello* or *balle au tambourin* in France which, because they make direct use of a musical instrument to hit the ball, emphasizes the percussively musical character of the games in which the ball gets hit and the pleasure of the synchronism that they share with cinema's audiovisuality. Or Valencian pilota, which is still played with bare hands today, or squash, speedball, or some others.

Because the most important thing is to understand their common origins. All of them come from real tennis, which was born in France in the thirteenth century, and until the time of Louis XIV was both a popular sport, easily enough set up on town and village marketplaces, a court wall and the roofs of closed market stalls to create an improvised court (the outdoor game is called *longue paume*), and an aristocratic one that was played by all the kings of France and their court in numerous refined rooms (the indoor game is called *courte paume*). Louis XIV abandoned real tennis, the court followed him and so did the nobles. The game thus disappeared entirely in just a few years after completely dominating every other game for five centuries in France and having been exported elsewhere, most significantly to England. To start a game of real tennis, someone would say *tenetz*, (the imperative of the verb *tenir*, to hold, in French): this is where the English term "tennis" comes from. It is because of this background, which mixes common and community, the masses and the elite, the hand and the eye, rapidity and joy, that ping-pong and tennis speak to Daney. According to Charles Tesson, "he was fascinated by any sport in which the hand becomes a second eye, which does not automatically obey the other" (2001, 244). Ping-pong pushes this relationship very far.

One of its early names might point to it if we interpret it a little. It is more or less established that ping-pong was invented between 1870 and 1891—a time at which the pre-cinema devices started to appear—by English tennis players (possibly in the colonies) who wanted to keep playing tennis on rainy days, which is why it was initially called "table tennis." The rivalry with two other names "Gossima" and "ping-pong" (an onomatopoeia which comes from the double sound of the ball hitting first the racket, then the table), stopped when the English sporting federation settled on "table tennis" in 1921. "Gossima" disappeared while "ping-pong" was used to designate the leisure activity, without becoming completely taboo in competitive circles.

Gossima is thus the third and archaic name of ping-pong/table tennis, its lost or hidden name. It was a nineteenth-century commercial invention, which lasted around thirty years at the junction of the two centuries, more precisely a trademark registered in 1891 by the British company "John Jaques and son" on the advice of James Gibb, the engineer who imported the little celluloid ball. This name was probably trying to evoke the English word "gossamer," which suggests cobwebs, tulle, or other very fine and light fabrics all at once. This seems very likely considering the mythological image stuck to the top of the Jaques box: Peter Pan-type elves throwing round balls around above a huge cobweb, which is at the center of the composition. The first nets, made out of a very light fabric, can evoke gossamer. We can also consider the first rackets made out of stretched skin and the idea that one of the goals of the game is to make a ball flying like a fly be captured by the spider-net.

The invisible threads linking the eye, the hand and the moving object, this organic ensemble of semi-instinctive movements of the whole body and the central nervous system (I will not talk about the relationship of all this with post-cinema, the "ping" of computers and the video game-future of post-cinematographic animation, because that is another story), find a good allegory in the image of the spider's web. The gossima player is like a mobile brother of the cinema viewer whose eye is associated with a strong kinesthesia, but whose body is physically immobile. Cinema is an arachnoid game of real tennis. Thank you, Serge Daney, for letting me play this match with you.

Translated into English by Melina Delmas and revised by Kate Ince

References

Agamben, Giorgio. 1993. *The Coming Community*. Minneapolis: University of Minnesota Press.

Barthes, Roland. 1982. *The Empire of Signs*. New York: Hills & Wang.

Bazin, André. 2018. *Écrits Complets*. Ed. Hervé Joubert-Laurencin. Paris: Macula.

Daney, Serge. 1986. *Ciné Journal*. Vol. 1, *1981–1982*. Paris: Cahiers du Cinéma.

———. 1988. *Le salaire du zappeur*. Paris: Ramsay.

———. 1994. *L'Amateur de tennis: Critiques, 1980–1990*. Paris: P.O.L.

———. 2002. *La Maison cinéma et le monde*, Vol. 2, *Les Années Libé (1981–1985)*. Paris: P.O.L.

———. 2012. *La Maison cinéma et le monde*, Vol. 3, *Les Années Libé (1986–1991)*. Paris: P.O.L.

198   Pasolini, Pier Paolo. 2012. *Écrits sur le sport*. Trans. Flaviano Pisanelli. Paris: Le Temps des Cerises.

Tesson, Charles. 2001. "L'enfant de la balle." *Trafic* 37 (special issue "Serge Daney, après, avec"): 241–49.

A Few Diaries in the Early Volumes of *Trafic*

Simon Pageau

Several diaries were published in the early issues of *Trafic*; Serge Daney wrote some, as did Bernard Eisenschitz, while Jean-Claude Biette published a series of articles influenced by daily writing. We believe that the journal form is not an insignificant one. As a journal, *Trafic* allowed critics to catch up on memories, or, conversely, to write about the films of the present, but always with a desire to show another present, an "untimely" actuality it sought. This article focuses on three of these diaries, analyzing the inventions of forms in the writing as much as the modalities of a life experienced amid the images.

For someone of my generation, who was born in the middle of the 1990s and only encountered cinema and its literature around twenty years later, approaching the journal *Trafic* meant being faced with a visually impenetrable number of volumes. The collection's spine is the first thing one sees. It forms a block that is very homogenous and quite austere. Taken as a unit, the different volumes can only be told apart by their number. The scansion of the tens and the thickness of some milestone volumes (no. 37, no. 50, no. 100) are the only relief, whereas the repetition of the title—*Trafic*—the compactness of its stenciled typography, and the consistency of the sandy kraft paper binding are separate from the rigor of the dates of production. What is actually communicated first is what is hidden—*Trafic* might be keeping a secret. Mallarmé wrote that "carrying a secret is the prerogative of any folded sheet," and *Trafic*'s secret seems to be deepened by this mute façade, which is still expanding, since n° 107 came out not long ago.

The word "secret" might be a little too heavy, a little too romantic. But it could identify this invisible and fleeting thing: this deliberately hidden object, whose work is nonetheless communicated through the weight of all these volumes. The word secret is also a way of inserting myself in a history that is not mine. Because a secret is never shared without an audience, it is never impersonal, or "loose," with a bit of play. On the contrary, a secret indicates a space of shared interests. It simultaneously names the parts of an exchange and establishes its rules. So if there is indeed a secret, uncovering it is my way of playing along. Understanding *Trafic*'s secret means finding myself in a position that enables me to understand this history and guarantees that I can understand this secret, almost 30 years after the creation of the journal. At least, a little bit. In short, it enables me to test *its sympathy.*

The early volumes of *Trafic* start with diaries: Serge Daney's diaries. Others accompany them, more will come later: Bernard

Eisenchitz's, Jonas Mekas's, Jean-Claude Biette's.[1] These diaries bear the trace of the time of the journal's creation, the early 1990s. A very "weak" (Daney 1991, 29) time according to Daney, but which despite all its spinelessness, presides over these cine-diaries. In *Trafic*, this time still watches over the passing of days—and thus exposes itself to the inevitable rhythm of the daily private diary. These diaries also depict individuals, characters, enthusiasms, or resistances, which are the traces of a certain method, often the critical method of being in the world with cinema, of a cinephilia.

A published diary is probably no longer private. Nevertheless, the type of free writing that mimics addressing yourself inevitably possesses personal echoes. For example, in his three diaries, Daney puts his body on display: he eats chocolate pralines to ward off fear in "Journal de l'an passé" (1991), he "eructates" (1992a, 14) when things are not moving forward in "Journal de l'an nouveau," he falls asleep and wakes up in front of his TV set in "Journal de l'an présent" (1992b). As for Eisenschitz, he talks about memories that come back to him when he visits places from his past, while Mekas even confesses that he no longer dreams. Thus, these texts are different from journalistic chronicles; different from a simple analysis of the state of cinema. In these diaries, we understand that the time of the journal will be that of everyday life, and that this everyday life is something thick in which the present is admittedly liminal, but always in dialogue with its deficiencies and its memory.

I became aware of this when reading the first of Serge Daney's diaries, the "Journal de l'an passé," which runs from April to November 1991. It follows Daney's life and current events through

---

1   Bernard Eisenchitz (1944–) wrote in the *Cahiers* in the 1960s but his collaboration ended in the "red years" of the journal for political reasons. Close to George Sadoul, he would become one of the great French cinema historians and translators. Jean-Claude Biette, critic and filmmaker, one of Daney's closest friends, wrote in the *Cahiers* in the 1960s, came back in the 1970s, and continued to write in the journal episodically until the 1990s.

 very scrupulously recorded dates. However, although the watch-word casts a wide net over the phantom of current cinema, in return, it is always about bringing it closer to an issue that marks a moral and memorial commitment with that cinema: that of its possible loss.

> Thus, the vapid questions which seemed that they *would never be asked again* come back. For instance: is cinema an art? Will it be kept: all of it or just a part? And what will happen to what we loved about it? And what about those of us who loved ourselves unduly through it? And what about the world it had promised us, of which we were supposed to be the citizens? Day by day, I take notes and note my takes. But I am now talking about Cinema in general and I talk to myself until I get sick of having talked about it so much. My leitmotiv could be "Were we dreaming?" And when I meet someone, I ask myself if this person was part of this "us," of this oral tradition that was the love of cinema. Because, of this, at least, I am sure: cinema cannot better endure forth-coming societies than Africa can find its place on the map of a world that works. (1991, 5)

Then, after this incipit, the diary starts and the days tally up. And thus the critical writing, which stays linked to contemporary events, always refers back to a broader memory. Daney uses notions from his own history as a critic, rehabilitating them to evaluate current events. This modus operandi is admittedly not new. But what changes in the *Trafic* diaries is the density of this memory in those constant back-and-forths between present events and past systems of thought. Of this memory, I ought to say here that it becomes denser and larger. It is no longer there only to maintain the coherence of a way of thinking that has been upset by its contemporary objects, but because this memory is in danger and it is already dying. It is about signaling its revitalized presence through a sort of active mourning—it is about trans-mitting cinema "with its loss" (Interview with Serge Daney and Jean-Claude Biette, no date, probably January 1992) according to

Daney. "With its loss"—in other words as if molded in the work of memory, a starting point towards which all the presents are coming back to from now on. To transmit cinema "with its loss," or else not being able to transmit it at all. But this gesture is not insignificant. It engages writing in a vertical dynamic, which was already present in Daney's critical analyses, but which became even more prominent from then on. Let us be clear, transmitting cinema, *passing it on*, will not mean making it History here. It will not mean arranging dates according to a linear axis, onto an effective materiality that is smoothed out by the arrangement of events. It will not be like going the length of the event of History. To take up Charles Péguy's expression it will truly mean, "being inside the event, [making sure] above all not to get out of it, but to stay inside, and to climb back into it from within," contrary to a historical history which "passes alongside" it, that is to say "passes it by" (1931, 229).

Generally speaking, this memorial style of writing is that of a diary one writes to ward off the present time. Blanchot said that a diary is "a convenient way of escaping… silence." Because to write every day, he says, is "to place oneself temporarily under the protection of everyday time"; it means submitting one's writing to "this fortunate regularity that one undertakes not to threaten" (2003, 183). So, from one regularity to another, the regularity of the diary protects one from mundane issues of the present time, and the most distant thoughts can be maintained in the everyday life of its pages. Sometimes, the person writing the diary relies on the present in order to better escape from it. Under the tutelage of the passing days, the writing becomes freer to feel a path into memory's staircase for itself. Reading the diaries from the early volumes of *Trafic* is thus a means of understanding this memory and the vision of cinema it carries. It is a way of grasping the present of the journal's volumes, while keeping in mind the fragments of a preexisting time—scattered pieces of one of its secrets that have been found and made readable.

Jean-Claude Biette in Lyon, the Theater

It is significant that, amongst the early volumes of *Trafic*, the article by Jean-Claude Biette that bears the most resemblance to a diary is *Trafic* no. 5's "À pied d'œuvre." Actually, the series "À pied d'œuvre" as a whole could be linked to the genre of the diary, if we understand that writing is as linked to films as it could have been to days. It is through them that Biette's thinking forms and then aggregates. Biette considers films in the present tense of their filmmaker's vision, and he follows the critical approach he had already used in his chronicle "Les fantômes du permanent," published a few years earlier in the *Cahiers du Cinéma*. In a way, the articles in "À pied d'œuvre" are themselves cine-diaries, as the films are viewed one by one, as autonomous entities. For each film, its very own and identifiable governing principles prevail, which guarantee the truth of its experience. The overall progression of Biette's meticulous diary appears scattered, indifferent to any absorbing and premeditated coherence. However, he still finds coherence through implicit connections, larger and subterraneous movements, and through the interest he takes in characters. In the early volumes of *Trafic*, his style becomes more coherent and fluid as he finds a new flexibility in the text. He stops using his usual elongated sentences with many clauses separated by dashes and parentheses, sentences which suspend their objects then drop them within the body of a paragraph.[2] Through the pressure of the sentences coming one after the other, he carries away the center of a thought that always seems to follow the reader's eye.

However, the fifth article of these chronicles marks a departure. First, *Trafic* no. 5 is the first volume without a text from its founder. Biette who, until then, closed each volume, now has the difficult task of opening it and introducing contemporaneous

---

2   Mathieu Macheret perfectly described Jean-Claude Biette's writing in "Voyages en cinéma" (2016, 135).

objects to the journal. This is because the first text of a volume,
be it explicit or not, and according to Patrice Rollet, "engages"
(Interview with Patrice Rollet 2018) the journal. It engages it by
positioning it in a topicality that it cares about, sometimes dis-
tantly, but always with the attention we pay to the object that
concerns us. And secondly, it marks a rupture because it is not
current events that are being written about. Time's tremors are
a dead weight over which the writing stumbles, jeopardizing its
balance and lost peacefulness. And as the text proceeds, only the
agitation of films will make Biette gradually forget about time.
Thus, it would be fairer to say that this text is a diary despite
itself. "Despite itself," despite current events. This is shown by the
date that opens it: "December 12th, 1992, a Saturday in Lyon," a
date that is precise but already nearly distorted, as if dispersed
by the use of the indefinite article, which renders its unique
character colorless, and invites us to listen to a tale, to a fabulous
story, rather than to a chronicle.

At the beginning of this entry, we are in a theater, in Lyon. Biette
is replaying an encounter, a conversation between other guests—
he is a guest himself—and the few audience members present
at the screening of Jean-André Fieschi's film, *Pasolini l'enragé*.
Although traditionally the afternoon's discussion should open
with an exchange of perspectives and a critical confrontation of
ideas, this is not how it goes this time. Due to the direction taken
by the first questions, the discussion lingers more on the filmmaker's death, and the number of works he has written, as the
audience wants to know what they should read by this poet:

> we suddenly become guests of a TV program [Biette writes],
> in which interviewers and interviewees, putting on hold
> the modest but real uniqueness of their experience, must
> find a common denominator of depersonalized informative
> elements, which are communicable precisely because they
> can be quantified and therefore immediately digested by a
> computer. (1993, 6)

 Now we understand that televisual aesthetics dominate the rules of this dialogue. Next, a heavy and immediate present settles onto the theater, demanded by those asking questions, who expect not memory, but *information*. There are no questions *with* the work but only *about* it, in other words concretely, about Pasolini's death. So what is missing according to Biette—and what makes up the consternation in the opening of this diary—is the density of a time liable to create an experience. The interviewees lack adequate time to answer, and the people asking the questions are likewise not given enough time. Without a doubt, they are lacking this private, irregular, non-normalized time, which carries within itself an imagination able to preserve the character of an *addressed* story weighed by the person telling it, and which, for the critic, thus guarantees a certain responsibility. So Biette's point of view from this stage is strange and eagle-eyed, completely external to events despite his precise descriptions of his own position, of the other guests' position, and that of the audience as a few divided blocks. To quote Pierre Léon's introduction to his book on Biette, if it is necessary for the latter to rely in his works on friendship, "in the meaning of it understood by ancient philosophers, in which the elements are holding together and the reason why they hold together is friendship" (2013, 8), it is clear that there is not much friendship here. Thus, it is from outside the event that Biette brings back cinematic names and considerations (Godard's for example) so that these elements can stick together.

Then the rest of the article progressively goes deeper into a type of writing closer to its object, in the sense of a cinema object, which, step by step, frees itself and supplants television. It only half does this at first, with André Antoine's *La Terre*, where restoring the film and screening it with live music maintains cinema in a sling since, for Biette, this "double sacralization" can only give rise to a fervent respect that is "anesthetized" (1993, 8) to the film. Accurate history is much more present than the film itself, and that demonstrates how distant we are from the images—*it distances us from them*—whilst the music, which is inadequate, separates the film from its own continuity. The way the screening is staged impedes the positive reception of the movie all the more because there is another obstacle: the theatrical set-up. This is internal to the film's dramaturgy, which restricts the actors, and can only offer tropes. Here I am roughly summarizing Biette's more complex analysis.

Then comes Boris Lehman's *L'Homme de terre*. This is also a silent movie, but the marriage of the live music and the images is more harmonious this time, more effective. So that critical writing no longer stops on the threshold of the images. This time, if we review the internal construction of the film's shots, it is clear that music—which is the starting point of Biette's critique—is actually the glue. It unites the filmmaker, who appears in the film, with the subject of his topic, the making of a statue. From the start, the music harmonizes Lehman's face with the statue he is filming, giving to one what it has taken from the other, namely the modelling of clay at work, and then the fear of this work.

> Here [Biette concludes], music does not overwhelm the film, nor does it smother or culturalize it. It does not detract from its message, but it *keeps us* [my emphasis] on the path of its internal violence … It is the least appealing and the least anecdotal part of the written language of Lehman's cinema. (1993, 10)

This music thus offers a return to cinema in that it brings the film's elements together and ensures the harmony of its geology. It "holds" the audience's attention in the film's work—in all its violence—yet this work is somehow the only thing able to deliver signs of its expressive truth. It is also via the music that the writing of this diary exposes itself differently. The description of the film becomes more attentive, more fluid too, switching from one proposal to the other—from the man to the statue and from the soundtrack to the image—with the new-found flexibility of its long sentences juggling with the shots, as they are certain to be supported by the film's matter which they are patiently moving, out of respect for the one effacing himself behind the object he is accompanying.

I will quickly gloss over the last part of the text. Cinema, once it is found again, is described from the eternally focal point of its images. The film Biette discusses is Ritwik Ghatak's *Reason, Debate and a Story,* which was programmed in Valence by Françoise Calvez and Raymond Bellour. From this patiently told story, Biette deduces the presence of a filmmaker, Ritwik Ghatak, as well as the reality of a world that breathes as if on its own, as it is filmed by a man who knows how to make us forget the artifices of his language. This is not far from the theories that will appear in "Qu'est-ce qu'un cinéaste?" (*Trafic* no. 18), even if, here, it is the film that is talking as it is the first witness of its own image event—a definitive actuality behind which the writing finally manages to carry itself.

Bernard Eisenschitz in Moscow, the Rain

One of the questions asked by the early volumes of *Trafic* could be: how to create a community now? How to assemble a group around a journal that is open to the desire of writing about cinema, but which does not have a full editorial board? In fact, in the first year (the first four volumes), more than forty different authors were published in *Trafic*. Although these collaborators for the most part had a shared past, all being Parisian cinephiles from the 1960s and 1970s, and possessed some common interests—Godard, Hitchcock, Lang, Renoir, or even Ford are the filmmakers that they most often quote—*Trafic*, a journal that chooses to embrace a certain disruption of the norm, does not hide that continuity is very important to it as well. A homogenous body for the journal is also created through writing, the kind of counter-society with bootlegger airs that was so beloved by Daney. This is apparent in their subtle way of quoting other members or referring to them by initials, which plays on the mystery of the identity of the group's actual members and is also found in the way they address one another or bring others of the group into their own thought. From the very beginning, *Trafic* is the journal of the "I"—written in the first person singular—in which however no one writes alone: one's words are always directed to someone else and, often, they are mulled over as a group. But even more than that, *Trafic* becomes the space in which news is shared and, through this, news from the world and other people is cross-pollinated too. And if letters—there are many of them in the early volumes—are a privileged place for these exchanges, the cine-diaries also participate in this sharing of inclinations, vision, and knowledge.

Amongst the early volumes of *Trafic*, "Boris Barnet: journal de Moscou" (Eisenschitz 1993) is a traveler's diary. Written between September and October 1992, it appears in *Trafic* no. 5, during the winter of 1993, and gives to the Russian autumn the gray shades of a risk of refreeze. Because, according to Bernard Eisenschitz, it is urgent to take hold of Soviet cinema while, after the collapse of the Soviet Union, it is opening up but already at risk of forgetting itself, as noted by the historian at the beginning of his diary:

> The bookkeepers of this memory did nothing to preserve it nor to examine it in detail (except as a gallery of master-pieces), and it would have gotten lost before any of this was even attempted. At the same time, it looked like archives were opening up and that people felt the urgency to talk more. It was the right time to try and preserve that—for us, not for the Soviets: if they had done it, it would not have mattered much, but it seemed that it was not the memory of this wealth and of this continuity that they wanted to keep. We are the ones who need to make our position on this Soviet cinema clear: why it mattered, what we liked about it, and beyond that, what we have to do with the Communist dream that it embodied again. (1993, 117)

 "We are the ones who need to make our position on this Soviet cinema clear": this weighty sentence gives momentum to the diary. With it, we understand who is talking to us. This "we" which is both impersonal and transparent—this "we" which is very much in line with the tone of the *Cahiers*—this "we" carries within it a heaviness of time from which the ashes of past dogmas and their barely extinguished beliefs are still gleaming. With this sentence, we also understand where this diary is going; towards a forthcoming community, towards its reinvested history. Towards the starting point of a dream that is now stateless except in the memory of films which, if they too may have imagined it, may have done so less than those who saw them, than those who made them, and those who keep them. Here, we are reminded of Daney in *Persévérance* who, after having mentioned his shared Maoist past with the *Cahiers*, wrote about China: "When I first went there in 1980, I truly felt—which is ridiculous but real—as if I was the only one from the *Cahiers* to come apologize, as if by coming, I was saying: I apologize" (1994, 146). Here, Daney was talking about an acquittal, a duty to go to China as a way of giving back to the place an old stolen desire that was not its truth. This is definitely not Eisenschitz's approach. But it is still about going somewhere, as one could do, to "check" (as Deleuze put it), to check if we have been blinded by images (for Daney), and to check that this is also why they deserve to be watched (for Eisenschitz). And also going there to protect them.

> At first, it was about seeing and listening as much as possible [the historian continues]. Films, people, documents. Films first, because it is the primary reason to get attached to this one rather than another one: Boris Barnet, whose film *Au bord de la mer bleue* had been screened again and again by Langlois at rue d'Ulm and had totally shaken up our idea of freedom in cinema. And because [he adds] misunderstandings always seem to happen about films.

Eisenschitz went to Russia to see a retrospective of Barnet's films. On the day he arrived, Friday 25 September, he went straight

to the cinema, quietly entering during the screening of *Nuit de*
septembre. The next day, he started searching the archives and
compiled a list of people to meet—either friends of Barnet or
people who worked with him on his films. The encounters come
one after another in his diary: naturally, some are very fruitful
whereas others are less so. Just like his films, since Barnet, an
erratic filmmaker, also shot some bad films. First because of
political contexts; secondly because of his inconsistent personality, showing enthusiasm for joining the Party while seeming
ignorant of politics himself. This is why some of his films seem
to dodge the issue and are at odds with contemporary viewers'
expectations, either too close to the Party's instructions or
struggling to adapt to them. His heroic films are clumsy, and his
realistic films lack plausibility. However, it is in this discrepancy
that Eisenschitz would find the greatness of Barnet's films; in
their inability to create stereotypes and through their too pure
characters which are almost too transparent; in the blind vol-
untarism which fitted the needs of his time and thanks to which
"unamendable" life seems to flood his films. "If there was an
image of the century [Daney taken up by Eisenschitz], it would
be Gene Kelly singing in the rain. *Le Bonheur n'a rien à vendre*,
or (he added) *Au bord de la mer bleue*" (1994, 130). This is understandable, as it is by rewatching films that Daney proceeds. He
mocked those who found this useless and opened his visions to
very free analogies inherited from his cinephilic history—Henri
King for example, but also Griffith and Hitchcock. "Watching and
rewatching films, the only proof that cannot lie" (1994, 125).

While the Barnet retrospective is at the heart of the diary, the
latter also reveals the historian's modus operandi:

> How to proceed? This is often the most exciting part, this first
> moment, listening to people's stories … It seems to me that
> documents have to go hand in hand with people's accounts.
> Both are inaccurate at best, probably dishonest, and first off,
> my only solution is to gather as many as I can, without too

much critical filtering, to attempt to understand them, to get them to talk. (Daney and Toubiana 1994, 125)

Filled with people, this "journal de Moscou" shows a network of knowledge building itself peacefully as days go by. It is constantly a question of letting people talk, of trusting them, because this vivid speech guarantees that the speaker will take a position towards history, towards the Party, and towards cinema. It guarantees national specifics, which are also the plane against which Barnet must stand out if we want to understand the dynamics of his swerves; these swerves are all the more important for presenting a memory that is still active and surfaces back to talk with the contemporary world of this diary. For the large network stimulated by Eisenschitz, from Moscow to Saint Petersburg, appears to be stratified. It is made up of different intertwined time layers that show the harshness of the country and follow Russia's turmoil. Indeed, during autumn 1992, Russia was caught between huge contradictory forces—carried away by the opening of its economy to the free market, but still marked by the vivid colors of its history and near past. The never-ending avenues inherited from Communism's functionalism open both onto overflowing train stations, freed from police and its checks, and onto museums that are indifferent to the time's moods and unchanged for many years. Caged in this arrhythmia, Russian cinema from the early 1990s did not seem to find its own identity. Disinterested in politics and lost in the affected mimicry of Tarkovsky's films, filmmakers were no longer grasping at reality, forgetting even the urgency of current affairs; for example, the war that was starting in Georgia.

Thus, the writing style of this diary responds to the temporal division related to Russia's states and that finds echoes in some of Barnet's films. Eisenschitz had been writing dryly for a long time already, using simple and concrete things to start his ideas off and then develop them. In this "journal de Moscou," however, this style seems assured. One is struck by the short sentences that set the scene with places and objects that are really present:

an interview at home, a visit to the museum, or walking along a long avenue in drizzle. We rediscover a great clarity and this Muscovite diary becomes more assured, where it was already holding up under the days' patience, never getting ahead of the research's results but waiting for the course of time to ultimately and peacefully grant it character. And thus, in turn, time expresses its density, which is made of divisions that Eisenschitz does not fabricate, never makes up, but that he reveals by writing: he only describes them, expressing them by describing places. Amongst these places, there is one that channels the contradictory flows of Russian life particularly exactly: the underground station. Here you come across beggars as well as antique dealers, a couple busy behind a car window, as well as many books being bought keenly, those dusty books getting wet with rain in the meantime.

Underground stations are a privileged space in this diary. Thanks to them, the author moves throughout the city and goes to film screenings, meeting their audiences. It is also through them that time layers get superimposed. And if present time speeds up to the point of forgetting itself, the dust sleeping on book covers protects from memories which, under the passengers' eyes, are still keeping watch and not getting lost.

Serge Daney in Paris, the Snow

Keeping a diary also means holding onto spaces of transit that indicate a dynamic and, more particularly, demarcate a desire. So that the passage sometimes opens the diary onto the ever-escaping world it is trying to contain (its "outside," let us say). And, in "Journal de l'an présent," there is a space of transit that is not really chosen but seems to appear on its own. This space, despite Daney's promise to stop talking about it, is television.

In "Journal de l'an présent," Daney's third diary, the omnipresence of television, and the domestic imaginary it brings with it, immediately implies a certain fixity of the critic's body. Since "Journal de l'an nouveau," it seems that Daney no longer travels.

216 The Rolle dinner with Godard and Toubiana, which opened his
second diary, happened in 1990, and the rest of his thematic
reflection on the cinematic character only tightens the geography
offered by films, going back in time to the contemporary present
of the *Trafic* releases. Daney watches Sirk's films on TV, and
Pialat's *Van Gogh*, on which his reflection ends, is a current
release that he probably saw in a Parisian cinema. Following
the same structure, the "Journal de l'an présent" opens on the
memory of a trip to Valence. Daney replays a conversation with
someone called Missika, before quickly abandoning this for an
observation about the becoming-spectacle of the image which
leads to the possibility of the absence of the image, this "Blanchot
effect" as Daney calls it, a very cinephilic effect, which draws on
a literary tradition, but which, in the early 1990s, is running on
empty. He thinks that, in the future, humanitarian aesthetics will
replace it, as this aesthetics of presence has become too full, and
now, illegible.

> Will he go back to the publicity of taking up again … the
> medieval tradition of the dance of death [Daney writes]
> or the Baroque tradition of the *vanitas*? … Meanwhile, it's
> not surprising that Luciano Benetton is a candidate in the
> Italian elections. This kind of icon manipulator can only be a
> genuine political animal. A strange feeling actually, that all of
> this is coming back from far away and that Italy is where it is
> coming from. [And he concludes a little while later:] What if,
> for the second time in our history … Italy was the laboratory
> in which, faced with the imminent rule of the visual and its
> simulations, we worked on new postures? (1992b, 6–7)

Here, we can be struck by the centrifugal nature of this commentary, the particular way of pointing out a memory before
reactualizing it in a form that better fits the era's demands.
Writing seems to possess a plural time with layers of memory
that all converge towards the present, which appears on its
last legs and as deaf as an imperative. Generally speaking, the
"Journal de l'an présent" is also constituted of these vertical

blocks of time, which pile up, asymmetrical and disparate blocks
that give the writing a scattered cohesion. To illustrate these
pages, I like to think of the shape of a bunch: a bunch of flowers
in which the flowers take root in the water of memory and, one
by one, open in the passion of a newborn day—although, in this
diary, days no longer actually matter. This was already the case in
the "Journal de l'an nouveau," which was more directly thematic
and in which paragraphs were separated by titles rather than by
dates. It is again the case in the "Journal de l'an present." Here,
however, the common thread seems much more erratic.

Usually, the calendar gives the writing of a diary its tempo.
However, when writing emancipates itself from time, it
paradoxically becomes calmer, a calm in which all the words from
the past come back and are mixed together with the fortuitous
event of the day, which appears as if twinned with its ghost of
ideas. The diary detaches itself from the assurance of everyday life, but gains in prudence what it loses in safety; and this
prudence is the burden of the past. This is the reason why the
"Journal de l'an présent" seems more frantic, the way its parts
are organized seems more instantaneous, decided by Daney himself in his interactions with the world or subjected to his TV set
through which the world comes to him, as shown by the following
passage about Bertrand Tavernier entitled "THE SNOW," which I
am quoting here in full:

> I had once again dozed off opposite my friends Bang and
> Olufsen, when some sort of vociferation woke me up. I
> realized it was a talk show and that Bertrand Tavernier was
> talking about his latest film, *La Guerre sans nom*. He was
> explaining that the Algerian War, because of its length and
> of the mountainous nature of the country, had also been a
> war in the snow. And that putting these words together—
> "Algerian War" and "snow"—was enough to create a new
> vision, a brand-new idea, a simple and daft desire to *see that*.
> I am not sure that, despite his shouting, Tavernier convinced
> the audience but, for once, he did move me. In fact, only a

filmmaker can still marvel at the possibility of an image that contradicts clichés. An image that is a little more precise or a little more exact, which gives a kind of desire to see, to check, for example, if the Algerian snow from the Aurès mountains was similar to the snow in an Anthony Mann western. All in all, cinema might just be clarifications of this kind: "less vagueness," in exchange for "more pleasure." Marveling at the pleasure of logical reasoning or at the pure and simple exercise of imagination, this exercise that little John Mohune was right to find "rewarding." (Daney 1992b, 9–10)

This excerpt follows Daney's critique of the televised broadcast of the closing ceremony of the Alberville Olympic Games, the 16th Winter Olympics. This gives the impression that Daney fell asleep in front of his TV between two paragraphs. By staging this awakening through writing, it gives the illusion of a real temporal continuity between the two paragraphs. The continuity is even stronger as it blends into a wintery atmosphere, which helps to envision the author's numb body. The snow on the TV, which is no longer broadcasting except for the little imagination it acquired through cinema, and the snow of the static kind on the screen, which gives a name to the interrupted image flow or (quite the reverse) signals that this flow is continuing for the solitude of the channel surfer during his sleepless night (1988); this snow now *awakens*. It allows us to see; it stops the flow of television with the presence of cinema.

In the first paragraph, he writes in the past tense, which is the tense of the somatic. Daney is looking at himself and he is staging a memory, the memory of a motionless stance, which is that of the *"passeur"* who points out what cinema is in televisual drowsiness. In the second part, he writes in the present tense. This is the moment when Daney seems to pick up the memory where he left off, and also when, beyond the TV program, cinema comes back. Here, the reflection goes back to a more general present that wishes to describe a piece of truth unalterable to its images—cinema as a precise gesture: on the basis of a current

event, Tavernier becomes a filmmaker for a short time. From this **219**
generic present, Daney pulls out a collective memory, through the
image of little John Mohune from *Moonfleet*. This childhood image
is omnipresent in Daney's last works and embodies this cinephilic
"we"; this "we" that returns to a hallucinated past and has become
nearly timeless. Motionless, Daney binds himself to a collective
history that he makes emerge within himself, through himself,
following the very permeable distinction between individuals
and group that would result in "Le Travelling de Kapo" (*Trafic* n°
4), and in one of his best remarks during a carte blanche session
in Marseille, in December 1991: "cinema taught the inhabitants of
the twentieth century to search and find themselves, one by one,
on a screen held out to everyone" (Daney 2015, 123).

In his book *Clio*, written in 1931, Charles Péguy helped to find
another image, a precise concept, to describe exactly the
movement of this "Journal de l'an présent" in which Daney,
between two sleeps, and through an accomplished experience of
cinema, closes the loop on his cinephile history and recaptures an
image from his childhood. This word is: "senescence."

> To age is to pass. To pass from a generation to another, from
> one time to another. … *To become* another generation, from
> another time … To age is not *having changed age*; it means to
> change age or, rather, it means having stayed too long in *the
> same* age. … Ageing is essentially an operation of return, one
> filled mostly with regret. Return within oneself, on oneself,
> on one's age, or rather, on the age preceding what becomes
> one age, one's actual age. … Ageing is mainly a memory
> operation. (Péguy 1931, 226–28)

In the "Journal de l'an présent," Daney could simply be ageing,
bringing to his future self some images from his previous age
that protect him from the present time and make him continue
meeting the world. His actual age, the time he wrote his diaries,
becomes this mix between old age and new presences that
awaken the undying images of his cinephilia. Through Tavernier's

 words, John Mohune appears, creating a community whose members, scattered in space and time, finally get together in this off-camera space of thought called upon by *the snow*, to start an exercise of "wonderment," of "precision," that is above all "rewarding"—"the pure and simple exercise of imagination" gifted in cinema. Daney *ages*; and all the more so because, since the creation of his new journal, he ages with other people. Through him, and his constant link to a larger group, a community that is admittedly very lively though hidden, *Trafic* is a journal in which names age together; in which the "return within oneself, on one-self" exposed by Péguy is a secret way of more aptly giving others news about one's era. And the *Trafic* diaries are a way of saying of this era—that it is still the same, still the one of little John Mohune.

Translated into English by Melina Delmas and revised by Kate Ince

References

Biette, Jean-Claude. 1993. "À pied d'œuvre." *Trafic* 7: 110–18.

Blanchot, Maurice. 2003. *The Book to Come*. Standford: Stanford University Press.

Daney, Serge. 1988. "En attendant la neige." In *Le salaire du zappeur*, 241–44. Paris: Ramsay.

———. 1991. "Journal de l'an passé." *Trafic* 1: 5–30.

———. 1992a. "Journal de l'an nouveau." *Trafic* 2: 5–18.

———. 1992b. "Journal de l'an présent." *Trafic* 3: 5–24.

———. 2015. "Carte blanche à Serge Daney." In *La Maison cinéma et le monde*, Vol. 4, *Le moment Trafic (1991–1992)*. Paris: P.O.L.

Daney, Serge, and Serge Toubiana. 1994. *Persévérance Entretien avec Serge Toubiana*. Paris: P.O.L.

Eisenschitz, Bernard. 1993. "Boris Barnet: journal de Moscou." *Trafic* 5: 117–35.

Interview with Patrice Rollet. 2018.

Interview with Serge Daney and Jean-Claude Biette. no date. Interview by Laura Laufer. Accessed September 17, 2020. http://www.lauralaufer.com/spip/IMG/mp3/_Daney_Biette-mp3-2.mp3.

Léon, Pierre. 2013. *Jean-Claude Biette, le sens du paradoxe*. Paris: Capricci.

Macheret, Mathieu. 2016. "Voyages en cinéma." *Trafic* 100: 135–39.

Péguy, Charles. 1931. *Clio*. Paris: Gallimard.

Serge Daney and *Trafic:* Round Table with the Members of the Editorial Board

The round table took place at the Institut National d'Histoire de l'Art (Paris), on September 28, 2018. Arranged by Pierre Eugène.

Serge Daney and *Trafic*

Patrice Rollet [PR]: I got to know Serge relatively late, when I was literary director at *Cahiers du cinéma* and he was at *Libération* and would stop by on his way home. He would talk for hours every time and we would let him cheer himself up in this way. I'd heard about a journal project at the time, the "Ur-*Trafic*" or "paléo-*Trafic*," a project he'd had in 1987 or 1988 for a journal that would be produced by a cinema producer (Paolo Branco) rather than published by a publisher. I don't know where the discussions got to; Branco would know. Raising this possibility again with Serge, our first thought was to make *Trafic* a quarterly supplement to *Cahiers du cinéma*. Paul-Raymond Cohen's initial draft was indeed developed at the desk of the editorial team of the time. The project was already very clear in Serge's head. As you know, he then fell ill. And he decided to stop everything, including the *Trafic* project, in order to concentrate on a book that would have been a written form of *Persévérance* (not just the interview he did with Serge Toubiana). That then lasted a few months. I remember that the first design for which Serge wrote a kind of summary of the first issue of *Trafic* dates from the end of June or early July of 1991. Then, after two or three months, his desire to go ahead with *Trafic* returned, but this time with the decision to cut the umbilical cord between him and *Cahiers*. At this point he looked for a publisher, and through Leslie Kaplan who wanted to get him to write a book for P.O.L., he met Paul Otchakovsky-Laurens. He gathered a few people around him who he felt would be compatible: Raymond for everything he could offer theoretically and for his connections with the world of contemporary art and installations; Jean-Claude Biette, a longstanding comrade from *Cahiers*; me more for my editing work at *Cahiers du cinema* that he liked; also Yann Lardeau, who did not become involved at all, and Sylvie, whom Serge called upon very early on.

So we met up. Discussions were held about what *Trafic* was to be. It was clear to him that that he would write the introductory text but that it wouldn't be an editorial—which is where the fake-real diary form of the first three issues came from. At the end of the issue, Jean-Claude was to write a text "responding" to the introductory text. The texts are actually much more out of sync with one another than that when you read them, but that was the initial idea.

The journal was conceived as very open to the art world, from prehistoric painting right up to contemporary art. What seems very important to me is that at the moment that he launched *Trafic*, Serge was effecting a return to cinema and to cinema as a point of view on the world. And that this was to be the "DNA" of *Trafic*, as he put it.

Raymond Bellour [RB]: When Serge found out he was ill, we really had to persuade him to carry on. We saw him one by one, talked to him, and promised to support him, to work with him

and to be fully involved. Doing this helped us to feel comforted **225**
ourselves, and gave this "year of *Trafic*" the particular color of an
existential commitment that forged a very strong bond between
us, one that continued even after Serge died.

Serge used to insist on the fact that the verb "revoir" [to see
again, review, revise] is related to the word "revue" [journal,
review]. That the journal would be concerned with current events,
but that current events implied two things: both the films coming
out and being made and the festivals taking place, but also the
concern of each of the editors with what was current for them
personally. In other words, if Patrice, Sylvie, or I were to wake up
one morning saying "I'd like to talk about Stroheim," our current
interest was just as valuable as the most recent film released by
a known director. I'll read you the last part of the statement of
intentions written by Serge, which describes what will be in the
journal:

1. Very personal articles that follow current events in the cinema
   from day to day
2. "Letters from" written in a deliberately epistolary style from
   distant friends in isolated locations
3. French and non-French texts from cinema's past that have
   remained unpublished for explicable or dubious reasons, or
   that have become unavailable
4. Texts by filmmakers representing different stages of their
   work, such as notes, appraisals of progress, or work-in-
   progress drafts
5. Texts dedicated more precisely to the adventures of art in
   general
6. Freely written essays by philosophers, writers, and novelists
7. One-off cinephilic essays that are untimely or unwelcome

We more or less stuck to this program. In spite of the years that
have passed and of predictable evolutions, I have the feeling that
it's still the same journal. I always wrap an issue up by asking
myself what Serge would have thought of it.

Sylvie Pierre [SP]: I'll start by saying that I can't put the feelings that tied me to Serge, which were essential, into parenthesis. He was a friend and partner in crime in the *Cahiers* context from 1967 on, a friendship that became firmer when I returned from a five-year stay in Brazil. I don't say this to talk myself up, but the global dimension of cinema—the fact that we had to travel to discover it worldwide—was very important for *Trafic*. How we became a global limited circulation journal has become a joke I often make! It's the same conviction Daney had and was emphasized by Patrice when he edited Daney's writings and entitled the collections *La Maison cinéma et le monde*—Serge's 'post card' dimension, which was central rather than incidental to the way he worked.

So I was a close friend of Serge's, and when he fell ill, it became a personal thing. I saw him every day and we had extremely important conversations. I was looking after his *Trafic* project at the moment he became certain that he had AIDS and knew he was terminally ill. That context of urgency was extremely important in the creation of the journal and marked the birth of *Trafic* with a necessity—one of publishing texts that their authors really needed to get published, that were vitally important for them. Although in this crisis, some bad infinites were avoided: "academicism" in the bad sense of the word, pomposity, the dominance of knowledge...and that other bad infinite, the kind of subjective untidiness that lacks knowledge, properly corrected writing, and precise articulation. It's not the cult of Daney that interests us: we prefer to be of his religion than of his cult, if I may put it that way! We did this journal in the best way we could to be worthy both of him and of ourselves. Serge successfully put a team together that is holding good and whose members respect one another despite our often fairly considerable differences in sensibility. This is what makes us mutually complementary.

Marcos Uzal [MU]: When *Trafic* was born, I was on the other side—a reader. I heard about it on the radio: "a journal has just appeared created by Serge Daney with a poem by Godard" and I rushed out to buy that issue. And I remained a reader of *Trafic* for a long time, with the feeling that it was to some extent "my journal." It was a continuation of the story of *Cahiers du cinéma* that had been so important for me, even if I continued to read *Cahiers*. I felt closer to *Trafic* when I did a masters degree on Franju supervised by Jean Narboni, and he told me to write it up and send it to *Trafic*. I wasn't faint-hearted and sent it to Patrice and Jean-Claude Biette. And Patrice called me and said "we'll take it," which was a very important moment in my life. After that I wrote very regularly in *Trafic* until Raymond, Patrice and Sylvie asked me to be on the editorial board, around 2010, and more recently to join them on the executive. What I must say where Daney is concerned is that in 1991 Daney was extremely active for a young cinephile. It was known that he was going to die and that he was preparing his legacy, by creating *Trafic* and also by doing *Itinéraire d'un Cinéfils*, a very important moment. He was speaking in the past tense about a life experience that was his and was part of an era, and yet, because he was a young cinephile in 1991, you could identify with his mode of cinephilia as an existential experience. I'm the only person in the masthead who didn't know Daney. I haven't felt the need to hero-worship Daney because he doesn't call for that at all. His writing is so lively, diverse, and engaging. There are contradictions in it and you can disagree with him. You can extend the stimulating side of his writing.

Jean-Claude Biette

PR: Out of all of us, Jean-Claude Biette was the closest to Serge. They spent the last year of his life phoning each other to share live commentaries on the film each of them was watching!

RB: it was Jean-Claude who came up with the journal's title, spelt with one "f" but alluding to the English word "traffic" with two 'f's, which was important. There were five of us to start with, sadly soon reduced to four. We thought about stopping after Serge died, and then the sudden death of Jean-Claude left a huge hole in terms of friendship, affection, and everything he constantly brought to the journal. And it also took us a while to ask Marcos to join us. To start with, at Paul Otchakovsky-Laurens's suggestion, we created the *Trafic* editorial board, the people making up what Serge called the "inner circle," people he had wanted to write from the start but who for various reasons remained peripheral: Jacques Bontemps, Leslie Kaplan, Pierre Léon, Jacques Rancière, Jean-Louis Schefer, and Jonathan Rosenbaum.

SP: Jean-Claude would make crazy plays on words that made us die laughing. He had a gift for defusing any potential conflict he saw emerging, including amongst us. Because this was linked to his very specific economy of friendship, which for me was a model. In his exchanges with other people he was one of the most thoughtful and subtlest people I've ever met. I think that what Jean-Claude had that was important, apart from his very long friendship with Serge, was the fact that they were both gay, which also created a profound complicity between them. Jean-Claude was a filmmaker and writer-critic, and when he was talking about films, he had a way of examining the famous alchemy of the auteur. Not only because the auteur had a universe of his own but because he was in touch with his actors and his crew, and so on. As a filmmaker himself, he was familiar with that kind of contact; he knew what it meant to make films. I remember a text of his I found outstanding, in his "*à pied d'oeuvre* [ready for work]" series around a magnificent Fellini film called *Il Bidone* [*The Swindle*] and the relationship between Fellini and Broderick Crawford. He spoke with extraordinary depth about what an auteur director is in his relationship with an actor. At *Trafic* we have always had difficulty finding texts by filmmakers that speak intelligently, sensitively, and precisely about their work. And that ability was what Jean-Claude represented.

With and after Serge Daney

RB: The list of points I referred to earlier corresponds to the direction of a program we stuck to. There's only one point we

didn't manage to stick to regularly: letters by filmmakers. On the
other hand, I did manage to create interest in letters offering news about cinema from many different countries of the world, for nearly five years.

PR: Daney thought that we shouldn't do interviews any longer because all the interviews were too formulaic. We had to get filmmakers to write. He succeeded, and we succeeded, in getting some filmmakers to write. And we very quickly realized that documentarists wrote much more readily than fiction filmmakers. A certain number of filmmakers who had previously been critics would cut short their critical period at the moment at which they moved into directing. And filmmakers who continue to do both are very rare.

SP: Serge had a very deep-seated intention to inscribe something in time. To create an important object that would mark its era and that would *last*. And to move from journalism (obviously without scorning journalistic writing) to a journal, to something more serious. He insisted absolutely on this existence of the written object. Journals are markers of this kind: *Esprit, Les Temps modernes*…there are journals that mark national cultures.

PR: Part of Serge's idea of what a journal should be was also to establish a journal in the format of a literary review. Blanchot's *NRF* was important for Daney. There's another journal that didn't last long, Jean Louis Schefer's *Café*. We accepted several of Schefer's illustrations into *Trafic*, which were line drawings he had done in caves. It was a principle of *Café* that the only illustrations were line drawings.

The Organization of Texts in *Trafic*

RB: Serge had a deep reverence for the solitary text. By this I mean that when *Trafic* began, the texts were essentially fundamentally solitary. This applied up to issue 11, at which point a strange thing happened: we simultaneously received a text from Alain Bergala about *A Day in the Country* and one from Alain Fleischer who had restored the film and at the same time re-edited the rushes. Two texts about the same film, but from such different points of view that we could bring them together. And an idea came to me: in my cupboards I also had a marvelous little Astruc text that he had previously given to me, called "Sylvia Bataille, my actress." So we put the three together. And from that moment on, this represented a real change of policy in our way of working; we began to organize little curated groups of texts on a particular national cinema, a particular filmmaker, a particular film or trend, etc. We tried to construct little systems of echoes.

PR: There were special issues on Lang, Hitchcock, on Serge… Serge didn't want the thematically organized kind of cinema journal of which a number existed at the time, even though he knew that this complicated things for us commercially. What happened is that we did a set of texts on Walsh, by commissioning each one of us. We are pragmatic, we want to do things as straightforwardly as possible. One thing that has to be emphasized is that *Trafic* doesn't have a discernable editorial line, more what could be called "thresholds" of quality for the texts selected. This was an important thing for Serge and for Jean-Claude: the text is all that counts. We sometimes published texts about films we had reservations about or were indifferent to, if the text was sufficiently illuminating. On the other hand, you have to be careful about the risk of academic wrong turns; there have to be committed positions. When Serge founded the journal, his state of health meant that he couldn't go to the cinema very much, but one or two films was enough for him to take a stance.

SP: This question of the journal's editorial line put me in a temper every time we were reproached for not having one. A journal's line or editorial policy is like a party's line, to be found on the horizon, like an ideal. It's pointless to proclaim it if the real-life acts that prepare for and constitute it are not up to the mark. In our case, these acts are the texts, which say (each in their own way, according to each author's own will): this is the direction we want to go in together. So I wouldn't say that *Trafic's* editorial line makes itself: it is made with every quarterly issue by our way of preparing our groups of texts. One is paired with another when the texts reach us, either spontaneously through authors' suggestions or because we have commissioned a text on such or such a subject, for example one linked to current events. Patrice's work is essential here: he is the one who organizes the logic of our tables of contents. As far as our special issues are concerned, we do not write an editorial: we write a brief text that is a sort of statement of collective intention.

PR: After Serge died we wondered how we were going to go on. Did we need a chief editor, or two chief editors? In the end we said we were going to function as a collective; I used to like saying that were "the last soviet" (the 1905 one). We know that we have tastes and estimations of things that are sometimes unusual, but we have found a kind of enduring balance, and that really means something.

MU: Also, a kind of "politique des auteurs of the text" (Daney's expression) exists. There are texts on films or filmmakers who we would not on the face of it have published anything on, but on which a writer important to us sent us a text, and it matters to us to know what that author is going to say about that film.

SP: What interests me about *Trafic* is the freedom to write that it offers. Without formatting constraints, for example; a long or a short text, depending. We respect different styles and forms of freedom. After Serge died we didn't even want a chief editor any more. In each of our texts the author has constructed their own guiding principle and we have asked ourselves, either in our own writing or about the texts we have accepted "is this for us?", "does this correspond to what we are trying to find together?" We trust each other and this allows us to breathe, to talk freely about the cinema we love in the way we want to talk about it. This freedom is an amazing and incredible opportunity.

MU: I wrote for *Vertigo* for a long time. It was an extremely constraining journal in comparison to *Trafic*, because we started with a theme—so the wrong way round, for me, for whom the desire to write came after rather than before thematic ideas. We did some fine things, but the problem was the constraint of the theme, which I ran away from, literally. What is good about *Trafic* is that we can write about whatever subject we want to. The last film we saw or John Stahl…

PR: There is a loyalty from regular authors, such as those who come from *Cahiers du cinéma*, but there are many young authors who send us texts. Recently I published two texts by an author I don't know and with whom I only spoke on the phone. He is called Paul Choquet and wants to become a filmmaker. He sent us his texts, we liked them, and we're publishing him[1]; this author just happens to be young!

RB: Two or three months ago I received a short 7 or 8-page text from someone I didn't know in the slightest, which was about Chantal Akerman's *Rendez-vous d'Anna*.[2] It took off from a very understated line in the film. And this person had been so seduced by this line that he had traced a corresponding delicate logic back through the film. And I found this text extremely original, as it reminded me of the way I'm often touched by films. But what touched me the most is that in the email accompanying his text, he wrote that he had been present at the meeting we had held at Serge's bookseller's shop in the rue Traversière when *Trafic* was set up, that he had been a subscriber to start with then had lost contact with the journal as life went by. Then one day he had sent us this text, *Trafic* being the only place he could send a text about an unimportant line of dialogue at the origin of passion for a film.

---

1   Paul Choquet, "Personnages en quête de lumière. *En attendant les barbares d'Eugène Green*" ["Characters in search of light in Eugène Green's *Waiting for the Barbarians* (2017)"], *Trafic* 105 (Spring 2018).

2   Gabriel Franck, "S'il vous plaît—en pensant à Chantal Akerman, aux rendez-vous d'Anna" ["Please—thinking of Chantal Akerman, of Anna's rendez-vous"] (1978), *Trafic* 110 (Summer 2019).

And indeed, I find it hard to see where else he could have got such a text published.

PR: When I commission a text, I like to ask the author for a text that is sufficiently idiosyncratic and personal for him to say that he would not be able to publish it elsewhere than in *Trafic*. At the moment *Trafic* was created I was in three different places: at *Cahiers du cinéma* as an editor, at *Vertigo* (I edited an issue about cinematic letters), and at *Trafic*. At *Cahiers* cinema was talked about a great deal, all the time, and at *Vertigo* it was possible to conduct a project on a particular subject semi-autonomously. But *Trafic* was the kind of freedom you dream about; there was no editorial constraint even if there were real, high expectations.

Question from Pierre Eugène [PE]: Is there a notion of balance between texts about authors from the past and those who are opening onto something new—a new relationship to the image, new images…is this an important dimension for you?

RB: It is of course an important dimension, but it is implicit, and never really preconceived. If you pay attention, though, you notice that each issue contains a balance between contemporary concerns and theoretical problems, groups of texts on a particular filmmaker, etc.

SP: For the next issue,[3] our idea is to investigate the question of conserving and restoring films, by looking into cinematheques, digital restoration, and broadcasting. We're asking for texts from people who have an eye in the past, the present, and the future, because it's a very urgent question: digital, analog, what are we doing? Raymond has coordinated this collection brilliantly, and it's a fine example of what you ask about.

RB: I had a first text I spoke to Patrice about, who suggested that more similar ones could be put with it. And in the end we have gathered a fine group of five texts by directors of archives

3   *Trafic* 108 (Winter 2018).

 and cinematheques and a German critic-historian who is very interested in these issues.

The Making of the Journal

RB: To start with we had planned payment by the page. The first two issues of *Trafic* had sold so well that Serge even briefly entertained the idea of bimonthly publication. We quickly realized that this would be madness and that paying by the page would quickly bankrupt the journal. So we created the system of paying a single, modest fee for any text longer than ten pages, without any discrimination between authors.

SP: But within this economy, translators are paid by the page! We cannot ask too much of our publisher, but we negotiate with him and we have a network of excellent translators. We pay for the texts: I'm totally hostile to the idea of not paying authors at all for them, as if we were saying "consider yourself honored to be being published in *Trafic*…"[4]

PR: I'd like to go back to the question of democracy. It was a founding question in the early days of *Trafic*. We decided that all authors should be paid the same, whoever it was and however long their text. But another, typographical question also gave rise to real discussions among us and between us and Serge early on—the question of whether texts should be laid out in one or two columns per page. And we took the stance that all texts would be in one column, that there would be equality between them. There is of course a structure for the issues, with an introductory text sometimes requested from external authors, which we are fairly vigilant about. That's a text that we consider binds us all to *Trafic*.

RB: The monologic structure of *Trafic* (if we can call it that) is one of the things that makes the journal very difficult to put together.

4   From 2019 onwards, the journal no longer remunerated authors.

Because we have no notes or images and a fixed number of pages (this is our commitment to the publisher) and we never cut the texts. On occasion we have had to completely reorganize an issue's Table of Contents because we couldn't get everything we wanted into it.

PR: The journal is difficult to put together particularly because of two sets of choices, one to do with policy, the other editorial: we can't use advertising (there is none, not even for other journals we think highly of) and we can't use illustrations either. Serge began with the idea that we would only illustrate "if necessary," which depended on what authors wanted. Sylvie, incidentally, wanted illustrations in the first issue. When Serge thought "if necessary," he was thinking very precisely of Godard's *Letter to Jane* published in *Tel Quel* 52 (1972), which had published the text of the voice-over and reproduced the photo of Jane Fonda in Hanoï as a thumbnail image on each page. This kind of idea excited Serge: his desire was that the writing itself should reproduce the temporality of the shots, the scenes and so on. The text by Godard called "La paroisse morte" [The dead parish] that appears several times across the first issue of *Trafic* is rather like the *Letter to Jane* photo in *Tel Quel*. Serge had sacrificed many things for *Trafic* and had very precise ideas about what it should be, but when I suggested to him that not illustrating was a stronger stance to take than a few measly photos in a few texts, he could understand the advice.

The *Trafic* Collection

PR: The collection arose from a desire of Paul Otchakovsky-Laurens as a possible extension of what was being done at *Trafic*. He has always kept *final cut* on books, whose titles we suggested to him (I'm not talking here about Daney's *La Maison cinéma et le monde* volumes, a title chosen by him and Jean-Claude Biette). I suggested a certain number of American authors to Otchakovsky-Laurens, such as Manny Farber, whom I already wanted to publish in *Cahiers du cinéma*, and who was very complicated to translate. A lot of translators ran away, until Brice Matthieussent, a literary translator, agreed to do it. Raymond published his book *L'Entre-Images 2*, then Jonathan Rosenbaum and Mark Rappaport in the collection, which has produced about two books per year.

Question from PE: To go back to the very early days, Serge Daney brought together in extremis a project he had thought about a great deal but which he knew would last. But the surprising thing is that it has lasted so long.

PR: It has lasted because *Trafic* was very well conceived by Serge initially. The balance between the attention to contemporary issues and to cinema history was the real principle of how *Trafic's* contents were organized. Carrying on in the same way was enough. The only change was related to each issue's introductory text, and I think we were intelligent enough not to want to take Daney's place, and to rotate authorship of this introductory text by appealing to people who really wanted to tackle cinema's present. Serge was also a very pragmatic person. Something he always used to say was "the succession of a journal has to be *taken*." He had the desire to do something of historical importance, but his books also mattered. He was extremely demanding when putting together his own collections; the editing of his texts was the guiding principle of each book. The *Persévérance* project was quite different, thanks to Serge Toubiana who helped him to carry it out differently. It's true that where *Trafic* is concerned, we said to one another that we felt obliged to carry on even if he had given up on the book project. He gave us the weapons to carry on, and we have had an extraordinary publisher. Without the greatness and loyalty of P.O.L. a project like *Trafic* would not have been born and would not have lasted. When Serge suggested it to other publishers it wasn't accepted.

On Current Events

Question from PE: Something struck me at the time of the issue of around 11 September 2001, and especially the cover photo which was not from a film but from TV news. I'm wondering what state of mind you were in at that time: did you want to cover current affairs or take the time to understand them?

RB: We were lucky enough to have an American author called Kent Jones who was in New York on 9/11 and who had the intelligence and imagination to write a text which was of course inspired by that day's events, but which undertook an archae-ology of them from inside American cinema itself. An American photographer was close to giving us an image free of charge, but his agency wasn't willing, so we made do with a more con-ventional image. In this way we did treat this burning topic of the time, a harrowing and all-consuming one for cinema.

SP: I wrote a text about 9/11 whose title was a sort of Anglo-French play on words: "would this God who injures some bless others?" A play on words not intended to make people laugh, of course. I watched the television news in horror, like every-one else. The shock was worldwide, and it was relayed largely by shocking images, about which the least we can say is that they were unprecedented and constituted an audiovisual as well as a geopolitical event. It was a totally unique audiovisual event, terribly upsetting, a real-life fiction. We're not slaves to current events in *Trafic*, but we are necessarily connected to them. And where strictly cinema-related current events are concerned, we like to be attentive to them. Current events were one of Serge's priorities. Getting ready to write about a big retrospective or a big festival is good. But we prefer the notion of presentness [*présent*] to current events [*l'actualité*], because presentness looks both back and forward at the same time. And so we are sympathetic to all work that can take account of evolving work on today's audiovisual matters.

RB: And sometimes we have strokes of luck. An example is when I saw Philippe Grandrieux's *Sombre* at the Locarno festival, wrote an essay that came out in the December issue, and the film came out in Paris on 15 December.

MU: There's something else about current events [*l'actualité*]: the idea of afterwardsness, of looking again. Having the time to return to things and see them again puts you more in the present [*présent*] than in current events. As everything—film releases, festivals—is going faster and faster, there's the idea of putting things into perspective.

RB: On the road you sometimes see that lovely sign that says "slow down, work in progress." This is *Trafic*'s motto.

Translated into English by Kate Ince

DIGITAL DANEY

Serge Daney's death in the summer of 1992 occurred just as the internet and mobile phones, two major technological upheavals that have connected people worldwide as part of a global digital network, were about to emerge. Increasing democratization of video, photographic, and sound recording tools took place over the same period, hugely developing the capacity to watch and to share subjective visions of the world. Although he died too early to analyze it fully, Daney wrote a lot about the accelerated mediatization of our lives through television and publicity, as well as the important changes these media made to the creation and perception of cinema. These issues have reconfigured cine-philia and its ways of expression in the contemporary digital era, and the three essays in this section aim to (re)think them "after Daney."

Pierre Eugène

TELEVISION
___

MACHINES
___

ROBOTS
___

COMPUTER
___

POST-MODERNITY
___

[11]

Serge Daney and the Robots

Pierre Eugène

By reviewing a number of Serge Daney's articles, this essay looks at how the critic experimented with computerization in the 1980s, notably at his workplace, the newspaper *Libération*. It considers the notions of computers, machines, robots, and computer-generated images in relation to changes in the status of cinematographic and televisual images during the 1980s–1990s—and our own relationship as viewers to images, characters, and reality.

A Dedication

The readers of Serge Daney who have looked at his book *Le Salaire du Zappeur* ("The Zapper's Wages"; Daney 1993a) may have wondered about the dedication of the book: "To Mister Atex."

 Who is this man? Not a human being in fact, but a computer; or rather: a complete computer system, including a large central unit (today we would say a "server") to which a myriad of small independent terminals were connected, into which the reporters of the newspaper *Libération*, from 1986, would type their texts directly, which would then be sent directly to photocomposition. This system, called "ATEX," created by a subsidiary of Kodak, began to be used in the early 1980s in the American press. It was quickly adopted by *Libération*—always in search of innovative solutions and economic aims—which envisaged it as a means of eliminating, over time, the long and expensive process of unautomated production, but also of receiving news agency dispatches and articles by journalists sent abroad with small portable computers (the Tandy 200) through a modem connection.[1] The first tests began in September 1986 in the Lyon edition of the newspaper and the practice was extended to the whole company when the Parisian head office moved to a new address at the end of July 1987. This IT transition was not without difficulties, and Daney's dedication to "Mr. Atex" could be an amused (if not ironic) echo of the consequent technological upheaval that cannot have facilitated the daily life of the newspaper.

In addition to this wink of complicity to his colleagues at *Libération*, the dedication of *Le Salaire du Zappeur* undoubtedly takes another sense in this collection intended to republish the major part of a column with the same title by Daney in *Libération*, which he wrote every day (except Sunday) between September 14 and December 24, 1987, about the mythologies, the effects, and the bestiary[2] of French television, which was then in full expansion.[3]

1   On this subject: Guisnel 1999, 242–44.

2   A long analysis of this column can be found in Joubert-Laurencin 1988.

3   The three channels of French television were entirely under state control before 1981. François Mitterrand, elected in 1981, allowed the creation of private radio and television channels: the fourth channel (Canal+) was created in 1984, the fifth (La Cinq) in 1986, the sixth as well as local and cable channels in 1987. Also in 1987, the first channel (TF1) was privatized.

This column would be published in a paperback, under the same title, in 1988.

Looking at television with "cinema's eyes," Daney organized his interest in the small screen around three main areas of interest. First the aesthetic and "market shares" competition between television and cinema in the field of images. Second, the fact that television was a privileged place of observing French political and social life, as well as a glimpse of the French vision of the world: debates about ideas, the treatment of information, the appearance of speakers or men of power, the "democratic" vision of people on the screen. Finally, television interested Daney in the way it reconfigured the division between public and private, outside and inside: how the world network of the "global village" (theorized by Marshall Mac Luhan) had echoes with the private life of a consumer of images "at home."

In this sense, the dedication to "Mr. Atex" is Daney's understanding of the increasingly massive incursion of information technologies into the private, intimate, but also professional life of individuals, transforming their perceptions of life. To personalize the computer, to give it a "Mr.," was to recognize that people would quickly have to "deal" with these technologies; and also that the generalized mediatization, which had inscribed the small screens in homes, now affected the professional world, as well as—undoubtedly an essential point—the intimate activity of writing. Writing on a computer is kind of a farewell to the materiality of handwriting (even the typewriter included the materiality of the sheets of paper). From now on, articles would be written on the screen of a word processor (*Libération*'s was called "*Le Rédacteur*": "The Editor") and immediately networked through the ATEX system. This "other" screen of writing, which did not belong to cinema or television, but to a third party, the computer, was not long in imposing its considerable role.

Daney was more melancholic than nostalgic. He never rejected the era in which he lived, but kept a fundamental distance, a "memorialist's" gaze at the events of his time, without really participating in them. Working at a newspaper, directly connected to all kinds of news, Daney not only experimented with the technological developments in his office, but also was kept informed of all innovations. Some of his articles echo scientific events, the awarding of Nobel Prizes or the parascientific debates around the "memory of water," for example (Daney 1997).[4] Traveling light and owning only a few things himself in his Parisian apartment (according to testimonies), Daney did not have a fetish for technology and very little appetite for gadgets. At the end of his life, his mobility severely impacted by AIDS, he equipped himself only with a *nec-plus-ultra* Bang & Olufsen stereo system, and a television set. Arlette Bonaud, Serge Daney's cousin, told me about his difficulties with electronic devices. She recalled in particular an answering machine that Daney couldn't get to work, and which he finally threw away. These difficulties may have been overcome with computers, because in addition to his articles for *Libération*, Daney wrote from day to day, between 1988 and 1991, various small texts on a personal computer: ideas, drafts of articles, intimate accounts and self-analysis, reading notes and various lists: all kinds of notes that he used to write by hand in the many intimate notebooks that followed him everywhere, in Paris or on trips.

"Our writing tools are also working on our thoughts," wrote Nietzsche in a letter (quoted by Kittler 1999, 200). We don't know exactly how the computer "changed" Daney's writing. But the computer, undeniably, is a sedentary, cumbersome, unwieldy tool, a tool for the home or the office, not for the street or for light travel. It can then be opposed to the notebooks of a declared walker and traveler, notebooks of all formats and styles (school notebooks from all over the world, diaries, bound notebooks...) that had accompanied Daney since his adolescence on all his

---

4   "Le cinéma et la mémoire de l'eau", originally published in *Libération*, December 29, 1989.

peregrinations. Daney started writing personally on a computer shortly after his "Salaire du zappeur" column in *Libération*. Hence, perhaps, another meaning of the dedication: after having written on the "small screen," the meeting with "Mr. Atex" would have engaged him to write directly on another "small" screen. And if the typewriter can be qualified as a "miniature printing press" (Hubertus Streicher quoted by Kittler 1999, 22), Daney's intimate writings on the computer repeat in miniature his writings at *Libération*; they take over from them as well as being their destiny. In the computer writings, the *marginalia* (drawings, calligraphy essays, and theoretical sketches) that sometimes adorned his old notebooks disappear, as the computer only records *printable text*. P.O.L. Editions would print these computer notes of Daney's in 1993, finding after his death the diskettes on which he had recorded his notes and publishing these under the title *L'Exercice a été profitable, Monsieur* (Daney 1993b). In this title chosen posthumously by Jean-Claude Biette from a line in Fritz Lang's *Moonfleet* (1955), a film that Daney loved, the "Monsieur" here is not supposed to be "Mister Atex," but Jeremy Fox, to whom little John Mohune is speaking.

"Chose" and "Machin"

In 1983, Daney dedicated his first book, *La Rampe* (Daney 1983), as follows: "Pour Chose et Machin" ("For Thing and Thingy"). In the first of the two terms, the "Chose," one can hear the Lacanian "Thing" ("Das Ding"), the unconscious, and at the same time the "real" object (in the Lacanian sense) which insists in perception without one being able to grasp, to understand, or to assimilate it; the "Machin" (word derived from "machine"), on the other hand, is a rather trivial object: a gadget, a machine. Both *chose* or *machin* can designate a person in French, and we also use "machin chose" to designate someone whose name we have forgotten. In the first edition of the book, which includes several pages of film photographs next to the texts, one can find an illustration of "Chose" and "Machin." The top of the page (Daney

 1983, 23) shows the two strange twins from Tod Browning's *Freaks* (1932); at the bottom of the page, in the same symmetrical posture, in mirror image, two cosmonauts in the spaceship of Stanley Kubrick's *2001: A Space Odyssey* (1968). Above: two "freaks," two *unheimlich* bodies caught in the "originary world of impulses," in relationship with the "naturalism" that Gilles Deleuze evokes in *The Movement-Image* (Deleuze 1983, 133). Underneath, Kubrick's "thingy," clean and technological. Between the two images, between the 1932 film and the 1968 film, the history of cinema unfolds. We can see the passage from the burlesque, trivial, circus-like age of early cinema (which was the argument of so many of Browning's films) to the modern, intellectual and technological age of the 1960s and after[5]. In Daney's work Godard is perhaps the filmmaker who best questions these two trends. One thus finds in *Numéro deux* (also evoked by Daney in *La Rampe*) both the "obscene" part of the body and the technical procedures needed to capture them (a recording and video studio; Godard names it in his film, saying *"machin, machines"*). Also in *Numéro deux*, Godard prints sentences on the screen with a computer, which we can see reproduced on another page of *La Rampe* (Daney 1983, 79), printing a photogram of the film, a real piece of film roll.

The "machin" and the "machine" are without doubt the strongest signs of modernity for Daney. In his texts from the 1960s to the 1970s, the word "machine" is implied first of all in the "production machines," Hollywood being the first of all. Then, at the beginning of the 1980s, he evokes (Daney 1983, 157–63)[6] some small French author-producers (notably Éric Rohmer, Paul Vecchiali…) who invented their own means of financing and directing their films by making themselves production "machines" (Les Films du Losange

---

5   In a postcard to his mother (Anvers, Belgium, July 17th, 1980) representing two orycteropes (very strange animals), Daney wrote at the back : "have you recognized Chose & Machin? It's them!".

6   "Le cru et le cuit.", originally published in *Cahiers du cinéma* 323–24, May, 1981.

for Rohmer, Diagonale productions for Vecchiali). "Machines" must also be understood in the sense of Deleuze and Guattari's "desiring-machines" in *Anti-Oedipus* (Deleuze and Guattari 1983). Under Daney's pen, at the end of the 1970s, humanity is divided between the mechanical (*machin*) and the animal body (*chose*). According to Daney, Jacques Tati created a type of comic character based on the fact "that there is no longer any human peculiarity" (Daney 1983, 117);[7] man becomes partly a thing among things, a quasi virtual figure. Bresson, for his part, shows in his "models" what links them to the "mechanical": "What's modernity in cinema? At the time of [World] war [II], the decision of some filmmakers to follow the human body and its activities in their *mechanical becoming.* Any action undertaken is dedicated to its 'unfolding' which implies reflex, repetition, *automaton*, in short: the non-human at the heart of the human. The human specificity is the exit of this 'becoming', it is the signifying rupture: miracle, encounter, salvation, event. It is undoubtedly Bresson who had the most exact awareness of this: the 'devil's share' is the share of the machine, of the machinic (as opposed to the 'game')." Bresson, playing on unthinking human gestures, puts on screen characters conceived as human automatons.

A Synthetic Reality

One of the central questions in Daney's articles during the 1980s is precisely that of the cinematic character. It resonates with the question of the "individual," this new being, an effect of the new age of capitalism and marketing. What is a character, a cinema character? wonders Daney, who finds in his articles "avatars," "Identikit," incarnations of actors, but stumbles on this untraceable figure of the character, which would emerge from the actor and distinguish itself from his "role" as written in the screenplay. A few months before his death, the idea of character

7   "Éloge de Tati.", originally published in *Cahiers du cinéma* 303, September, 1979.

 will be the explicit subject of his second article in *Trafic* (Daney 1992).

In a famous article from 1981 on *Wir Kinder vom Bahnhof Zoo* (Uli Edel, 1981), which dates from his arrival at *Libération*, Daney draws out the difference between character and "Identikit"—which is called in French *portrait-robot*, "robot-portrait." The film is an adaptation of Christiane Felscherinow's autobiographical story, that of a young girl who fell into drugs and prostitution. Speaking of the main character, Daney writes:

> What's the use of the real Christiane F.? It was enough to put all the literature on the subject into a computer, from the confessions of former drug addicts to the confessions of drug dealers, not to mention the police files and medical reports, *to obtain* Christiane F, the harmless little girl of thirteen, the identikit [*portrait-robot*] of a fallen child, the sociological sample we needed to illustrate the standard scenario, the robot scenario of the film" (Daney 1998, 33).[8]

The "robot" is to be understood as that which constructs a character *from the outside*. If Daney speaks of a creation by "computer," it is because the character of Christiane F in the film is a representation formed from *information*, from *data*—just as an avatar or a pure virtual reality creation are created from programmed codes. An identikit also keeps a resonance of the police, thus the threat of an "art police." Between the character and the code, it is the whole range of the unforeseen, of what escapes the code that disappears. A "real" character embodied in an actor's body should surprise, go beyond his sociological profile, make him more ambiguous, gain through the filmmaker's mise en scène a "margin of indeterminacy" (as Bresson would say).

What Daney observes throughout the 1980s, and in particular through television, is the emergence of an increasingly coded cinema, with a simplified grammar, and for the spectator, the

---

8   Originaly published in *Libération*, August 14, 1981.

recognition of "sociological" clichés for constructing identities that are always formatted. The most representative filmmaker of this type of film is Jean-Jacques Annaud. Daney describes him as a "post-cinematographer, that is, one who knows nothing of what cinema has known" (Daney 2015, 156).[9] That is to say, he knows nothing of the capacity of cinema to record, *nolens volens*, things that cannot be mastered, coded, or decoded. Daney devoted one of his very last texts in *Libération*, a few months before his death, to *L'Amant* (1992; the adaptation of the novel by Marguerite Duras). In this dark, violently polemical and somewhat desperate article, Daney writes of Annaud that he is "in fact, not just anyone, but the first non-cinephile robot in the history of cinema. One feels … that he will always know what it should look like, the 'rendering' of human behavior and emotions. But that's all he knows: he has the knowledge of a robot who doesn't know that he doesn't know everything" (Daney 2015, 157). Criticizing the system of a film that asks the spectator to "initial" each of the images it shows him, a film that sells each of the objects and beings contained in the film as in an advertisement to a "poor spectator-decoder," Daney ends up questioning Annaud's filming in Vietnam: "what risk was he running that his camera, for a moment, might record by chance a few grams of reality that was not pre-made?" But, concludes Daney: "In the age of synthetic images and emotions, the chances of an encounter with reality have become quite minimal" (Daney 2015, 160).

About Luc Besson and the success of *Le Grand Bleu* (1988), Daney writes in his notes to *L'Exercice*: "The future is always a certain mutation of the image, a becoming of the image, a technological redefinition. So let's say that Besson's cinema, from the beginning, is a cinema of the time when the idea … of the computer-generated image makes all the other images fall into the past" (Daney 1993b, 358). Besson would have public success

9 "Lire notre critique ci-dessous.", originally published in *Libération,* March 31, 1992.

 because it would anticipate the synthetic becoming, the loss of real inscription of every image. Daney adds:

> The synthetic image is an image that does not come from the gaze (print what one has seen) but where the gaze comes afterwards (sees what has been printed, "what it gives"). ... It is because he [Besson] raises the technique of shooting ... to an impressive level that we are grateful to him for producing a fundamentally synthetic image of the world. The Besson effect would not exist if ... we showed ["*exhibait*"] the capacity of computers to produce images comparable to those of the cinema. (Daney 1993b, 358)

It is the "unsynthetic" reality that interests Daney, who has always confessed his lack of interest in (more than his aversion to) a cinema that would stray too far from the recording of cinema: animation cinema, computer-generated-imagery, mannerist or overly formalist films, experimental cinema... This personal disinterest in these types of cinema did not prevent him from publishing texts in *Trafic* about these domains, nor from twice receiving on his radio program Microfilms Philippe Quéau, director of the Institut National de l'Audiovisuel between 1977 and 1996, and a promoter and theorist of computer-generated-imagery (then in full development). Quéau was also one of the pioneers of the Internet in France, developing one of the first French web servers. Writing on television in *Le Salaire du Zappeur*, Daney refuses the easy opposition between cinema and television, noting that the great filmmakers, the inventors of forms, also made links to a "history of communication": "the real impact of filmmakers like Vertov, Rossellini, Bresson, Tati, Welles, Godard, or Straub (among others) was their unstable situation between the poetic requirements of cinema and the progress of the mass-mediatization of the world" (Daney 1993a, 186–87). But they used their reflection on media in their own medium: to transform it, deconstruct it. As far as television is concerned, it's another story.

During a trip to Japan in December 1982, at the time the country of advanced technology and gadgets, Daney wrote a series of columns for *Libération* evoking the specificities of Japanese culture (from manga to cinema, from the red-light district to *kawaii*). Arriving in Osaka, Daney writes that the city looks like "the museum of everything that has been invented, attempted, taken up, failed, copied, quoted, and re-cited in terms of urban décor since the war" (Daney 2002, 646)[10]. He describes the city as a "dictionary of quotations" of a decor that "does not quote anything, it does not celebrate anything, it has forgotten what it quoted: it is *a* decor, it is *a* simulacrum." Five years later, writing about the figure of city in cinema, Daney recalls Osaka and remarks that "Japanese films resemble Japanese comics (manga), because they are cross-linked, framed, fetishized, drawn to the point of disgust. … Any human being with a camera brings back a reasonable harvest of pre-framed images, focused on signals and fetishes, visual operating instructions, living prayers for insertion. Japanese postmodern space (the hallucinating journey from Tokyo to Narita, for example) is *over-marked*" (Daney 2012, 282).[11] The "post-modern" city is already an image for the tourist, who can find nothing original in it, only "pre-framed" images, a set of exposed signs, suitable only for decoding. During his trip to Japan in December 1982, Daney also tested a capsule hotel, and described the experience of watching television in the miniaturized box: "Until two in the morning, a few hundred yen slipped into the television slot are the sad cord that umbilically connects the small capsule to the great Japan. Everything is small: colored corpuscles play baseball, … miniaturized announcers smile indulgently" (Daney 2002a, 650).

Through these various examples, one understands that Japan, the postmodern and technological country itself, is undoubtedly the place par excellence of the *screen*. "Screen" in the sense that

10   "Osaka, sublime mocheté.", originally published in *Libération*, December 18, 1982.

11   "Ville-ciné et télé-banlieue.", originally published in Grenier 1987.

 Daney gives to this term in December 1988 in an interview, at the time of the publication of *Le Salaire du Zappeur*: "We are in the culture of the screen, not of the image. There are screens everywhere, but the screen does not necessarily imply the image. It implies it only as far as it is easy to decipher" (Le Grignou 1988). He adds that "the screen of the television is a shop window, one passed from representation to presentation." In Japan there are omnipresent televisual screens, but also a "city-screen" whose profusion of (advertising) signs crushes and hides individualities, preventing any encounter with an ambiguous reality and unforeseen characters.

Solitude of the Viewer

This technological modernity, such as Daney analyzes it in his trip to Japan or in the evolution of television in France, has another point in common as well as the problem of coding and decoding: the solitude of the spectators, abandoning the public cinema for the private home space of the television (even if Daney does not directly make this parallel). In the afterword to *Le Salaire du Zappeur*, he remarks:

> It appeared to me at first that all that was hateful on TV had a common point. Dispensers of 'culture' or entertaining hosts … made us feel that without them, we would be nothing. They made us feel that real life was no longer 'elsewhere' … They made pass for greatness of soul and concern for the other the monopoly that television has on the solitude undergone by its viewers. (Daney 1993a, 187)

In the capsule hotel in Osaka, Daney talks about that "sad cord that umbilically connects the small capsule to the great Japan" and a televisual world where everything is reduced, miniaturized, adapted to an *individual* scale, far from the great collective seizures of the cinema. In his notes to *L'Exercice*, Daney describes this historical evolution: "If the person was a node of forces in a network, man a circle with a core and a periphery, the individual [that of the 1980s] is a kind of faceted polyhedron, exposed in more facets to more stimuli from outside, capable of more connections but *more superficial*. Our world is more superficial because *there are more surfaces that are all interfaces*. The heart is bald, the core not hard but empty (this would be the nipponization of our cultures)" (Daney 1993b, 172). The screen is a surface which becomes an interface, on which the spectators *project* their own tropisms, but they do not receive anything from the outside, if not *recognized* codes.

Images without Bodies

Writing about John Badham's *War Games* (1984), Daney evokes the loneliness of the teenager in the film, a budding hacker who unknowingly starts off a thermonuclear war. Daney compares him to the hero played by Cary Grant in Hitchcock's *North by Northwest* and ends his article on his 1980s alter ego, a "kid who knows how to do everything, a snoop who has become a ferret, always capable of fixing his own escape" (Daney 2002, 206).[12] It is the solitude of this teenager hungry for video games and computer manipulation (more than for television or cinema) that makes this teenager the new spectator of the 1980s.

We can see in this film how the young hero has no body and how the computer in his bedroom can be assimilated to masturbation. We learn in one scene that he does not know how to swim, while his high school classmate, who flirts with him, is very athletic. In *L'Exercice*, Daney writes out a quote from a book by Marc Guillaume, *La Contagion des passions, essai sur l'exotisme intérieur*:

> Interfaces, screens, and more generally prostheses (of language, knowledge, intelligence) take charge of the spectral individual, dispensing him from bodily presence and consequently from the rituals that regulate the confrontations of

12   "*War Games*: Guerre et puce.", originally published in *Libération*, December 14, 1983.

bodies, enabling him to avoid committing the totalitý of his personality in exchanges with others … The elision of a part of the being is what allows … easier connections.

When Daney was chronicling television in *Le Salaire du Zappeur*, he was interested in an announcer entirely made up of computer-generated images, who first appeared in the United Kingdom: Max Headroom, who presented a program of musical clips. "There are dogs to guard houses, why shouldn't there be image robots to announce programs and tell the news?" (Daney 1993a, 145)[13]. In fact, added Daney, since "the traditional image of the human body is so little exalted by the small screen … it is perhaps reasonable to leave it to the cinema (or to the great occasions of live recording) and to switch resolutely towards *images*" (Daney 1993a, 146). Images become autonomous, outside the human world, managing the images themselves. Daney had this formidable prescience, I think, of what would become computer algorithms governing our relationship to images for several years (on social networks or Google, for example): "Just as, for a long time, machines have replaced us (without causing great suffering), it is also possible to imagine images that would do the housework in our stead in the world of images" (Daney 1993a, 146).

Ecology of Images

A vision of an autonomous world of the pure, synthetic image, definitively distant from the human world. But is this really possible? A passage from *L'Exercice* has always fascinated me, because Daney evokes the Internet before it existed. Reacting to an article published in *Libération*, Daney writes: "The connection, via the telephone and the computer, of all people with all other people is less and less unimaginable. Someone will be able to fax

13   "Mac Headroom, créature télévisuelle.", originally published in *Libération*, November 26, 1987.

his diary from a favela in São Paulo more easily than he will be admitted to the presence of the powerful of this world, or to the management of his living conditions. In the same way that television has been considered as a substitute good, an enchantment of the world for the underprivileged, general communication can very well be considered as a hypnotic-entertainment rattle that allows the poor to inhabit—even—the world" (Daney 1993b, 338–39). The article Daney mentioned, written by François Ascher (Professor at the French Institute of Urbanism), evokes how in a world entirely governed by "virtual" information, real presence could become a social and financial value: "The possibility of seeing and hearing each other without intermediaries, but also of touching, smelling, tasting will designate real wealth, and will define the new social and geographical inequalities" (Asher 1991). What is interesting is precisely that François Ascher is not a specialist of media or computing, but an urban planner. He thinks of social interactions in relation to the territory, to the concrete landscape. And indeed, the interface promised by the networks, as Daney notes it, is not fundamentally different from television reception (and we could think of the way western citizens experienced the health crisis in 2020 and 2021: looking at screens). In his last article at the end of his "Le Salaire du zappeur" column, Daney referred to television in terms of ecology: "it should be possible to say that we live in houses that have water, gas, electricity, and image. … The water (one says) is more or less pure, good, or chlorinated. This is the central question of television and it is more a question of ecology than anything else" (Daney 1993a, 183).[14] The question that Daney bequeaths to us is this one: who manages our environment of images politically, with the codes and the signs that they carry? Daney's column on television should be reread freshly to question the Internet. There, he interrogates more than the quality of images: he also questions the

14   "En attendant la neige.", originally published in *Libération*, December 24, 1987.

relationships that we weave with them and the way we are in the middle of images.

Translated into English by Pierre Eugène and Kate Ince

References

Asher, François. 1991. "Villes: le paradoxe des télécommunications." *Libération*, June 4.

Daney, Serge. 1983. *La Rampe*. Paris: Cahiers du cinéma/Gallimard

———. 1992. "Journal de l'an nouveau." *Trafic* 2: 5–18.

———. 1993a. *Le Salaire du zappeur*. Paris: P.O.L (first edition 1988. Paris: Ramsay).

———. 1993b. *L'Exercice a été profitable, Monsieur*. Paris: P.O.L.

———. 1997. Devant la recrudescence des vols de sacs à mains. Lyon: Aléas. (first edition 1991).

———. 1998. *Ciné journal, vol. 1, 1981–1982*. Paris: Cahiers du cinema.

———. 2002. *La Maison cinéma et le monde: Les années Libé (1981–1985)*. Paris: P.O.L.

———. 2012. *La Maison cinéma et le monde: Les années Libé (1986–1991)*. Paris: P.O.L.

———. 2015. *La Maison cinéma et le monde: Le moment Trafic (1991–1992)*. Paris: P.O.L.

Grenier, Lise (ed.). 1987. *Cités-Cinés*. Paris: Grande Halle de la Vilette & Ramsay.

Guisnel, Jean. 1999. *Libération, la biographie*. Paris: La Découverte.

Kittler, Fredrich. 1999. *Gramophone, Film, Typewriter*. Stanford: Stanford University Press.

Deleuze, Gilles 1986. *Cinema 1: The Movement-Image*. Minneapolis: University of Minnesota Press.

Deleuze, Gilles, and Guattari, Félix. 1983. *Anti-Œdipus: Capitalism and Schizophrenia*. Minneapolis: University of Minnesota Press.

Joubert-Laurencin, Hervé. 1988. "Dictionnaire des idées zappées." *Vertigo* 2: 137–50.

Le Grignou, Brigitte. 1989. "Entretien avec Serge Daney, Libération." *Quaderni* 8: 87–93.

VIDEOGRAPHIC CRITICISM

SPECTATORIAL MEMORY

CINEMA EXPERIENCE

FEAR AND TRAUMA

A Video Exploration of a Viewer's Account: *L'œil était dans la tombe et regardait Daney*

Chloé Galibert-Lainé

This article reflects on the production of a videographic essay exploring and responding to Serge Daney's text "The Eye Was in the Tomb and Stared at Franju." I argue that transposing Daney's written memory of Franju's *Eyes Without a Face* onto the screen offers an original and sensitive way to access the practice of criticism and the multiple temporalities which it encompasses, all the while exploring in a performative way the gap which always exists between a film and the manner in which it is remembered. I also show how creating the audiovisual essay helped me to break out of the sole analysis of Daney's text to reflect more generally on the different ways this text can be read today.

 On September 25th, 1986, Serge Daney published a short text in *Libération* entitled "L'œil était dans la tombe et regardait Franju" (reprinted in Daney 2012, 145–47) in which he discussed his memory of Georges Franju's *Les Yeux sans visage* (1960). It was common for Daney to write about films that were not current. More than critiquing new releases, he liked to observe, through a retrospective, a TV rerun, or a new cinema release (as was the case for *Les Yeux sans visage*), how the films he had enjoyed survived (or did not survive) the passing of time. Some of his most touching texts were born of out this attention paid to what happened to films from his past. A good example of this is the melancholy incipit of his "Journal de l'an passé," in which he discusses Michael Curtiz's *Robin Hood* (2015, 53–82)[1] as Kevin Costner announced his intention to make a remake. Or the more cheerful dialogues in which he stages himself in conversation with different films as if they were old friends.[2]

"L'œil était dans la tombe et regardait Franju" fits into this corpus of new critiques of old films. Contrary to the previous examples however, its aim was not to determine if Franju's film had suffered from the passing of time (the question gets answered right away, and the answer is no). It is Daney's opportunity to share his personal memory of the film that he had kept for twenty-six years and, on the occasion of the film's re-release, to confront his memory of it with what is actually on the film roll. Some interesting questions arise due to this essay's status as a "memory text."[3] To what extent can a film be distorted in viewers' minds over the years as it takes root in their memories and gets entangled with their own personal stories? At the cost of what compromises and approximations can writing about a film grasp

1   It was originally published in *Trafic* 1, Winter 1991, pp. 5–30.

2   See, for instance, the dialogue between Daney and Vincente Minnelli's *Celui par qui le scandale arrive*, reprinted in *La maison cinéma et le monde* 3: 163–65.

3   I borrow this term from Annette Kuhn's *An Everyday Magic*, which is an essential methodological reference to analyze a corpus of cinema viewers' memories.

a past viewing experience? And what can reading these accounts provoke in viewers from a different generation, who probably have a different relationship to cinema?

To explore Daney's text, I used an experimental method inspired by work that has been conducted for several years in the field of "videographic research" in cinema studies.[4] This research practice consists in studying films, not only by describing them and analyzing them on paper, but by putting them back on the editing table and producing a video analysis. This allows the film medium to be explored endogenously, and reduces the distance between the study and the object studied in a productive way (a distance that was discussed by Raymond Bellour in his 1975 article "Le texte introuvable"[5]). According to Catherine Grant, one of the pioneers in this field, this practice comes directly from Brad Haseman's proposal in his "Manifesto for Performative Research" (2006). Haseman invited his readers to adopt in their research "the same medium or the same mode as the object of their research; that is to say, in the case of films, television, audiovisual art, or internet videos, [to conduct their research] *audiovisually*" (Grant 2016). Pushing this reasoning even further, I wanted to explore Daney's experience as a viewer in a performative way, by producing a new viewing experience for a contemporary audience, which would shed a critical light onto Daney's account and make each viewer reflect on their own memory mechanisms. This research led me to create a ten-minute-long audiovisual essay entitled *L'œil était dans la tombe et regardait Daney* (Galibert-Lainé 2017).

In this article, I propose to return to the creation of this film, concentrating on the different ways of studying a corpus of viewers' accounts. What emerged from this video exploration of

4   The website [in]Transition, edited by Catherine Grant, Chiara Grizzaffi, Christian Keathley, and Drew Morton, is one of the most complete resources on this topic at the moment: http://mediacommons.org/intransition/resources (all the links were accessed on 10 July 2019).

5   Originally published in *Ça cinéma* 2 (7–8), May 1975.

 Daney's account regarding how viewers' memory works and the stakes of creating accounts of cinema's memories? This article will have two parts. First, I will argue that transposing a viewer's account onto the screen offers an original and sensitive way to access the practice of criticism and the multiple temporalities it encompasses, all the while exploring in a performative way the gap that always exists between a film and the manner in which it is remembered. Then, I will show how creating this audiovisual essay helped me to break out of the analysis of Daney's text to reflect more generally on the different ways this text can be read today. This will lead me to present the videographic approach as a way to bring back the memory account into a double present: both the present experienced during the screening and the present of our contemporary era, in which it is important to keep alive the memory of these accounts and the films they refer to— because archiving and studying past viewing practices can help to understand present and future viewing experiences.

Exploring the Multiple Temporalities of Memory Accounts through Film

In his diary, which was published posthumously under the title *L'exercice a été profitable, Monsieur*, Serge Daney wrote:

> Things imprint themselves twice: once on the film roll and once in the viewer. … There is the roll's developing time (rushes) and the time it takes for the film to mature in the body and nervous system of a viewer in the dark. It might be this relationship to time which allows for some people (including me) to go from passively watching a film to actively writing about it. … Writing is acknowledging what has already been written. In the film (films being an organized sediment of signs) and in me (organized by a sediment of mnemic traces which, over time, constitute my story). Before: one is written (worked on). After: one is writing (working). Thus,

writing is unwriting (rewriting with visible ink on invisible ink). (1993, 20–21)

This very rich passage deserves to be analyzed in more detail than this article allows. What I am most interested in is the way Daney insists on the importance of the *time* spent "in the dark." The viewers' "exposure time" to the film (to extend the photographic metaphor) would be what makes an impression on their mind and imprints the film in their memory. According to Daney, this length of time is the condition for recollection to be possible, and thus for critique to be possible. But if we re-read the paragraph carefully, we can see that at least four different temporalities are evoked, and the relations between them are far from being resolved. First, there is what Daney calls "the time of the film" (1999, 82), which corresponds to the actual length of the film roll. This time is immutable, metronomic, fixed forever at the time that the film was edited. There is also the time that viewers experience when watching the film. This "dream time" can correspond very closely or very loosely to the "time of the film." With a film, "which confuses the art of editing shots together with the art of creating time" (Daney 1999, 82),[6] the time measured by the clock in the cinema auditorium and the time experienced during the screening by the viewers will be very similar, whereas, watching a film, "which manages to have time on its side" (Daney 1999, 82), objective and experienced time can differ enormously. Then, there is the time that occurs between viewing the film and recalling and writing about it. This period of time can span a few hours for the critic who needs to send his text back right after the end of the screening—or several years. Here, Daney only briefly touches on the various metamorphoses that the film can go through while maturing like this "within" the viewers, but elsewhere he did describe these transformations very precisely.[7]

6   Daney uses this expression about *La Vérité sur Bébé Donge* (Henri Decoin, 1952).

7   *L'exercice a été profitable, Monsieur* is very rich material to do research on this as the reader can observe how the memory of some films evolves page after page, nearly day by day.

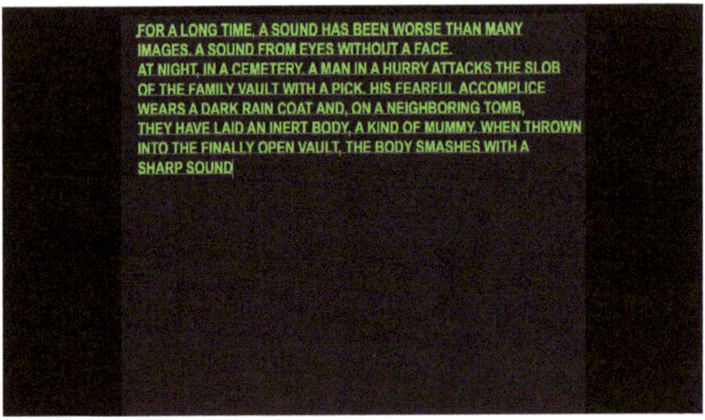

[Fig. 1] Reenactment of the writing process of Daney's text (Source: Galibert-Lainé 2017)

And, finally, there is the time of writing, which the reader usually knows nothing about, but which Daney suggests would be superimposable on the time spent "in the dark" facing the film, since writing would mean "rewriting in visible ink" what the film has already written (or "imprinted") on us during the viewing. However, here Daney chose not to mention the fact that these invisible notes might have been largely erased and rewritten over the years.

Is it possible to distinguish the traces of these four distinct temporalities within the text "L'œil était dans la tombe et regardait Franju"? This is one of the first questions I asked myself when I created my film. Or, to be more precise, I started from the following intuition: if we accept the idea that cinema is "the art of inventing time," it is probable that exploring a memory account through the means of cinema will allow light to be shed on the different time strata in a productive way.

L'œil était dans la tombe et regardait Daney starts with a long writing sequence. Daney's text appears, word by word, in green on the black screen[8] (fig. 1). A typing error, a minute of hesitation, give the viewer the impression of discovering the text as it is being written. Several viewers described having the same impression when watching this sequence, it can seem as if we are looking over the shoulder of the critic while he is at work. While the text is appearing, the original soundtrack of the scene Daney is describing from memory is being played in real time.

By putting myself in Daney's shoes in a completely fictitious way when I filmed this passage, trying to guess the words on which he could have stumbled, I also had the very striking feeling of "rewriting with visible ink on invisible ink." Because I was literally writing over Daney's words by copying them from the book onto my computer screen. But also because, as the words were transiting through me, I realized how debatable each one of them was, how radically subjective the text was, beneath its apparently relatively objective description of the content of the film (how the characters are acting, what they are wearing…). Thanks to this exercise, I acquired a sensitive and intimate understanding of what the passage quoted above is trying to explain. Describing a film from memory, even without trying to intentionally insert one's own affects, always means writing over in visible ink, that is to say translating into a language understandable by all, the subjective, incomplete, and largely non-verbal traces the film has imprinted upon us during the viewing.

This opening sequence explores several tensions. First, there is the confrontation between the time of Franju's film (the one that is imprinted on the film roll, or in this case, in the audio part of the .mp4 file), and the time of critical writing. Since the way my film is edited means they happen at the same time, viewers are invited to notice the gaps: the times when describing the noise takes more time than the actual noise itself, or, on the contrary,

---

8   I chose these colors to recall the screen of the Apple II computer Daney probably had at the time (according to Pierre Eugène, to whom I am very thankful for this information).

the times when the writing ignores some elements of the sound-track and anticipates the arrival of a significant sound event. These gaps also reveal the subjectivity at work when writing a text. I think it is also possible to perceive what I became aware of when I shot this sequence while watching the film. By confronting the memory with the object it recalls, the editing invites people to reflect on how each word chosen by Daney matches the sound it describes. Is the sound of the dead body hitting the bottom of the vault really "sudden"? Is that the term you would have used? If not, does that mean Daney is not remembering it correctly, or simply that this noise evokes a different network of mental associations for you? Besides, memory accounts sometimes omit some elements, the importance of which is only revealed afterwards. For example, the way my film is edited allows viewers who are familiar with Daney's text to realize that he is not talking about the blaring throbbing of the plane flying over the cemetery during the scene, although he will conclude his memory account on the image of that specific plane, the sound of which he has forgotten (this "amazing shot," this "purely poetic" move).

The videographic exploration of Daney's account offers the possibility of confronting three texts in a synchronous way: the filmic text, given to read in all its sensitive and symbolic density (although the fact that there are no images here makes it easier to read by forcing viewers to focus on the soundtrack alone); Daney's memory text, which demonstrates both his subjective perceptions during the screening and the way these perceptions have matured in his memory over the years; and a third virtual text, the one you would write yourself if you were free to choose your own words to describe the scene you can hear, and of which you might already have a personal memory. The different public screenings of *L'œil était dans la tombe et regardait Daney* have given me the opportunity to observe the performative efficiency of this sequence, which can be measured through the fervor with which, each time, at least one member of the audience took the mic to tell "their" version of *Les Yeux sans visage*. In this sense, I think that the film constitutes a *performative* study of Daney's text. It offers an analysis of the memory mechanisms which underpin the critic's account whilst inviting the audience to observe the ways in which these same mechanisms are at work in their own memories of the film.

The Future of Viewers' Accounts: Reading and Memorial Transmission

It is because the memory text has this *contagious* quality—because we have all experienced how difficult it is, when listening to someone's personal memory, not to start looking for the memory of a similar experience in our own mind—that the analysis of Daney's text made me think more generally about the different possible modes of reception of this type of account. What effect can this type of text have on contemporary readers? What can they learn from it, even if—particularly if—they are not familiar with Franju's film? I was all the more interested in this question since, as I said in the film, I had myself never seen *Les Yeux sans visage* when I first came across Daney's text. So, I had to find out how to document the way in which my intimate knowledge of Daney's memory account would inform my discovery of the film. I took inspiration from methods developed by auto-ethnographers Carolyn Ellis and Arthur P. Bochner. In my film, I tried to produce an "aesthetic and evocative thick description of [my] personal and interpersonal experience" (Ellis, Adams, and Bochner 2011) when I first watched *Les Yeux sans visage*. The aim of that explicitly auto-reflexive sequence was, once again, to invite my viewers to engage themselves into introspective work by thinking about the way Daney's words, which they were (re)discovering on the screen, informed their perception of the images on screen.

It is at this stage of the research process that the fact that *Les Yeux sans visage* is a terrifying movie became very important. Intuitively, I thought that out of all the emotions that a film can

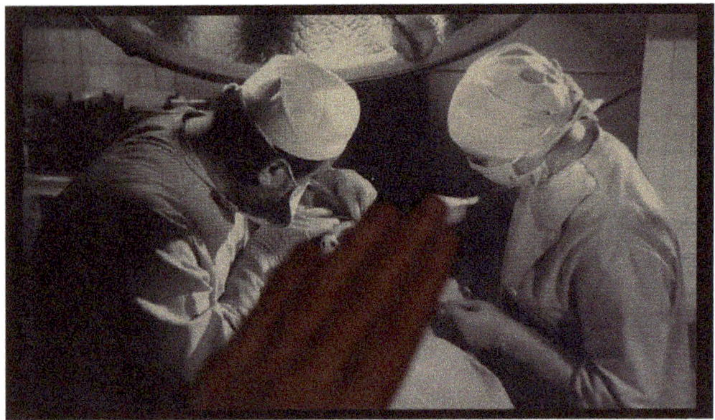

[Fig. 2] The graft scene from *Les Yeux sans visage* seen through the prism of Daney's memory (Source: Galibert-Lainé 2017)

produce, fear would be the most likely to be negated by a precise knowledge of the events happening in the film. By recounting the two most frightening scenes of the film (Daney relates not only the cemetery scene but also the scene of the face graft), did Daney not make me immune to the fear they are supposed to create at the risk of ruining my pleasure as a viewer? Or, on the contrary, would it intensify my experience by making me *anticipate* what would be shown (and heard)? Jean-Marc Leveratto et Laurent Jullier claim that some "negative emotional states such as disgust or fear" can become "delectable" if "their structure is brought to consciousness rather than being buried and working mysteriously" (2010, 7). Thus, would Daney's account paradoxically turn the fear Franju's film creates into a pleasurable experience, whereas it would have been difficult to watch other-wise? The central sequence of my film shows this experience as well as the strategy of visual obstruction I adopted because of the anticipated fear created by Daney's text (fig. 2).

What I experienced when I shot this sequence is that Daney's text had not ruined my discovery of Franju's film in any way. However, it had undeniably modified its parameters by influencing my horizon of expectations and directing my attention towards some

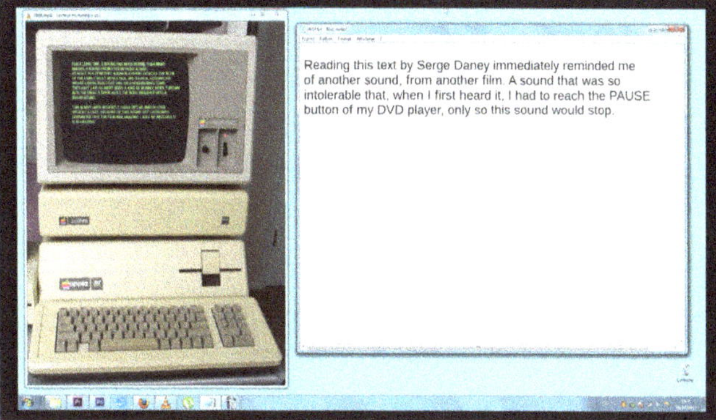

[Fig. 3] Two memory accounts, separated by 30 years of technological evolution
(Source: Galibert-Lainé 2017)

details that I might have ignored otherwise. Nevertheless, I must
say that Daney's text did not guide my reactions in a deterministic
way. As I said in the film, I realized in retrospect that I had
unintentionally modified Daney's account, that I had *remembered
it incorrectly*. I had made his memory mine. My sensations as a
viewer were thus enriched, not directly by Daney's, but by the
feelings and thoughts I had had when reading his text.

Regardless, after shooting *L'œil était dans la tombe et regardait
Daney* and screening it at various events, I became aware that
there is something else at stake linked to the reading and transmission of viewers' accounts. They can of course enrich the way
we perceive old films, but they can also provide us with tools to
understand more contemporary films and media. I previously
mentioned how, at every screening of my film, a member of the
audience would take the floor to tell their own version of Franju's
film. But, oftentimes, someone would take the floor to talk
about another film. This might be because, in my film, I respond
to Daney's text with a personal memory linked to my viewing
experience of Danny Boyle's *Shallow Grave*, released in 1994 (fig.
3). Once, someone talked about the sound of the boots in the
opening scene of Jean-Pierre Melville's *L'Armée des ombres* (1969);

 another time, a young woman talked with emotion about how terrified she was by the clinking sound of the were-rabbit in Nick Park and Steve Box's *Wallace and Gromit* (2005).

It might be irreverent to compare *Les Yeux sans visage*, a film that is so important in the history of cinema, to *Shallow Grave* or *Wallace and Gromit*. As far as I am concerned, I must admit that I was quite embarrassed to realize that Danny Boyle's film played, in my cinema education, a similar role to the one *Les Yeux sans visage* played in that of Daney. But this is something that Daney had anticipated himself. Indeed, at the beginning of his diary, he wrote:

> Children who were born with television will never have the same relationship to cinema [that we have]. … It's silly to think that during each new period in the (materialistic) history of perception, old things are not re-discovered nor reconsidered. As if we should be ashamed to have dis-covered Keaton without live piano music in the room. The saddest part (for me) would be if, for these young people, cinema had completely turned into Culture, and would thus only be consumable in a commemorative way, like a *son et lumière* show. Conversely, the greatest thing would be the need to re-read Eisenstein for a music video. (1993, 42–43)

This excerpt shows how wrong the people are who make Daney the representative of a nostalgic cinephilia and someone who is utterly pessimistic about the future of film forms. This excerpt also makes me feel that it is carrying the work initiated by the critic, by using his text about Franju to give an opportunity to a contemporary viewer to reflect on the impact *Wallace and Gromit* had on the little girl she was in 2005.

At the end of this reflection, it seems to me that exploring a memory account like Daney's videographically allows us to reactivate its *presence* in our contemporary era in different ways. First, it is about sharing the experiential present of the moment Daney is recalling in the film. Replaying the writing process allows us to create a situation, maintained over a certain time, in which viewers can become aware of the memory process which is at the origin of the text. As they are invited to compare each word chosen by Daney to the sounds he aimed to describe, viewers become aware of the gap between the film and Daney's memory account of it—a gap that can be explained both by the difficulty of verbally translating a sound object and by the disconcerting liberties Daney's memory sometimes took. Shooting this audiovisual essay also gave me the opportunity to measure, both empirically and intimately, how much reading a viewer's account can inform a future viewing experience by creating a context in which the film is loaded with all the meanings the first viewer invested in it, and enriched by the expectations that the account will have created in the second viewer's mind. The observation my video essay ends on brings up a useful analogy. Previous viewers, whether they are on the screen or have been members of the audience before us, influence the way we, in turn, perceive what we know they have perceived first. Finally, I want to argue that these memory accounts, by Daney and others, are not only supposed to be read reverently or to enrich our understanding of the great films in the history of cinema. We are allowed to divert them from their primary goal, to take them out of their socio-historical context, and to use them to shed some light onto our contemporary viewing experiences, even if it is through uncertain analogies. Daney himself would probably be happy that his story is being used. Indeed, in May 1992, during the meeting with *Trafic* at the Jeu de Paume, he said the following words, in which it is hard not to perceive a testamentary intention:

> As for memory, if it only serves to cultivate the nostalgia of what was before and how much better it was, then I hate it. Memory only makes sense if, suddenly, someone says: "Oh, your story is interesting. I need it for...". (2015, 37)

Everyone can finish this sentence as they wish: for *what* do we need these viewers' accounts? "I need it..." to try to grasp what cinema represented to a generation of viewers I have not known, in the hope of enriching our collective understanding of the relationship we have today with the images and the sounds we consume and produce.

Translated into English by Melina Delmas and revised by Kate Ince

References

Daney, Serge. 1993. *L'exercice a été profitable, Monsieur*. Paris: P.O.L.

———. 1999. *Devant la recrudescence des vols de sacs à main, cinéma, télévision, information: 1988–1991*. Lyon: Aléas.

———. 2012. *La Maison cinéma et le monde*, Vol. 3, *Les années Libé (1986–1991)*. Paris: P.O.L.

———. 2015. *La Maison cinéma et le monde*, Vol. 4, *Le moment Trafic (1991–1992)*. Paris: P.O.L.

Ellis, Carolyn, Tony E. Adams, and Arthur P. Bochner. 2011. "Autoethnography: An Overview." *Forum: Qualitative Social Research* 12 (1). Accessed July 10, 2019. doi: 10.17169/fqs-12.1.1589.

Galibert-Lainé, Chloé. 2017. *L'œil était dans la tombe et regardait Daney*. Accessed July 10, 2019. https://vimeo.com/212253201.

Grant, Catherine. 2016. "The Audiovisual Essay as Performative Research." *Necsus European Journal of Media Studies*, Autumn 2016. Accessed July 10, 2019. https://necsusejms.org/the-audiovisual-essay-as-performative-research/.

Haseman, Brad. 2006. "A Manifesto for Performative Research." *Media International Australia Incorporating Culture and Policy* 118: 98–106.

Leveratto, Jean-Marc, and Laurent Jullier. 2010. "L'expérience du spectateur." *Degrés* 38 (142): 1–16.

FANDOM

CINEPHILIA

FAN ART

CALL ME BY YOUR NAME

Cinephilic Fandom

Philipp Dominik Keidl

Using Luca Guadagnino's 2017 film *Call Me by Your Name* as a case study, this essay investigates the phenomena of cinephilic fandom and cinephilic fan art. It argues that cinephilic fandom represents a specific form of film spectatorship, characterized by an engagement with cinephilic debates through practices that are usually associated with fandom. Cinephilic fan art is defined as the drawings, videos, and self-made merchandise that are inspired by "cinephiliac moments." As such, this essay argues, cinephilic fandom has the potential to introduce new voices, practices, and interpretations into debates of cinephilia.

In Luca Guadagnino's *Call Me by Your Name* (2017), toward the middle of the film: 17-year-old Elio (Timothée Chalamet) steps from a dark corridor into his bedroom, which is currently being loaned to his family's house guest, Oliver (Armie Hammer), a 24-year-old graduate student from the United States. He softly closes the door, careful to make no sound, looks around, and begins snooping through Oliver's belongings, which are spread across the room. Elio picks up Oliver's drying red swimsuit from the bed frame and sits down on the squeaky mattress. Only his naked back is visible, but the sound of the synthetic material and the slight tilt of his head and subsequent inhalation presents him exploring the bathing suit with all of his senses. He throws the shorts on the bed, turns around, gives them a brief pensive look, and puts them over his head. Spreading his legs and pushing his upper body up so that he is on all fours, he arches his back and gently moves back and forth until the trunks fall off his head. For these short 10 seconds, Elio's growing love and lust for Oliver is captured by his fleeting body movement, the crackling noise of synthetic fabric, and the rustling of wind in the trees outside the room.

Interpretations of this scene have circulated in different forms and formats online, demonstrating the impact that it has had on many viewers. For instance, a drawing named "Lust" depicts in warm colors Elio's sexual arousal when his head is immersed in the smell and feel of the swim trunks.[1] Despite the painting's stillness, it provides the impression of a continuous time span in which Elio moves on the bed tenderly, but with determination. Other works take more liberty with their depictions of the scene. One Kawaii Chibi–style sticker, available for purchase on Etsy, shows Elio with the trunks on his head and provides a glimpse

[1]   See: Aloysius J. Gleek, "Re: Armie Hammer & Timothée Chalamet find Love in *Call Me by Your Name* (November 24, 2017)," *BetterMost* (forum post). Accessed February 14, 2020, https://bettermost.net/forum/index. php?topic=53351.540.

of how he might have blushed while on all fours.[2] Finally, the red shorts are featured on a poster with more than sixty objects from the film, also sold on Etsy. Even if the objects are devoid of their diegetic contexts, they evoke memories of concrete scenes, such as Elio's trip into Oliver's room, or the film's aesthetic and atmosphere of 1980s' Italy as called forth, for instance, by more marginal props such as a cigarette pack, newspaper, and bus ticket.[3] These different examples all enable one to (re)experience *Call Me by Your Name* beyond the moving image through their attention to minute details.

The artistic responses to *Call Me by Your Name*, this essay argues, are the result of *cinephilic fandom*, a specific disposition of film spectatorship that cannot be reduced to either cinephilia or fandom. Neither of these concepts remains productive in and of itself for the analysis of cinephilic discourses that are strongly influenced and driven by practices usually associated with fandom. Consequently, the analysis of the phenomenon of cinephilic fandom requires film and media scholars to combine theories and methods from cinephilia and fan studies. By bringing together the two subfields, this essay follows the idea that "just as there have been many 'cinemas' over the course of the history of the medium, there have also been many 'cinephilias'," and that there is a need to "multiply a diversity of voices and subjectivities, and a plethora of narratives about cinephilic life and experience" (Shambu 2020, n.p.). The aim of this argument is to assign new value and use to ideas, methods, and voices that have been excluded from discussions of cinephilia

2   See: MewtantArt, "Call Me by Your Name Kawaii Chibi Stickers Set of 11," *Etsy*. Accessed September 18, 2020, https://www.etsy.com/listing/781338717/call-me-by-your-name-kawaiichibi?ga_order=most_relevant&ga_search_type=-all&ga_view_type=gallery&ga_search_query=call+me+by+your+name+sticke rs&ref=sr_gallery-1-20&organic_search_click=1.

3   See: JordanBoltonDesign, "Call Me by Your Name Pos-ter, Artwork by Jordan Bolton," *Etsy*. Accessed September 18, 2020, https://www.etsy.com/ca/listing/694768656/call-me-by-your-name-poster-artwork-by?ref=shop_home_active_15&crt=1.

because of their impulsive subordination into the categories and norms of fandom. This subordination is caused by predetermined categorizations of cinephiles and fans, based on cultural hierarchies that draw artificial but nevertheless sharp lines between high art (cinephilia) and popular culture (fandom) without examining in more detail the kind of debates in which fans and cinephiles engage.

Moreover, cinephilia is defined by "watching but also thinking, reading, talking and writing about cinema in some form, no matter how unconventional" (Shambu 2020, n.p.). Yet the plea for unconventional practices is rarely extended to the production of creative content beyond the written word. While video essays have found their place in discourses about film, allowing for more leeway for visual and formal experimentation (Smith 2011; Keathley, Mittell, and Grant 2019), written criticism continues to be considered the backbone of cinephilia.[4] In turn, transformative creative works that take more artistic freedom and (re)interpret, expand, and mash up films with other media content—often acting outside the intended meanings of film and media producers—remains neglected if not shut out from discussions on cinephilia. At best, such works are labeled as "fan cult cinephilia" (Elsaesser 2005, 36) but without considering questions of what motivates and characterizes fandom or what fan studies can offer to the study of cinephilia. The idea of cinephilic fandom is an attempt to overcome these theoretical and structural barriers of cinephilia and fan studies; it is also an attempt to widen perspectives on who can say something about film and cinema, what they can say, and how they can say it.

As the first section argues, the cinephilic fan is both fluent in subcultures and characterized by thinking about cinema and engaging with cinephilic discourses through activities and media

4   For examples, see: "Video Essays," *Project: New Cinephilia* (blog post). Accessed October 27, 2020. https://projectcinephilia.mubi.com/resources/video-essays/.

production associated with fandom; fandom and cinephilia can
be seen as two ideal positions on a spectrum of film spectatorship that are united by affect and productivity. The second
section defines the appropriations and reinterpretations of film
into other media as a form of cinephilic fan art: works that translate cinephiliac moments (Keathley 2006) into media ranging from
videos to drawings, posters, mashups, or self-made merchandise.
Finally, the third section maintains that the cinephilic fan is them-
self evidence of the continuous transformation in the way film,
cinema, and knowledge is discussed and diffused through diverse
practices among different communities.

Cinephilic Fandom

Asked in an interview what distinguishes cinephilia from fandom,
Henry Jenkins concludes that at "the end of the day, they're doing
exactly the same thing" and "the line [between fandom and cine-
philia] blurs very quickly" (Jenkins 2015, n.p.). Jenkins is certainly
not the only scholar who questions the "too-tidy division of fan
and cinephilic discourses into separate camps" (Keller 2020, 77).
Discussions about new configurations of cinephilia in the age
of digital reproduction and a growing love for cinema beyond
the structures established in pre-war and post-war France have
diversified the concept (de Valck and Hagener 2005; Balcerzak
and Sperb 2009; Balcerzak and Sperb 2012). Research on queer
and feminist cinephilia (Hallas 2003; Kim 2005; White 1999),
techno-centric cinephilia (Klinger 2006; Hudson and Zimmermann 2009), and globalized and transnational forms of cinephilia
(Rosenbaum and Martin 2003; de Valck 2007; Bhattacharya Chairs
2004; Trice 2015; Vidal 2017) are only a few examples that broaden
the definition of cinephilia as cultural practice and theoretical
concept to varying degrees and question its assumed univer-
salism by underlining the multiplicities and approaches that
it constitutes. Still, even though similarities between fandom
and cinephilia are stressed regularly, the differences seem to

 outweigh them to the effect that a tidy division between fans and cinephiles continues to be made in film and media scholarship.

Of course, there are considerable differences between cinephiles and fans as well as cinephile and fan studies, both historically and today. The notion of being a fan refers to a much broader field of culture than cinephilia, with its narrow focus on film and cinema. One can be a fan of television, video games, sports, comics, literature, opera, dance, theatre, celebrities, politicians, toy lines, themed environments, or animals, for example. As such, fan studies can be applied to a much wider field of discourse and practices (Booth 2018; Click and Scott 2018; Sarver Coombs and Osborne 2022). Even if we consider research on home entertainment and digital technologies (de Valck and Hagener 2005; Klinger 2006; Hudson and Zimmermann 2009; Balcerzak and Sperb 2009; Balcerzak and Sperb 2012), film and cinema remain at the core of cinephilia scholarship, whereby practices that deviate from it, such as cosplay or fan-made art and merchandise, get neglected.

Additionally, there are different dynamics among academics and non-academics, even though scholarship on both cinephilia and fandom habitually connect personal and theoretical perspectives (Hagener and de Valck 2008; Hills 2002). Whereas theories on cinephilia have always had a strong presence in public discourse outside of universities, with the effect that the concept had lost its bite for many academics for a time (Keathley 2006), fan studies does not receive similar interest and acknowledgment among fans themselves. "Aca-fans" have shaped the sub-field since the 1990s and collaborated with fans, but there are also fans who mistrust academics and dismiss their analyses and theories in their own discussions and writings (Neville 2018; Pignetti 2020; Hills 2002). Moreover, cinephilia and fan studies have dissimilar relationships to the study of the history of their object of study. Scholarship on cinephilia demonstrates great interest in theories and practices before the 1950s, such as the notion of "protocinephilia" and photogénie in the 1920s (Keathley 2006), whereas historical fan cultures and practices dating from before the second

half of the twentieth century continue to be unrepresented in fan
studies (Reagin and Rubenstein 2011).

Furthermore, fandom has different forms of institutionalization than cinephilia, therefore impacting the traceability of works and ideas and theories connected to them. Although they have similar infrastructures in the form of clubs, journals, magazines, blogs, and zines, many fans do not achieve the same name recognition as cinephiles. Whereas written criticism is more likely to tie specific ideas to identifiable authors, most notably in magazines like *Cahiers du cinéma* or *Senses of Cinema* or in the form of popular blogs, many fan writers and artists are often known only by pseudonyms, and works frequently circulate online without any reference to their makers.

Finally, although both are a global phenomenon, cinephilia as a practice and way of thinking about cinema began in France, whereas fandom and fan studies emerged in scholarship from the United Kingdom, the USA, and Japan. Add vernacular clichés and prejudices of high and low culture—the fan as a cultural dupe and cinephile as cultural elite, the former as someone who mindlessly consumes everything and the other a connoisseur of one art form—and the boundary between cinephiles and fans seems to reappear.

Yet, these differences often say more about scholars' attempts to establish universalized and naturalized categories about fans and cinephiles than about how individuals are inspired by film and cinema and participate in debates about it. Both cinephilia and fandom suffer from scholarly definitions that limit them to archetypes that are simultaneously too broad and too narrow. Definitions of cinephilia are broad in the sense that it is defined as a love for film and cinema as a whole, but narrow in the sense of which debates belong to the phenomenon and how they can be expressed. In fandom, definitions are narrow in the sense that fans are often reduced to one specific fandom and broad when it comes to the ways they engage with their object of fandom. To put it pointedly, one is either too dedicated to one medium or too indifferent to medium specificity. However, archetypical conceptions of fandom and cinephilia should be considered two ideal positions on a spectrum of interpretations of film spectatorship and the productivity of film spectators. This spectrum is united by two aspects that differentiate fans and cinephiles, and everyone in between, from regular audiences. The first common denominator is affect. Consider Sarah Keller's definition of cinephilia:

> First, *cinephilia is an affect*, something that derives from feeling and is therefore personal and subjective. Second, *cinephilia is an extension of affect into actions*: it manifests itself (makes itself visible) in such actions, especially through but not limited to writing. Third, cinephilia depends on displacements in time and space. As a partial result of this dependence, it tends to be nostalgic. Another result is that it is interested in relationships between past and present. Finally—the thing that undergirds the three previous categories — *cinephilia is fundamentally anxious*. (all emphases by Keller 2020, 15)

Her description of cinephilia resembles the emphasis put on the affective qualities of media fandom (Grossberg 1992), fans' participation and productivity (Jenkins, 1992), the complex relationship between past and present (Geraghty 2014), as well as the anxiety over loss that shapes fandom and some of its expressions (De Kosnik 2016). This also becomes evident in Jenkins's early definition of fandom as "a particular mode of reception … set of critical and interpretive practices … base for consumer activism … forms of cultural production, aesthetic traditions and practices [and] alternative social community" (Jenkins 1992, 284–87). These observations resonate with Keller's evaluation that cinephilia "often depends on a sense of other movies … inspires a drive to connect to other things and products … is interested in the material, technological, aesthetic, social, or other qualities specific to itself … and fixates on strong feelings, frequently mixed between good and bad" (Keller 2020, 15).

Definitions of cinephilia and fandom also highlight the spectrum's second common denominator: productivity. Fans and cinephiles are both "undisciplined spectators" as they easily switch between being immersed in a film's narrative, as the filmmaker intends, and a "panoramic perception" (Keathley 2006), with which they look at the screen with more distance and their own agency in determining what is of most interest to them. The result is the discovery of details that have minimal or no narrative purpose, but nevertheless capture their attention and interest. Fans often explore these details in their own fanfiction, to name only one example, in which they develop the backstory of minor characters or explore parts of the hyper-diegeses not depicted in the film (Hills 2002). Among cinephiles, the fetishization of moments that are visible for all but only provocative to a few are described as "cinephiliac moments" (Keathley 2006). When encountered in a film, Christian Keathley explains, expanding on Paul Willemen's concept, cinephiliac moments "spark something which then produces the energy and the desire to write, to find formulations to convey something about the intensity of that spark" (2006, 140). Writing represents a means to share and extend these experiences as "cinephiliac anecdotes," personal recollections of cinephiliac moments, and the sensation when something captures your interest (Keathley 2006, 140–52). In the case of the cinephilic fan, however, writing is only one of many media interpretations into which this energy is channeled.[5]

5　Adapting Willemen's terminology, Keathley uses the term "cinephiliac" over "cinephilic" in order to stress the overtones of necrophilia in cinephilia. However, even though a complex relationship to the past is evident in both fandom and cinephilia, this essay does not consider necrophilia to be a defining aspect of cinephilic fandom. While some individuals may engage with themes of death, the overall dynamics of cinephilic fandom demonstrate more diverse dynamics.

Cinephilic Fan Art

Cinephiliac moments are "a reminder that films are themselves made up of fragments" (Keathley 2006, 38), and cinephilic art, much like cinephilic writing, also reflects the fragmentary nature of filmmaking. Consider the following three drawings. Elio is lying on his back with the red shorts, first all over his face, and then, in the second picture, with them covering his mouth. Finally, the last drawing shows him taking them nearly off of his face completely.[6] These three drawings make direct reference to the film and to Elio playing with Oliver's shorts, although the artist took the liberty of presenting an alternative version of the film scene. In the drawings, Elio is wearing the same shorts and no shirt, but he is resting on his back instead of being on all fours. With Elio's relaxed body posture and flushed cheeks, this image depicts an idea of how the scene of Elio with the swimsuit can be read as a post-masturbation blush. Although more consequential than how Elio is shown to act on his fantasies in the film, the drawings retain the same narrative in suggesting his longing for Oliver. Yet, by offering a different perspective on Elio's actions, rearranging how he moves in space, and implying that he lingers longer on Oliver's bed than he does in the film, the drawings emphasize that Guadagnino's directorial choices for framing and editing represent only one possible way to tell the story. Cinephiliac moments, and the art inspired by them, therefore enable awareness of the restrictions imposed upon them by framing and editing, always limiting the visible to what the filmmaker has chosen (Keathley 2006).

This extends not only to aesthetic and narrative questions, but also points toward criticism of the film for teasing audiences

6   See: Paolacosette Vica, *Pinterest*. Accessed September 21, 2020, https://www.pinterest.ca/pin/249246160613294791/; Madeline Bass, *Pinterest*. Accessed September 21, 2020, https://www.pinterest.ca/pin/249246160613294794/; Paolacosette Vica, *Pinterest*. Accessed September 21, 2020, https://www.pinterest.ca/pin/249246160613294801/.

with several scenes of uninhibited kissing and foreplay but
ultimately shying away from showing explicit images of the
couple having sex—even though Elio is shown having sex with
a girl. For instance, some drawings frame the scene differently
and show Elio's backside or partly reveal his penis while they are
having oral sex. They foreground Guadagnino's complicity with
directors of other mainstream gay-themed movies by "limit[ing]
the visibility of gay male sex, whose depiction is scrupulously
kept from approaching the explicitness reserved for hetero-con-
summations" (Miller 2018, n.p.). Other examples go even further,
such as re-edits of the film that integrate pornographic scenes,
mix stills from the film's non-explicit sex scenes with porn shots,
place sex noises over shots from the film, or play the film's soundtrack over animated porn.[7] While D.A. Miller argues in his review
of the film that Guadagnino uses the beauty of Italy to distract
from the physical aspects of gay relationships, the added images
and sounds of the porn versions provide an explicitness that the
film denies its audiences. Cinephilic fans create those scenes that
the director chose to exclude from the script;[8] or, as Miller puts it,
"the gay sex scene that [the film] spent well over an hour making
everyone anticipate, a scene that might have taken our breath
away for real" (2018, n.p.). In other words, cinephilic fandom is

7   See: Rob Gee, *Pinterest*. Accessed September 20, 2020, https://www.
pinterest.ca/pin/784330091336821122/; Rob Gee, *Pinterest*. Accessed
September 20, 2020, https://www.pinterest.ca/pin/784330091336820956/;
Rob Gee, *Pinterest*. Accessed September 20, 2020, https://www.pinterest.
ca/pin/784330091336822189/; "Call Me by My Name Gay Sex Scenes," *Cloudy
Girls*. Accessed September 20, 2020, https://www.cloudygirls.com/porn/
call-me-by-my-name-gay-sex-scenes.html; "Elio and Oliver Part 2," *Pornhub*
(video). Accessed September 18, 2020, 03:37min, https://www.pornhub.com/
view_video.php?viewkey=ph5e2d19c6f1ac4&utm_source=PBWeb&utm_
medium=PT&utm_campaign=PBWeb; "Call Me by Your Name-Porn Version,"
Pornhub (video). Accessed September 18, 2020, 04:53min, https://www.
pornhub.com/view_video.php?viewkey=ph5e8e3db63e5ee.

8   Screenwriter James Ivory criticized the lack of nudity and camera pans away
from the lovers (Brockington 2018) and the removal of much more sugges-
tive scenes from the original script than those featured in the film (Wheeler
2018).

  expressed in the production of new scenes that are inspired by the film and that fans would have liked to see in the original version.

The selection of cinephiliac moments is as subjective as their reinterpretation into other media, and cinephilic fan art brings the active eyes of different spectators together and makes these moments perceivable. By definition, cinephiliac moments may not be intended to be memorable and therefore escape the attention of the general audience, but this does not mean that several individuals cannot share one and the same fascination (Keathley 2006). Two kinds of questions need to be asked when talking about the cinephiliac moment: "what" has one seen and "how" have they seen it? Just as critical writing on cinephiliac moments is one means to establish connections to the personal, fan art provides "information about how [the artists] read, interpret, and use the text" (Cherry 2016, 39). Aquarelle paintings, pencil drawings, comics and manga, stickers, and abstract posters all show subjective approaches to a scene. Crucially, fan communities have always had the "centrifugal" approach to cinema (Shambu 2020, n.p.), and built contact zones for remixing (Hudson and Zimmerman 2009) all forms of culture that conceptions of cinephilia in the digital age aim to institute. Cinephilic fan art establishes connections beyond film culture and history, drawing from a much broader intertextual repertoire: it reimagines scenes from *Call Me by Your Name* as a Studio Ghibli production, places shots of Oliver and Elio in impressionist paintings, produces mash-up trailers to foreground homoerotic subtexts in contemporary television shows, sketches images of the couple in the style of manga or Young Adult fiction cover art, materializes them as puppets, draws them as Furries, or recreates dialogues from the films by creating playlists with songs whose titles match the words spoken in certain scenes.[9] If cinephiles build on their

9   See: @bibbongtsubibo, *Twitter*. Accessed September 20, 2020, https://twitter. com/bibbongtsubibo/status/961539447874404352; Rachel Thompson, "Genius Instagram account merges 'Call Me by Your Name' Scenes with

personal preferences and memories of their previous cinema-going experiences, always analyzing the place of individual films in film history, cinephilic fans establish connections across media. Such cross-media cinephilic fan canons are highly personal and individualized, and challenge those engaging with cinephilic fan art to constantly test their pop cultural knowledge, researching references they may not yet know as they are "moving across different fandoms… moving across these different forms of fan knowledge" (Hills 2015, 158–59). Resistance to medium-specific canons, especially in a time of media convergence, participatory culture, and transmedia storytelling (Jenkins 2006), bears the potential to rethink earlier cinephile canons and to bring them into dialogue with the popular culture of their time.

The intertextuality of cinephilic fan art also redirects attention away from questions regarding film's ontology, which have been central in cinephile debates and scholarship (Keathley 2006; Keller 2020). Although there have been prominent claims about

Monet Paintings," *Mashable*. Accessed March 15, 2018, https://mashable.com/2018/03/15/call-me-by-monet-instagram/?europe=true; Robazizo's Tumblings, *Tumblr* (post). Accessed September 21, 2018, https://robazizo.tumblr.com/post/178316216644/call-me-by-your-name-manga-illustrated-by-yamimaru; "Great Showdowns by Scott C.", *Tumblr* (post). Accessed September 20, 2020, https://greatshowdowns.com/post/174601335819/call-me-by-your-name-and-ill-call-you-by-mine; Mediodescocido, "Elio & Oliver / Call Me by Your Name." *Flickr* (post). Accessed April 10, 2018, https://www.flickr.com/photos/mediodescocido/26507452597/; StarFrom-Phoenix, *Pinterest*. Accessed September 20, 2020, https://fi.pinterest.com/pin/585679126520889193/; Grace Pagdanganan, *Pinterest*. Accessed September 20, 2020, https://www.pinterest.it/pin/480407485253228641/; Baranorgi, "Fan Art/ Call Me by Your Name," *Furaffinity* (forum post). Accessed September 20, 2020, https://www.furaffinity.net/view/31737877/; planetvcr, "So Call Me by Your Name-," *DeviantArt*. Accessed September 20, 2020, https://www.deviantart.com/planetvcr/art/so-call-me-by-your-name-829882093; Jindo K, "Call Me by Your Name (but it's The Office)," *YouTube* (video). Accessed September 20, 2020, 02:09 min, https://www.youtube.com/watch?v=o9clKgoooYc&t=31s&ab_channel=Jindok; See: Dark Alex. "Call Me by Your Name TikTok Compilations," *YouTube* (playlist). Accessed September 20, 2020, https://www.youtube.com/playlist?list=PLxa5T9k6fZYFQI7nLrTe9SSO4li1TeaWC.

film as a photographic medium having a privileged relationship to reality, others have begun to reexamine if this was ever really the case (Keathley 2009). Indexicality also only plays a minor part in cinephilic art, but connections exist nevertheless. This becomes especially evident in the many forms of fan tourism and pilgrimages (Williams 2017) to Italy, shared in the form of videos, slide shows, or individual photographs. One of the most popular endeavors of this kind has been a photo project that matches film stills from *Call Me by Your Name* to their original shooting locations, merging stills from the film (shot on 35mm) with the fan's own (digital) photos taken at the shooting locations.[10] A more abstract take is represented by art engaging with the depiction of landscape and nature in the film. Landscape and nature "have long been sources for cinematic splendor and cine-philia" (Keller 2020, 130) and this becomes evident in collages pairing photographs from the film together with impressionist paintings. By placing Elio and Oliver in paintings by Monet, among other painters, the collages emphasize—as well as replicate—the excessive use of rustling trees, whipping grass, and splashing water to represent the inner tension of the characters.

Crucially, however, fans document their own moments of film reception and art production. In regards to the former aspect, some fans record videos of themselves watching trailers of or scenes from the film, thereby capturing ephemeral and fleeting moments of the affective film experience.[11] In terms of the latter,

10   See: Jacob Shamsian, "A Fan Flew to Italy to Seamlessly Match the Most Romantic Scenes in 'Call Me by Your Name' to their Real-Life Places," *Insider*. Accessed January 18, 2018, https://www.insider.com/call-me-by-your-name-real-life-italy-vs-movie-photos-2018-1.

11   See: Winchester Twin, "We Watch Call Me by Your Name for the First Time," *YouTube* (video). Accessed June 6, 2023, 20:39 min, https://www.youtube.com/watch?v=jK2GW4Nc0kc&ab_channel=WinchesterTwins; Sue 101, "Call Me by Your Name Best Moments: Reaction," *YouTube* (video). Accessed June 6, 2023, 14:39 minutes, https://www.youtube.com/watch?v=wkhrffTyDdk&ab_channel=Sue101; ZZAVID, "Call Me by Your Name *Re-Reaction* *Commentary*, *YouTube* (video).

they document the making of their fan art, in some cases with the film or its soundtrack playing over the video.[12] These videos make transparent the decisions that were made and methods used to produce the final work, preserving affective reactions to the film turned into actions, and making them accessible in the present and future for additional reflection in the form of comments and appreciations about the impact the film had on viewers. In this regard, cinephilic fan art is shifting attention from what happened in front of the camera to what happens in front of a screen and during a screening respectively.

By trying to capture the uncapturable—time and affect—cinephilic fan art brings out the fraught relationship between past, present, and future. Home entertainment caters to the desire of the "fetishistic spectator" to "stop, hold and to repeat" a film (Mulvey 2006, 173). Cinephilic fan art is the result of a viewer's in-depth scrutiny of images, characters, and storyworlds that circulate cinephiliac moments across media in a more flexible manner, as well as a reading of them against the grain. They can be experienced as desktop background or screen saver, inserted in notebooks and calendars, or hung up on walls as posters and prints. Moreover, if DVDs, Blu-Rays, or digital files are some of the many ways that film can be owned and integrated into the home (Klinger 2006), cinephilic fan art provides fans the opportunity to have *Call Me by Your Name* and the particular scenes that are dear

Accessed September 20, 2020, 31:05 minutes, https://www.youtube.com/watch?v=obXc72nxwCo&ab_channel=ZZAVID.

12 See: Jellyfish Tea, "Call Me by Your Name Fan Art," *YouTube* (video). Accessed September 20, 2020, 03:06 minutes, https://www.youtube.com/watch?v=-cr--JEIT_iw&ab_channel=JellyfishTea; mgxaz, "Call Me by Your Name Fanart," *YouTube* (video). Accessed September 20, 2020, 04:10 minutes, https://www.youtube.com/watch?v=x5hV_E4_Qgc&ab_channel=mgxaz; koikawas, "Call Me by Your Name Speedpaint Except You Can Hear Elio Crying in the Background," YouTube (video). Accessed September 20, 2020, 06:08 minutes, https://www.youtube.com/watch?v=nkoW6vke1nw&ab_channel=koikawas, blubibo, "Call Me by Your Name Fanart || Paint with Me," *YouTube* (video). Accessed September 20, 2020, 07:17 minutes, https://www.youtube.com/watch?v=xDsIJ8c_z6s&ab_channel=blubibo.

to them in a vast variety of objects, given that fan art is available for purchase on sweaters, shower curtains, mugs, and mobile phone cases, among other products.[13] They allow their makers and owners to express their appreciation for the film and engage with the characters and storyworlds in all aspects of their everyday lives and routines, be it in their homes, at school, or in their office (Geraghty 2014; Affuso 2018; Santo 2018).

The dynamic between past, present, and future that emerges out of this availability is also crucial to understanding how a feeling of collectivity can emerge out of subjective and personal selections. Although new technologies always provide different opportunities for watching a movie over and over again, any expectation of experiencing it in the same way as the first time will be unfulfilled. Every time one watches a movie the reception differs, be it the result of personal developments or the setting and contexts in which the film is re-watched. Cinephilic fan art balances the old and the new, as the discoveries of new fans allow established fans the opportunity to recollect their previous film experiences while also seeing the film with new eyes because of a different form and format. This process combines what is already known with the anticipation of new interpretations. As sites on Pinterest and Tumblr dedicated to *Call Me by Your Name* indicate, cinephilic fans are collectors of their own cinephilic anecdotes as well as those of others—in the literal sense that freely available fan art can be downloaded and archived and in the metaphorical sense that they create new affects that may lead to further actions. In short, the making, watching, and collecting or curating of fan art counteracts anxieties about the loss and disappearance of, the affection for, and one's personal memories of a film.

13   For example, see the *Call Me by Your Name* products offered on Etsy and Redbubble.

Cinephilic Fan Criticism

Although a critical and box-office success, *Call Me by Your Name* was also criticized as being an inauthentic, apolitical, and historically unlikely depiction of gay life and sex. In addition, critics voiced concerns about the romanticized sexual relationship between a teenage boy and a man seven years his senior, as well as the celebration of white masculinity in its stylized and bourgeois depiction of 1980s Italy (Galt and Schoonover 2019; Branciforte 2022). Following these concerns, some of the fan art discussed in this essay could also be criticized as reinforcing youth and whiteness as the ultimate in desirability in gay culture (Tortorici 2008) or as being complicit with "gay mainstream" cinema and its normative depiction of queer lives. Still, other examples could be interpreted as actually highlighting the whiteness and tamed depiction of gay sex in *Call Me by Your Name* by positioning and connecting Elio and Oliver to queer culture beyond the mainstream. Neither completely transformative or affirmative, or progressive or regressive, art about *Call Me by Your Name* reflects the many possibilities and conceptions of what it means to be queer, which results in works that can conform but also challenge dominant formulas and canons. As such, neither fandom nor cinephilia—and hence also not cinephilic fandom— is neutral but instead resonates with the social, cultural, and political contexts in which they are practiced and the subjectivities of their practitioners.

No matter how the politics of these artworks are interpreted, however, by acknowledging fan practices as cinephilic, new "perspectives on what qualifies as *valuable* or *useful* criticism" (de Valck 2010, 134, emphases in original) also emerge. Cinephilic fan art can challenge what participation in cinephilia looks like and what forms it can take, placing the creation of drawings and mash-ups alongside written or video criticism. In some cases, cinephilic art seeks connections to established film canons. For instance, Studio Ghibli–style drawings of Elio and Oliver pay tribute to both Luca Guadagnino and Hayao Miyazaki, celebrating the style of both filmmakers by bringing them together in art and imagining a collaborative approach by two prolific directors. But not every juxtaposition of films, styles, and directorial sensibility is celebratory. Consider the example of the mash-up trailer of *Call Me by Your Name* and the comedy *Stepbrothers* (Adam McKay 2008).[14] Here, the soundtrack of the former is used to reimagine the latter, a goofy comedy, adding sensitivity where brute humor previously set the tone. The mash-up trailer can be seen as a reinforcement of the division of filmmakers into *auteurs* and *metteurs-en-scène* (Sarris 1963). Hence, even if fan art depends on preexisting images, narratives, and characters, it is crucial not to confuse it with the uncritical embrace of an object or a film-maker's oeuvre; on the contrary, cinephilic fan art often trans-forms the content and style of a film and must therefore be seen for its critical potential that defies hierarchies between director and spectator.

Although auteur theory is less fundamental to contemporary cinephilia than it was in the past, the attention given to film directors as key indicators of value still shapes canons, festival programming, and the catalogues of boutique distributors. The rewriting and re-editing of scenes, or the remediation into other forms and formats, point to a different and shifting power dynamic between filmmaker and spectator. Traditionally, cine-philes appear as critics and are less inclined to create transfor-mative content such as writing alternative endings, "shipping" characters, or creating crossovers between different media texts, thereby challenging the interpretative authority of the film-makers over their work. In the tradition of cinephilia-as-criticism, hierarchies between directors as the makers of a film and the audience as critics of them remain intact. Fandom, in turn, is built to a great extent on individuals challenging filmmakers by

14   See: Alex Langosch, "Step Brothers/Call Me by Your Name Trailer Mashup," *YouTube* (video). Accessed September 20, 2020, 02.09 minutes, https://www.youtube.com/watch?v=hSrcu3l4Uag&t=30s&ab_channel=AlexLangosch.

producing their own works based on their favorite characters and storyworlds. If they do not like an aspect of the film, they correct what they deem to need improvement by producing their own media. Indeed, many fans consider themselves to be equal owners and co-producers of a storyworld whose interpretation of and playing with a text matter as much as the filmmakers' ideas (Fiske 1992). In other words, fans give themselves as much authority as the director over a film's narrative and style.

This struggle over authority becomes evident in the creation of explicit sexual content. Cinephilic fan art that focuses on Elio and Oliver's sex can also be understood as a critique of the film for shying away from more explicit depictions to meet the demands of rating systems, as well as the film's homonormative characters that seem to be detached from the queer culture of their time well as from the homophobia of the 1980s. Arguably, this art provides more mature access to the men's sexuality than the hyped scene (as well as some fan art) of Elio masturbating and eventually ejaculating into a peach, a scene that reduces his mature sexual desires to a whimsical act one might associate with high-school comedies. Moreover, by translating the characters into drawings in the style of Boys' Love or the covers of YA queer fiction, the cinephilic fan art positions the film firmly in queer culture and similar narratives that deal with non-hetero-normative sexualities and explicitly address the continuing dis-crimination of queer youth.[15] Finally, the transformation of Elio and Oliver into drawings is of importance here, as many of them detach these characters from the heterosexual star personas of Armie Hammer and Timothée Chalamet. Among the fan art, one finds many examples in which the characters, but not the actors, are recognizable.[16] *Call Me by Your Name* followed the example of

15   The Tumblr blog-to-graphic novel-to-Netflix series *Heartstopper* (2022) is a
      recent example of YA fiction that addresses the effects of bullying and dis-
      crimination on queer youth.
16   See: Cam's art, "Call Me by Your Name//Fanart Speedpaint," *YouTube*
      (video). Accessed September 20, 2020, 03:53 minutes, https://www.

previous arthouse blockbusters, such as *Brokeback Mountain* (Ang Lee 2005), that cast straight actors in queer roles, and reinforced the actors' straight personas in promotional campaigns. By detaching the characters from the actors, and by visualizing their sexual encounters with less restraint, the artworks confront the media industries and their production schemes that determine what can and cannot be seen, always keeping in mind how to maintain the widest possible audience.

At the same time, the global digital circulation of fan works related to the film has the potential to create awareness for media productions beyond North America and Europe. For example, a drawing depicting the protagonists of the Filipino web series *Gameboys* (2020) in the style of the official *Call Me by Your Name* poster directs attention to non-western queer media as well as to a community and their fight for equality and civil rights.[17] As such, cinephilic fan art carries the potential to give voice to marginalized and underrepresented groups in a film culture dominated by white, straight men from Europe and North America (Shambu 2020, n.p.). Another example is the circulation of films on websites dedicated to porn such as xHamster.com. Alongside alternative fan-edits of films like *Call Me by Your Name*, users of streaming platforms upload select scenes or complete files of films such as *Hawaii* (Marco Berger 2013), *Fanatic Love* (Tingjun Du 2016), or *Phor lae lukchai* (Sarawut Intaraprom 2015). Some of the uploaded films may be programmed at festivals or distributed commercially, but it is through the labor of fans that they become available to a wider audience online and provide

youtube.com/watch?v=cmsq6r9Gc5o&ab_channel=cam%27sart; Madeline Bass, *Pinterest*. Accessed September 20, 2020, https://www.pinterest.ca/pin/249246160613304359/; Madeline Bass, *Pinterest*. Accessed September 20,2020; https://www.pinterest.ca/pin/249246160611548405/; Madeline Bass, Pinterest. Accessed September 20, 2020, https://www.pinterest.ca/pin/249246160613294779/.

17   See: geloxarts. "Gameboys The Series x Call Me by Your Name." *DeviantArt* (forum post). Accessed October 28, 2020. https://www.deviantart.com/geloxarts/art/Gameboys-The-Series-x-Call-Me-By-Your-Name-857024749.

access to queer films with limited or no international distribution.
Both of these examples demonstrate that social media and video
sharing platforms give audiences a certain degree of independ-
ence from release schedules and distribution strategies of
the media industries, allowing audiences to seek content and
establish connections between *Call Me by Your Name* and queer
cinema, television, and porn.

However, cinephilic fans are not operating completely outside of,
or in opposition to the media industries. Even the more critical
examples of fan art serve as publicity for *Call Me by Your Name*,
keeping the film fresh in the public's memory because of the
unpaid labor fans perform in their free time (Stanfill 2019). But
as the commodification of some fan art demonstrates, cinephilic
fandom can also be considered an economic activity that creates
an "alternative economy" and "a grey market, where produced
artefacts are exchanged as gifts and/or commodities" (Carter
2018, 13). For Carter, alternative economies are defined by three
features:

> firstly, the advancement of digital technologies enables
> audiences to become workers and entrepreneurs; secondly,
> produced texts are instead artefacts that are exchanged as
> both gifts and/or commodities; and finally, rules and regu-
> lations, such as intellectual property laws, are commonly
> circumvented, manipulated, and countered to allow enter-
> prise to take place. (15)

The first two features are of particular interest here, as they
point to questions of availability, accessibility, and participation
in fandom, cinephilia, and cinephilic fandom as well. Although
digital technologies offer new opportunities for many, not everyone can afford the technologies to access the Internet or produce
their own media. Moreover, even if access to the Internet is
available and images can be accessed and saved, not everyone
can afford to spend money on merchandise and shipping costs.
Neither should the time that goes into the making of fan art be

 underestimated. The time to create content and "lovebor," the act of visibly loving a fan object (Stanfill 2019, 165–66), is not available to everyone. Digital technologies and associated practices therefore provide *more* availability and accessibility to the film and cinephilic fan communities, although participation nevertheless remains restricted and not as inclusive as it may seem at face value.

Despite these exclusionary socio-economic dynamics, cinephilic fandom does provide *more* diversity and a different set of voices to cinephilia and can further problematize default notions of universal cinephilia that operates on exclusion rather than inclusivity. Again, the emphasis is on *more*, as fan communities themselves have a long history of racism, homophobia, sexism, and xenophobia. Fan communities are not categorically progressive and liberal. They replicate societal and cultural hierarchies and power inequalities. Even if this is not always perceptible in fan-made art, interaction among fans can be toxic in interpersonal as well as online interactions (Fiske 1992; Pande 2018; Busse 2013). While the examples of fan art discussed in this essay may celebrate the love between two men, homophobic tendencies may come to light in other forums. Moreover, fan art cannot provide empirical insights into who stands behind the abstract conceptions of fan and fandom. Reaction videos, video criticism, and other fan-made videos shared on YouTube and TikTok, however, provide insights into how fans engage with the film and connect it to their lived experiences. Their makers are young, queer, international, and racially and ethnically diverse, showing an equally diverse range when it comes to the expression of their ideas and emotions about the film through remakes, remixes, and commentaries. They operate outside international film festival and art house cinema circuits associated with classical cinephilia, displaying film culture as it is practiced in private and public spaces, alone or with peers, led by affect or critical thought. These videos show a generation that grew up with digital technologies as a means for media reception and production, and a transmedia culture in which cinema has always been thought of as being in dialogue with other media forms and formats, and the consumption of transformative fan-made works and criticism occurred alongside the consumption of legacy media.

Conclusion

In 1996, Susan Sontag famously claimed that if "cinephilia is dead, then movies are dead too," fueling premillennial debates about the death of cinema at the hand of digital technologies. Since then, cinema and cinephilia have continued to change, but neither has died. Indeed, alternative interpretations of cinema and cinephilia have emerged. The makers of the works discussed in this essay are a new generation of cinephiles rather than the living dead. Their practices redefine what it means to love and engage with film and cinema beyond moving images and medium specificity, echoing as loud reminders that audiences should not be forced into existing categories of either cinephilia or fandom, but that definitions of cinephilia and fandom change with the times and also merge. In the case of the cinephilic fan, this refers not only to new modes of production, distribution, reception, and criticism of feature films. It also reconceives cinephiles as creative producers, who extend and expand the films they love and criticize across media. Not only do they love to make films and other media themselves, as did cinephiles before them. Cinephilic fans love to (re)make the same film all over again across various media and formats. It is up to film and media scholars—and those interested in fandom, cinephilia, and audiences in general—to further examine how these works shape cinephilia.

References

Affuso, Elizabeth. 2018. "Everyday Costume: Feminized Fandom, Retail, and Beauty Culture." In *The Routledge Companion to Media Fandom*, ed. Melissa A. Click and Suzanne Scott, 184–92. New York: Routledge.

302 Balcerzak, Scott, and Jason Sperb, eds. 2009. *Cinephilia in the Age of Digital Reproduction: Film, Pleasure and Digital Culture*, Vol. 1. London: Wallflower Press.

———. 2012. *Cinephilia in the Age of Digital Reproduction: Film, Pleasure and Digital Culture*, Vol. 2. London: Wallflower Press.

Bhattacharya Chairs, Nandini. 2004. "A 'Basement' Cinephilia: Indian Diaspora Women Watch Bollywood." *South Asian Popular Culture* 2 (2): 161–83.

Booth, Paul, ed. 2018. *A Companion to Media Fandom and Fan Studies*. Hoboken: John Wiley & Sons.

Branciforte, Joshua J. 2022. "A Critique of 'Mascquerade': Homotribalism and *Call Me by Your Name*." *GLQ* 28 (1): 55–86.

Brockington, Ariana. 2018. "Screenwriter James Ivory Criticizes 'Call Me by Your Name's' Lack of Frontal Nudity." *Variety*, March 28. Accessed October 28, 2022. https://variety.com/2018/film/news/james-ivory-call-me-by-your-name-nudity-luca-guadagnino-1202738618/.

Busse, Kristina. 2013. "Geek Hierarchies, Boundary Policing, and the Gendering of the Good Fan." *Participations* 10 (1): 73–91.

Carter, Oliver. 2018. *Making European Cult Cinema: Fan Enterprise in an Alternative Economy*. Amsterdam: Amsterdam University Press.

Cherry, Brigid. 2016. *Cult Media, Fandom, and Textiles: Handicrafting as Fan Art*. New York: Bloomsbury Publishing.

Click, Melissa A., and Suzanne Scott, eds. 2018. *The Routledge Companion to Media Fandom*. New York: Routledge.

De Kosnik, Abigail. 2016. *Rogue Archives: Digital Cultural Memory and Media Fandom*. Boston: MIT Press.

De Valck, Marijke. 2007. *Film Festivals: From European Geopolitics to Global Cinephilia*. Amsterdam: Amsterdam University Press.

———. 2010. "Reflections on the Recent Cinephilia Debates." *Cinema Journal* 49 (2): 132–39.

De Valck, Marijke, and Malte Hagener, eds. 2005. *Cinephilia: Movies, Love and Memory*. Amsterdam: Amsterdam University Press.

Elsaesser, Thomas. 2005. "Cinephilia or the Uses of Disenchantment." In *Cinephilia: Movies, Love and Memory*, ed. Marijke de Valck and Malte Hagener, 27–43. Amsterdam: Amsterdam University Press.

Fiske, John. 1992. "The Cultural Economy of Fandom." In *Adoring Audiences: Fan Culture and Popular Media*, ed. Lisa A. Lewis, 30–49. London: Routledge.

Galt, Rosalind, and Karl Schoonover. 2019. "Untimely Desires, Historical Efflorescence, and Italy in *Call Me by Your Name*." *Italian Culture* 37 (1): 64–81.

Geraghty, Lincoln. 2014. *Cult Collectors: Nostalgia, Fandom and Collecting Popular Culture*. London: Routledge.

Grossberg, Lawrence. 1992. "Is there a Fan in the House? The Affective Sensibility of Fandom." In *The Adoring Audience: Fan Culture and Popular Media*, ed. Lisa A. Lewis, 50–65. London: Routledge.

Hagener, Malte, and Marijke de Valck. 2008. "Cinephilia in Transition." In *Mind the Screen: Media Concepts According to Thomas Elsaesser*, ed. Jaap Kooijman, Patricia Pisters, and Wanda Strauven, 19–31. Amsterdam: Amsterdam University Press.

Hallas, Roger. 2003. "AIDS and Gay Cinephilia." *Camera Obscura* 18 (1): 85–126.

Hills, Matt. 2002. *Fan Cultures*. London: Routledge.

———. 2015. "Fandom as an Object and the Objects of Fandom." Interview with Clarice Greco. *MATRIZes* 9 (1): 147–63.

Hudson, Dale, and Patricia R. Zimmermann. 2009. "Cinephilia, Technophilia and Collaborative Remix Zones." *Screen* 50 (1): 135–46.

Jenkins, Henry. 1992. *Textual Poachers: Television Fans and Participatory Culture*. London: Routledge.

———. 2006. *Convergence Culture: Where Old and New Media Collide*. New York: New York University Press.

———. 2015. "Fans and Cinephiles (Henry Jenkins Interview)." Interview with Edgar Pêra. *edgarpera.org*. Accessed October 28, 2022. https://edgarpera. org/2015/12/02/fans-cinephiles-henry-jenkins-interview/.

Keathley, Christian. 2006. *Cinephilia and History, or the Wind in the Trees*. Bloomington: Indiana University Press.

———. 2009. "Preface: The Twenty-First-Century Cinephile." In *Cinephilia in the Age of Digital Reproduction: Film, Pleasure, and Digital Culture*, ed. Scott Balcerzak and Jason Sperb, 1-4. London: Wallflower Press.

Keathley, Christian, Jason Mittell, and Catherine Grant. 2019. *The Videographic Essay*. Accessed October 28, 2022. http://videographicessay.org/.

Keller, Sarah. 2020. *Anxious Cinephilia: Pleasures and Perils at the Movies*. New York: Columbia University Press.

Kim, Soyoung. 2005. "'Cine-Mania' or Cinephilia: Film Festivals and the Identity Question." In *New Korean Cinema*, ed. Chi-Yun Shin and Julian Stringer, 79–91. New York: Edinburgh University Press.

Klinger, Barbara. 2006. *Beyond the Multiplex: Cinema, New Technologies, and the Home*. Berkeley: University of California Press.

Miller, D.A. 2018. "Elio's Education." *Los Angeles Review of Books*. February 19. Accessed October 28, 2022. https://lareviewofbooks.org/article/elios-education/.

Mulvey, Laura. 2006. *Death 24x a Second: Stillness and the Moving Image*. London: Reaktion Books.

Neville, Lucy. 2018. *Girls Who Like Boys Who Like Boys: Women and Gay Male Pornography and Erotica*. Cham: Springer International Publishing.

Pande, Rukmini. 2018. *Squee from the Margins: Fandom and Race*. Iowa City: University of Iowa Press.

Pignetti, Daisy. 2020. "'She's a Fan, but This was Supposed to be Scientific': Fan Misunderstandings and Acafan mistakes." *Transformative Works and Cultures* 33. Accessed October 28, 2022. https://doi.org/10.3983/twc.2020.1763.

Reagin, Nancy, and Anne Rubenstein. 2011. "'I'm Buffy, and You're History': Putting Fan Studies into History." In *Fan Works and Fan Communities in the Age of Mechanical Reproduction*, ed. Nancy Reagin and Anne Rubenstein, special issue, *Transformative Works and Cultures* 6. Accessed October 28, 2022. https://doi. org/10.3983/twc.2011.0272.

Rosenbaum, Jonathan, and Adrian Martin, eds. 2003. *Movie Mutations: The Changing Face of World Cinephilia*. London: British Film Institute.

304   Santo, Avi. 2018. "Fans and Merchandise." In *The Routledge Companion to Media Fandom*, ed. Melissa A. Click and Suzanne Scott, 329–36. New York: Routledge.

Sarris, Andrew. 1963. "Notes on the Auteur Theory in 1962." *Film Culture* 27: 1–8.

Sarver Coombs, Danielle, and Anne C. Osborne, eds. 2022. *Routledge Handbook of Sport Fans and Fandom*. London and New York: Routledge.

Scott, Suzanne. 2019. *Fake Geek Girls, Fandom, Gender and the Convergence Culture Industry*. New York: New York University Press.

Shambu, Girish. 2020. *The New Cinephilia*. Second Expanded Edition. Montreal: caboose.

Smith, Damon. 2011. "Eyes Wide Shut: Notes Toward a New Video Criticism." Blog post. *Project: New Cinephilia*. Accessed October 27, 2020. https://projectcinephilia.mubi.com/2011/06/10/eyes-wide-shut-notes-toward-a-new-video-criticism/.

Sontag, Susan. 1996. "The Decay of Cinema." *The New York Times*, 25 February. Accessed October 28, 2022. https://www.nytimes.com/1996/02/25/magazine/the-decay-of-cinema.html.

Stanfill, Mel. 2019. *Exploiting Fandom: How the Media Industry Seeks to Manipulate Fans*. Iowa City: University of Iowa Press.

Tortorici, Zeb J. 2008. "Queering Pornography: Desiring Youth, Rave, and Fantasy in Gay Porn." In *Queer Youth Cultures*, ed. Susan Driver, 199–216. Albany: State University of New York Press.

Trice, Jasmine Nadua. 2015. "Manila's New Cinephilia." *Quarterly Review of Film and Video* 32 (7): 611–24.

Vidal, Bélen. 2017. "Cinephilia goes Global: Loving Cinema in the Post-Cinematic Age." In *The Routledge Companion to World Cinema*, ed. Rob Stone, Paul Cooke, Stephanie Dennison, and Alex Marlow-Mann, 404–14. New York: Routledge.

Wheeler, André-Naquian. 2018. "Read the Tender Sex Scene Cut from 'Call Me by Your Name'". *i-D*, April 25. Accessed October 28, 2022. https://i-d.vice.com/en_uk/article/59j8az/read-the-tender-sex-scene-cut-from-call-me-by-your-name.

White, Patricia. 1999. *Uninvited: Classical Hollywood Cinema and Lesbian Representability*. Bloomington: Indiana University Press.

Williams, Rebecca. 2018. "Fan Tourism and Pilgrimage." In *The Routledge Companion to Media Fandom*, ed. Melissa A. Click and Suzanne Scott, 98–106. New York: Routledge.

Authors

Claire Allouche is currently Attachée Temporaire d'Éducation et de recherche at the Université Paris 8 Saint-Denis-Vincennes (France) and a PhD candidate under the supervision of Dork Zabunyan and Thierry Roche. She trained in Film Studies (Université Paris 8 and ENS Ulm in France, UNSAM in Argentina) and in the humanities and sociology of space at EHESS. Her doctoral research focuses on the process of creating fiction outside the traditional production centres of Argentina and Brazil between 2008 and 2019. She is also a critic (*Cahiers du cinéma*) and programmer (Doc&Doc, CLaP, Regards Satellites).

Raymond Bellour is a researcher, author, emeritus research scientist at the CNRS (Paris). He has been responsible for editing the complete works of Henri Michaux in the Pléiade (1996–2004) and has (co)curated several exhibitions (from *Passages de l'image*, 1990, to *Chris Marker*, 2018). His books include *L'Analyse du film* (1979); *L'Entre-Images. Photo, cinéma, vidéo* (1990); *L'Entre-Images 2. Mots, Images* (1999); *Le Corps du cinéma:Hypnoses, Émotions, Animalités* (2009); *La Querelle des dispositifs. Cinéma – installations, expositions* (2012), *Pensées du cinéma* (2016). He is a founding member of the journal *Trafic*.

Club Des Femmes are a queer feminist film curation collective, based in the UK and programming since 2007. We curate film screenings and events. Our mission is to offer a freed up space for the re-examination of ideas through art. In the age of the sound-bite Club Des Femmes is a much needed open platform for more radical contextualisation and forward-looking future vision: a chance to look beyond the mainstream. https://www.clubdes-femmes.com

Mélina Delmas holds master's degrees in Translation from Université Paris 3 and Université Bordeaux-Montaigne (France), as well as a PhD in Translation Studies from the University of Birmingham (UK). Since 2021 she has been working as a Research

 Assistant at the University of Warwick (UK) where she collaborates closely with Professor Jo Angouri on various projects relating to multilingualism, linguistic landscapes and pedagogy. Additionally, in her role as the Warwick local facilitator for the EUTOPIA alliance, Mélina works to support several EUTOPIA Learning Communities. Mélina has also worked as a freelance translator for various clients since 2014.

Garin Dowd is Professor of Film, Literature and Media at the University of West London, UK. He is the author of *Abstract Machines: Samuel Beckett and Philosophy after Deleuze and Guattari* (Rodopi 2007), co-author (with Fergus Daly) of *Leos Carax* (Manchester University Press, 2003) and co-editor (with Lesley Stevenson and Jeremy Strong) of *Genre Matters: Essays in Theory and Criticism* (Intellect) and (with Natalia Rulyova) of *Genre Trajectories: Identifying, Mapping, Projecting* (Palgrave Macmillan 2015). He is also the author of the chapter on Serge Daney in Felicity Colman (ed.) *Film, Theory and Philosophy: The Key Thinkers* (Acumen, 2009) and of "Pedagogies of the Image between Daney and Deleuze" in *New Review of Film and Television Studies* 8 (1), 2010.

Pierre Eugène is Lecturer in Film Studies at the Université de Picardie Jules Verne (Amiens, France) and a member of the *Cahiers du cinéma* editorial board since 2020. His research focuses on Serge Daney, cinema writers and film aesthetics. He has published articles on many European and American filmmakers, and co-edited *Jean-Claude Biette, appunti et contrappunti* (De l'Incidence, 2018) with Hervé-Joubert-Laurencin and Philippe Fauvel. His book *Serge Daney, Exercices de relecture* (Éditions du Linteau, 2023) has just appeared, and he is currently working on a book devoted to Paul Vecchiali's film *Femmes femmes* (1974) (Yellow Now Editions).

Chloé Galibert-Laîné is a French researcher and filmmaker. They hold a PhD from the Ecole normale supérieure de Paris and are currently working as Senior Researcher at the Lucerne School of Art and Design in Switzerland. Their video essays and desktop

documentaries explore the intersections between cinema and 307
online media, with a particular interest in questions related to
modes of spectatorship, gestures of appropriation and mediated
memory. They have taught courses and workshops at various
universities and art schools, most recently at the University of
Massachusetts, the Beaux-Arts de Marseille and the California
Institute of the Arts.

Theresa Heath is a post-doctoral researcher at Loughborough
University, London, researching disabled access at film and
cultural festivals and events. She has published articles and
chapters on women's and queer film festivals, representations
of chronic illness in cinema, and is currently completing a book
titled *Queer Film Festivals and Urban Space: Remaking the City* to be
published in 2024.

Kate Ince is Professor of French and Visual Studies at the University of Birmingham (UK). She has published books on the
performance artist Orlan (*Orlan, millennial female,* Berg 2000), on
French filmmakers Georges Franju (*Georges Franju,* Manchester
University Press, 2005; in French as *Georges Franju: au-delà du
cinema fantastique,* Paris, L'Harmattan, 2008) and Mia Hansen-
Løve (*The Cinema of Mia Hansen-Løve: candour and vulnerability,*
Edinburgh University Press, 2021), and developed a feminist
phenomenological approach to women's cinema in *The Body and
the Screen: female subjectivities in contemporary women's cinema*
(Bloomsbury plc, 2017). She has just completed an essay that
employs psychology and phenomenology in conjunction with
Céline Sciamma's *Petite maman* (2021).

Andrea Inzerillo is the artistic director of the Sicilia Queer Film-
fest. He has translated and edited the Italian edition of works
by Michel Foucault, Jacques Rancière, Gilles Lipovetsky, Pierre
Bayard, Madame de Staël, Douglas Sirk. He also recently edited
the book *Atlante del Cinema Queer Contemporaneo. Europa 2000–
2020 / Atlas of Contemporary Queer Cinema. Europe 2000–2020,*
published by Meltemi (Milano, 2023). A teacher of history and

308 philosophy in high schools, he has recently been a post-doctoral research fellow in cinema at the University of Palermo. He collaborates with periodicals such as *Alias – Il manifesto*, Fata Morgana, *Gli Asini.*

Hervé Joubert-Laurencin is Professor of Cinema Aesthetics at the University Paris Nanterre (France) and a member of the Institut Universitaire de France. His research includes Pasolini's work (films, theatre, literature, politics and poetry, including translations into French), André Bazin's writings (*Ecrits complets*, Paris, Macula, 2018), other *écrivains de cinéma* such as Jean-Claude Biette, Barthélemy Amengual, Serge Daney, André Martin, Glauber Rocha, and Animation theory. He realizes films with Marianne Dautrey (*Bazin roman*, 2018, *Fontaine. Trente-trois minutes à la documenta fifteen*, 2023) and is currently working on a long-term creative and research project focusing on four subversive filmmakers: Pasolini, Rocha, Fassbinder and Oshima.

Philipp Dominik Keidl is Assistant Professor of Screen Media in Transition at Utrecht University. His research on fandom, material culture, and film heritage is published in *Journal of Cinema and Media Studies*, *Film Criticism*, *Journal of Popular Culture*, and *The Moving Image*. He is the co-editor of "Institutionalizing Moving Image Archival Training" (*Synoptique* 6.1, 2018), *Pandemic Media* (meson press, 2020), "Fandom Histories" (*Transformative Works and Cultures* 37, 2022) and *Platforms and the Moving Image* (meson press, forthcoming).

Simon Pageau is a film critic. At university, between 2017 and 2019, he worked on *Trafic*, the magazine created by Serge Daney in the early 1990s; then he co-founded a magazine, *Apaches*, whose first issues, published between 2020 and 2023, were partly devoted to classic American cinema. He is currently working on a book on *Dodes'kaden* by Akira Kurosawa.

Sylvie Pierre-Ulmann was a critic for *Cahiers du cinéma* in the 1960s and 1970s, and has been a teacher, editor, translator, and member of *Trafic's* editorial board from the foundation of the journal in 1991 until its final issue in 2021. She edited Glauber Rocha, *Textes et entretiens de Glauber Rocha*, Paris, Éditions de l'Étoile/Cahiers du cinéma, 1987 and published « *Frontière chinoise* » *de John Ford*, Crisnée, Yellow Now, 2014.

Bamchade Pourvali holds a doctorate in Film Studies and has taught at the École Polytechnique and Gustave Eiffel University. He is the author of *Chris Marker* (Cahiers du cinéma, 2003), *Godard neuf zéro, les films des années 90 de Jean-Luc Godard* (Séguier, 2006) and *Wong Kar-wai, la modernité d'un cinéaste asiatique* (L'Amandier, 2007). His latest book is *L'essai au cinéma, de Chaplin à Godard* (Créaphis, 2023). Also a specialist in Iranian cinema, he runs the "Iran ciné panorama" website (www.irancinepanorama.fr).

Patrice Rollet is an essayist and film critic, an editor and teacher, and was a member of *Trafic*'s editorial board from its foundation by Serge Daney in 1991 up to its final issue in 2021. Literary director of *Cahiers du cinéma* in the 1990s, his publications include a collective book on John Ford (1990), the writings of James Agee (1991) and Stanley Cavell. For Editions P.O.L., in addition to his own books, he edited the writings of Manny Farber, Jonas Mekas, and the four volumes of the *La Maison cinéma et le monde* (2001-2015) collection of Serge Daney's articles. Latest publication: *Descentes aux limbes*, Éditions P.O.L, 2019.

Marc Siegel is Professor of Film Studies at the Johannes Gutenberg University in Mainz. His research and publications focus mainly on issues in queer studies and experimental film. His book *A Gossip of Images* is forthcoming from Duke University Press. He has also been active internationally as a freelance curator for film series, programs and performance festivals. He is a member of the Academy of World Arts and Culture in Cologne and the Berlin-based art collective CHEAP. He is currently working on a book about bathrooms in film and video.

Marcos Uzal has been editor-in-chief of *Cahiers du cinéma* since May 2020. He was a member of the board and then the editorial board of *Trafic* magazine, a critic for *Libération* newspaper and

310   a member of *Vertigo* magazine. He has co-edited books on *Tod Browning* (2007), *Jerzy Skolimowski* (2013) and *Guy Gilles* (2014), and is the author of an essay on Jacques Tourneur's *I Walked With a Zombie* (2006), for the Côté Film collection (Yellow Now Editions), which he directed from 2006 to 2020. He was also film programmer at the Musée d'Orsay in Paris from 2010 to 2020.

www.ingramcontent.com/pod-product-compliance
Lightning Source LLC
LaVergne TN
LVHW052235150726
843469LV00055B/2209